THE ORTHODOX ~~BIBLE~~ SERIES

The GOSPEL of MARK

THE SUFFERING SERVANT

by Fr. Lawrence R. Farley

Ancient Faith Publishing
Chesterton, Indiana

THE GOSPEL OF MARK:
THE SUFFERING SERVANT
© Copyright 2004 by Lawrence Farley

One volume of *The Orthodox Bible Study Companion Series*

Published by   Ancient Faith Publishing
                A Division of Ancient Faith Ministries
                P.O. Box 748
                Chesterton, IN 46304

ISBN 978-1-888212-54-9

Printed in the United States of America

Dedicated to
the worthy SERAPHIM,
Bishop of Ottawa and Canada,
and father to us all.

Table of Contents and Outline

❧ Introduction ☙

A Word about Scholarship, Translation, and Format

This commentary was written for your grandmother. And for your plumber, your banker, your next-door neighbor, and the girl who serves you French fries at the nearby McDonald's. That is, it was written for the average layman, for the nonprofessional who feels a bit intimidated by the presence of copious footnotes, long bibliographies, and all those other things that so enrich the lives of academics. It is written for the pious Orthodox layman who is mystified by such things as Source Criticism, but who nonetheless wants to know what the Scriptures mean.

Therefore, it is unlike many other commentaries, which are written as contributions to the ongoing endeavor of scholarship and as parts of a continuous dialogue among scholars. That endeavor and dialogue are indeed worthwhile, but the present commentary forms no part of them. For it assumes, without argument, a certain point of view, and asserts it without defense, believing it to be consistent with the presuppositions of the Fathers and therefore consistent with Orthodox Tradition. It has but one aim: to be the sort of book a busy parish priest might put in the hands of an interested parishioner who says to him over coffee hour after Liturgy, "Father, I'm not sure I really get what St. Paul is saying in the Epistles. What does it all mean?" This commentary tries to tell the perplexed parishioner what the writers of the New Testament mean.

Regarding the translation used herein, an Italian proverb says, "All translators are traitors." (The proverb proves its own point, for it sounds better in Italian!) The point of the proverb, of course, is that no translation, however careful, can bring out all the nuances and meanings of the original, since no language can be the mathematical equivalent of another. The English translator is faced, it would seem, with a choice: either he can make the translation something of a rough paraphrase of the original and render it into flowing sonorous English; or he can attempt to make a fairly literal, word-for-word translation from the original with the resultant Eng-lish being stilted, wooden, and clumsy.

These two basic and different approaches to translation correspond to two basic and different activities in the Church. The Church needs a translation of the Scriptures for use in worship. This should be in good, grammatical, and flowing English, as elegant as possible and suited to its function in the majestic worship of the Liturgy. The Church also needs a translation of the Scriptures for private study and for group Bible study. Here the elegance of its English is of lesser concern. What is of greater concern here is the bringing out of all the nuances found in the original. Thus this approach will tend to sacrifice elegance for literality and, wherever possible, seek a word-for-word correspondence with the Greek. Also, because the student will want to see how the biblical authors use a particular word (especially St. Paul, who has many works included in the canon), a consistency of translation will be sought and the same Greek word will be translated, wherever possible, by the same Eng-lish word or by its cognate.

The present work does not pretend to be anything other than a translation for private Bible study. It seeks to achieve, as much as possible, a literal, word-for-word correspondence with the Greek. The aim has been to present a translation from which one could jump back into the Greek original with the aid of an interlinear New Testament. Where a single Greek word has been used in the original, I have tried to find (or invent!) a single English word.

The result, of course, is a translation so literally rendered from the Greek that it represents an English spoken nowhere on the planet! That is, it represents a kind of "study Bible English" and not an actual vernacular. It was never intended for use outside the present commentaries, much less in the worship of the Church. The task of producing a flowing, elegant translation that nonetheless preserves the integrity and nuances of the original I cheerfully leave to hands more competent than mine.

A final word about the actual format of this work. In all these pages, the translated text is first presented in boldface type. Italics in this biblical text represent a word required by English syntax that is not actually present in the Greek.

The biblical text is followed by a commentary. In this commentary section, citations from the portion of text being commented upon are given in boldface type. Citations from other locations in Scripture are given in quotation marks with a reference; any reference not including a book name refers to the Gospel of Mark. In the commentary, italics are also used in the ordinary way—for emphasis, foreign words, etc.

The Writing of Mark's Gospel

The first century saw the creation of an entirely new literary genre. White-hot from the heart of the apostles, like a fire kindled on the earth, came something never before seen: a Gospel.

A Gospel is not a biography. It does not necessarily begin at the birth of the protagonist; it does not purport to tell all the significant details of the life (as would be normal in a biography); it does not pretend to historical objectivity. One might as well expect historical and dispassionate objectivity from a love poem. One does not write of the virtues of one's Beloved with cold and measured precision. Rather, one says, "You are all fair, my love, there is no flaw in you" (Song 4:7). The Gospel was an altogether new form of literature, written to meet an altogether new literary need—to describe the fair beauty and glory of the Son of God, in whom there is no flaw. It was a faith document, written to record the disciples' experience of Christ.

That is, it was written by the Church and for the Church, to rehearse for the generations to come the apostolic reminiscences of Jesus. The apostles were quickly dying and passing from the stage of world history. Their voices once related to the Church the stories of their time with the Master, but their voices were increasingly hard to find, as they scattered and were martyred. It became imperative, if these priceless stories were not to be lost, that they be written down and preserved.

So it was that Mark wrote his Gospel. Early tradition says that Mark was with Peter in Rome. Indeed, Peter, writing his first epistle from Rome (which city he styles "Babylon"), records that Mark was with him there (1 Pet. 5:13). According to a tradition preserved by Eusebius of Caesarea, the first church historian, the Christian people of Rome "resorted to appeals of every kind to induce Mark, as he was a follower of Peter, to leave them in writing a summary of the instruction they had received by word of mouth" (*History of the Church*, 2.15). Irenaeus, however, suggests that Mark wrote his work *after* the death of Peter, saying that "after the departure [i.e. death] of Peter and Paul, Mark the disciple and interpreter of Peter handed down to us in writing what had been preached by Peter" (*Against Heresies* 3,1,1). St. John Chrysostom records another tradition (in his first homily on Matthew's Gospel), that Mark wrote his Gospel "in Egypt" (i.e. in Alexandria). What are we to make of these various early traditions?

It would appear that Mark was indeed with Peter in Rome in the months preceding Peter's martyrdom. No doubt Mark was collecting material for his Gospel while Peter was alive, recording what he said, though not actually committing it to final edited form until after his death and martyrdom. Through Mark's flight from Rome to Alexandria, the Gospel received its widest distribution and publication from there.

Who was this Mark, the friend and "interpreter" of Peter? Tradition says that he was the "John Mark" of Acts 12:12, whose mother Mary opened her home in Jerusalem to the apostles for their use. Many feel that he was also the anonymous young boy of Mark 14:51, a youth of perhaps fourteen years, who followed the apostles at a distance as they entered Gethsemane and fled away naked from the ensuing fray, after the crowd sent to arrest Jesus seized his outer garment. Mark was the cousin of the Apostle Barnabas, and he accompanied Barnabas and Paul on their first missionary journey—and abandoned them to return home when things got rough in Pamphylia (Acts 13:13). Though Paul later quarreled with Barnabas and refused to take Mark along on a subsequent missionary journey (Acts 15:36–40), he was afterward reconciled to his young friend, requesting that Mark come to him in prison when he was facing his end (2 Tim. 4:11).

The Gospel of Mark therefore represents some of the earliest and most vivid eyewitness accounts of the words and deeds of Christ. It was written in the late sixties of the first century, with the tacit blessing of Peter, and after Peter's death it was distributed throughout the Church to be treasured at once as the authentic reminiscence of the apostle.

Key to the Format of This Work:

• The translated text is first presented in boldface type. Italics within these biblical text sections represent words required by English syntax that are not actually present in the Greek. Each translated text section is set within a shaded grey box.

> ॐ ॐ ॐ ॐ ॐ
>
> **16 And going along by the Sea of Galilee, He saw Simon and Andrew, the *brother* of Simon, circle-casting into the sea, for they were fishermen.**

• In the commentary sections, citations from the portion of text being commented upon are given in boldface type.

> He concentrates on the abruptness of their call and the completeness of their break with the world. They were in the midst of their daily occupation, **circle-casting into the sea, for they were fishermen.**

• In the commentary sections, citations from other locations in Scripture are given in quotation marks with a reference; any reference not including a book name refers to the book under discussion.

> In Jeremiah 16:16–18, God said He would "send for many fishermen" to fish in Israel—those who would judge them for their sins and "doubly repay their iniquity."

• In the commentary sections, italics are used in the ordinary way—for emphasis, foreign words, etc.

> The word translated *circle-casting* is the Greek *amphiballo*; it describes a particular kind of fishnet.

❧ I ☙

PROLOGUE
(1:1–13)

§I.1   The Forerunner

> ☙ ☙ ☙ ☙ ☙
>
> **1** 1 *The* beginning of the Gospel of Jesus Christ, *the* Son of God.

Mark's Gospel begins with the Baptism of Jesus, and not (like those of Matthew and Luke) with an account of His birth, nor (like John's Gospel) with a reflection on His eternity. That is consistent with Mark's purpose. He intends to share with the world ***the beginning of the Gospel of Jesus Christ***—that is, how this Gospel preached by the Church all began, and what happened when their Christ was first revealed to the world. It is, in fact, Christ's public appearance on the stage of the world that is Mark's concern. The events of His Birth (which were mostly hidden from the world at large) are not here in his view—nor are His final Resurrection appearances to His disciples (which were also not public events; Acts 10:40–41). Rather, Mark is presenting Christ to the world, and states that his purpose in writing is to preserve an account of the deeds the Son of God did before the watching world.

> ☙ ☙ ☙ ☙ ☙
>
> 2 As it is written in Isaiah the prophet, "Behold, I send My messenger before Your face who will build Your way,
>
> 3 "a voice shouting in the wilderness, 'Prepare

> the way of *the* Lord, make straight His paths!'"
>
> 4 John the Baptizer came in the wilderness, and was heralding a baptism of repentance for forgiveness of sins.
>
> 5 And there came out to him all the country of Judea, and all the Jerusalemites, and they were being baptized by him in the Jordan River, confessing out their sins.
>
> 6 And John was clothed *in* camel's hair and a leather belt around his waist and was eating locusts and wild honey.

The ministry of John the Baptizer is presented with an economy of words. The main thing to know about him, Mark says, is that he was the Forerunner long expected. Isaiah had written of him many centuries earlier, saying, **"Behold, I send My messenger before Your face who will build Your way, a voice shouting in the wilderness, 'Prepare the way of *the* Lord, make straight His paths!'"** The quote is actually from two Old Testament prophets—Malachi 3:1 (who writes of God sending His messenger before His way), and Isaiah 40:3 (who writes of the voice shouting in the wilderness to prepare the way of the Lord). Mark mentions only Isaiah, appending the citation from Malachi anonymously to its beginning (a practice not uncommon throughout the New Testament), for his point is not which prophet said what, but only that God had long prepared for this day.

In ancient days, roads were not kept up as they are now. If a king was intending to travel down a given road, the local people were required to **build** it up again, clearing debris, filling in potholes, leveling out bumps. Only then, when it was suitably **prepared**, could the king come. That is how the Church viewed these ancient prophecies—as speaking of the preparatory work of John.

John came as the head of a revival movement in Israel, announcing the imminent arrival of the longed-for Kingdom of God and calling Israel to repentance. Israel, he announced, was in no shape to receive the messianic King. If He came now, when they were in their sins, they would not survive His judgment. There was work to be done—debris to be cleared from the road, sins to be eradicated from people's lives. Just as unclean and sinful Gentiles who repented of their sins and joined the commonwealth of Israel were baptized, so the Hebrew people needed to be baptized too. Only then could they receive **forgiveness of sins**, and not judgment, when Messiah came.

This baptism which John proclaimed that Israel needed was very controversial. It was based, almost certainly, on the practice of Jewish proselyte baptism. In those days, when a Gentile wanted to repent of his sinful ways and become a Jew, he stated his intention to the local Jewish community, promising to keep all the Law. He then was circumcised and later, on healing, was baptized, immersing himself in water (just as Jews did to wash away ceremonial uncleanness; see Lev. 14:8), to wash away the stain of the Gentile world. He then was considered a Jew. Sometimes entire families would be converted in this way, with women and children being baptized at the same time.

It would seem that this was the source and model for John's baptism of his Jewish disciples. Though Jews, they were nonetheless in the same need of repentance and cleansing as the hated Gentiles. This was a bold proclamation indeed—and one that did not sit well with the religious establishment (see John 1:25).

It did, however, reach the hearts of the common people, and they responded. John's messianic movement sparked a religious revival, as most considered John to be a true prophet, sent at last to announce the imminent Kingdom. He **heralded** his message of repentance in the wilderness of Judea, and **there came out to him all the country of Judea, and all the Jerusalemites, and they were being baptized by him in the Jordan River, confessing out their sins.** That is, they acknowledged their basic sinfulness—that they were oppressive tax collectors or prostitutes, that they were proud and impious, that they were greedy, that they had shut God out of their lives. Here was not a quiet pastoral and private confession (such as is practiced in Orthodox churches today), but a public acknowledgment of public sin, a public acceptance of the label of "sinner," and a public and impassioned cry for the mercy of God. As for John himself, he stood among them as one of the prophets of old, **clothed *in* camel's hair** with **a leather belt around his waist**—every inch the picture of Elijah (see 2 Kings 1:8).

Like Elijah, John was a man of the desert. He lived in the deserts from his youth (Luke 1:80), eating the food of the desert—**locusts and wild honey**, depending on God and His Word for survival—not on man (Deut. 8:3).

This desert context was no accident, for the desert had always been the place where God took His people in order to reveal His power and teach them dependence on Him. He had brought Israel into the desert after their liberation from Egypt and, after their spiritual decline in the Promised Land, prophesied that He would return them to the desert to deal with them again (Ezek. 20:35; Hos. 2:14). John's desert location then was no accidental detail, but a sign that God was once again moving among His people to restore them. Indeed, even the choice of the Jordan River for baptism was significant—for the Jordan was famous in the history of Israel as the site where God first revealed His power in Canaan. It was the waters of the Jordan that knew the power and Presence of God, as He parted the waters to bring His people home (Josh. 3—4) —a sign and prophecy that through His Presence in the Jordan, at the Baptism of Christ, He would again bring Israel home into their promised provision.

ॐ ॐ ॐ ॐ ॐ

7   And he was heralding, saying, "The stronger One than I is coming after me, and I am not sufficient to stoop down and loose the strap of His sandals.

8   "I *myself* baptized you with water, but He *Himself* will baptize you in *the* Holy Spirit."

John's message was manifold and included a political component, as he rebuked the current ruler for his sin (6:18). Here, however,

Mark focuses on the main burden of his message, that of the imminence of the Kingdom of God and of Messiah. Like a herald, John
proclaims that Messiah, who is a **stronger One** than he, is coming.
So mighty is His Kingdom and so great is He that John is **not sufficient to stoop down and loose the strap of His sandals.** That is
greatness indeed! For it was commonly allowed that a Jewish slave
may do all manner of lowly tasks for his master, but a line was drawn
at loosing the straps of his sandals and taking off his shoes. That was
work even too menial for a slave—a man should take off his own
shoes! Yet, says John, I am not even fit to do that for Messiah, so
great is His coming Kingdom!

Messiah is the focus of John's mission. When John finds himself
criticized and condemned for his innovative temerity in baptizing
Jews, he replies, "I *myself* [the "I" is emphatic in the Greek] am only
baptizing in water—when Messiah comes, He *Himself* [once again,
the "he" is emphatic] **will baptize you in** *the* **Holy Spirit.**" He will
bring a new age, baptizing Israel in the fire of the Spirit—how then
can they criticize John for merely baptizing in water?

§I.2   The Baptism of Jesus

> ֍ ֍ ֍ ֍ ֍
>
> 9 **And it came about in those days, Jesus came
>   from Nazareth of Galilee, and was baptized in
>   the Jordan by John.**
> 10 **And immediately coming up out of the water,
>   he saw the heavens being split, and the Spirit
>   as a dove descending to Him,**
> 11 **and a Voice there was out of the heavens: "***It
>   is* You *who* are My beloved Son; in You I am
>   well-pleased.**"**

The Baptism of Christ, the revelation of the Trinitarian nature
of our salvation, is related with a minimum of detail. John said that
the stronger One "is coming" (v. 7); now it is recorded that **Jesus
came** (v. 9), and Mark means us to see this as a fulfillment of John's

words. In humility, Christ came to John after the pattern of all the other sinners and penitents, identifying Himself with the race of men He had come to save. It is to be noted, however, that unlike those men, He did not come "confessing out [His] sins" (see v. 5), for He had none to confess. It is simply recorded that, like the others, He too was **baptized in the Jordan by John**.

Why then was He baptized? This is the big question which many have asked, and which is answered by the Church in her hymns for the Feast of Theophany. Mark does not attempt a complete answer. Instead, he focuses on the one part of it which was immediately relevant to John: Jesus was baptized in the Jordan to reveal to John His identity as the designated Messiah.

After baptism, Christ came **up out of the water**, standing on the riverside and praying (Luke 3:21). It was then that John had a vision. John saw the heavens **being split**, revealing the glory and purposes of God. He saw the Spirit, like a harmless **dove, descending to Him** and heard a **Voice** from the heavens above him saying, "*It is* **You** [the "You" is emphatic in the Greek] *who* **are My beloved Son; in You I am well-pleased**." Here was Messiah, designated and revealed at last!

Why did the vision take this form? (see John 1:33)—for the dove was not a commonly acknowledged image for the Holy Spirit. Perhaps it hearkens back to original creation, where the Spirit of God was hovering (like a bird) over the face of the waters (Gen. 1:2); here is the Spirit hovering over the waters of the new creation. More likely, however, the dove is a symbol of purity, since it was known to be harmless and innocent (see Matt. 10:16). It meant that the One singled out by such an innocent Dove was Himself innocent—no guilty sinner like the others, but the Messiah in whom God is **well-pleased**—His Chosen One.

Later generations would delight to see the Trinity revealed—the Son in the waters, the Father bearing witness to Him, and the Spirit, as a dove, confirming the truth of that witness (see the Troparion for Theophany). Here, however, Mark focuses on the Son and how His Baptism revealed Him to John—and through John, to Israel—as the Son of God.

§I.3   The Temptation in the Wilderness

ॐ ॐ ॐ ॐ ॐ

12 And immediately the Spirit cast Him out into
the wilderness.

13 And He was in the wilderness forty days being
tested by Satan, and He was with the beasts,
and the angels were serving Him.

Immediately after His Baptism, the battle was joined. The Spirit who descended on Him at Baptism, and with whom He was anointed with the power to heal all who were oppressed by the devil (Acts 10:38), now **cast Him out into the wilderness**. The verb is a strong one—Greek *ekballo*—the same word used for Christ casting out demons (e.g. in v. 34). It is used here to show the strength of the divine inner compulsion of the Son of God in combating Satan—He did not casually meander into the wilderness to begin His ministry and His warfare. Rather, He rushed to the front line to meet the adversary.

The story of the Temptation (told in greater detail in the Gospels of Matthew and Luke) is here mentioned only briefly. What matters to Mark is that Christ instantly and strenuously took up the challenge. The wilderness here is the place of testing—Israel was tested in the wilderness for forty years (Deut. 1:1–3) and Christ was tested **forty days**, embodying and encapsulating the sacred history of Israel as her true King. The reference to **the beasts** is probably meant as a counterbalance to the reference to **the angels**. The wild **beasts**, the only dwellers in that dread wilderness, showed how dangerous it was there to man. It was in this dangerous and daunting landscape that the Son of God strove with Satan—aided only by the **angels**, who **served Him**, perhaps by fending off the brutes. Mark does not lift the curtain very much on that lonely drama. He mentions it only in passing, as a foretaste of the struggle to come.

ॐ ॐ ॐ ॐ ॐ

Notes for Section I:

_____

_____

_____

_____

_____

_____

_____

_____

_____

_____

_____

_____

_____

_____

_____

_____

_____

_____

_____

_____

_____

_____

_____

_____

_____

_____

_____

_____

_____

_____

_____

❧ II ❧

EARLY GALILEAN MINISTRY
(1:14—3:6)

§II.1 Entry into Galilee

❧ ❧ ❧ ❧ ❧

1 14 And after John had been delivered up, Jesus
came into Galilee, heralding the Gospel of
God,

15 and saying, "The *appointed* time is fulfilled, and
the Kingdom of God has drawn near; repent
and believe in the Gospel."

Mark now begins to describe the ministry of Christ, and he
begins at the point **after John** [the Baptizer] **had been delivered
up** and arrested. (That is, he omits the preparatory acts of Christ,
mentioned by John the Evangelist in John 2—3.) Mark's aim, while
not denying that Christ worked and preached *before* John's arrest, is
to focus on what Jesus did *after* He came into His own, emerging,
as it were, from the shadow of the Forerunner. At that time, Jesus
came into Galilee, heralding the Gospel of God. The word translated
heralding is the Greek verb *kerusso*, "to act as a herald," proclaiming
the words and deeds of a King. Like John before Him (see v. 7),
Christ came to announce the imminent arrival of **the Kingdom of
God.** The Jews long expected the Kingdom to come, when God's
Messiah would vanquish evil and bring righteousness to reign on
the earth. The **Gospel** or Good News (Gr. *evaggelion*) is that the
appointed time (Gr. *kairos*) has been **fulfilled**; this Kingdom **has
drawn near** and is even now at the point of breaking into human

history. What is required of the people is simple: they must **repent and believe** this message!

When one had faith in the message of John the Baptizer and heeded his call to repentance, one expressed that faith by receiving baptism. It would appear that it was the same for those who accepted Christ's message—that repentance and faith were expressed in being baptized. Thus it was that the Fourth Gospel could speak of Christ "making and baptizing more disciples than John" (John 4:1).

§II.2   Call of the First Disciples

> ॐ ॐ ॐ ॐ ॐ
>
> 16 And going along by the Sea of Galilee, He saw Simon and Andrew, the *brother* of Simon, circle-casting into the sea, for they were fishermen.
> 17 And Jesus said to them, "Come after Me, and I will make you become fishers of men."
> 18 And immediately leaving the nets, they followed Him.
> 19 And having gone on a little further, He saw James *the son* of Zebedee, and John his brother, and they *were* in the boat, restoring the nets.
> 20 And immediately He called them, and leaving their father Zebedee in the boat with the paid *servants*, they went away after Him.

Mark then describes the call of the first disciples. Jesus had known Simon and Andrew before (see John 1:35–42) and no doubt they knew of His desire to enlist them as His disciples. Mark does not relate this kind of prehistory, nor the story of the miraculous catch of fish that finally clinched their conversion (related in Luke 5:1–11). Rather, he concentrates on the abruptness of their call and the completeness of their break with the world. They were in the midst of their daily occupation, **circle-casting into the sea, for they were fishermen.** The word translated *circle-casting* is the Greek *amphiballo*; it describes a particular kind of fishnet—not the huge dragnet that was dragged behind a boat, but a smaller circle-net, weighted on the edges, which was thrown into shallower waters from near the shore. In the midst of this mundane life, He called them to **come after** Him and become His disciples. If they did that, they would **become fishers of men**.

The concept of becoming **fishers of men** now has a warm evangelistic feel about it, perhaps for some conjuring up images of tearful and heartfelt conversions to God. But the image originally had a more eschatological feel to it, one darker and more tinged with judgment. The fishing of men the apostles knew of from the Prophets was a fishing of judgment. In Jeremiah 16:16–18, God said He would "send for many fishermen" to fish in Israel—those who would judge them for their sins and "doubly repay their iniquity." In Ezekiel 29:4–5, God said He would Himself fish for arrogant Egypt, putting "hooks in your jaws and making the fish of the rivers cling to your scales" and giving you "for food to the beasts of the earth." Christ's image of becoming **fishers of men** meant that the disciples, by their proclamation, were to be conveyors of judgment as well as salvation in Israel—salvation if one accepted the Gospel, and judgment if one did not! Despite the greatness of the change in their lives, **immediately leaving the nets, they followed Him**.

The call of James and John is related as well, with similar brevity. When Christ found them, they were **in the boat, restoring the nets**, mending any torn places after a night of fishing (for the best fishing was done at night). Like their partners, they also responded to His call, **leaving their father Zebedee in the boat with the paid** *servants*. That is, their break with their old life, like that of Simon and Andrew, was complete. Mark relates their call in this way as an example for *all* Christ's disciples, for *all* Christians—whether apostles or not. Though all are not necessarily required to leave their jobs and families behind as these apostles did, all of His followers are required to make that inner psychological break with the world. After baptism, they now no longer belong to the world. Their heart's first loyalty and their destiny now lie with Christ.

§II.3   Teaching with Authority in Capernaum

ॐ ॐ ॐ ॐ ॐ

21 And they enter into Capernaum, and immediately on *one of* the Sabbaths, coming into the synagogue, He was teaching.

22 And they were thunderstruck at His teaching, for He was teaching them as one having authority, and not as the scribes.

23 And immediately there was in their synagogue a man with an unclean spirit, and he cried out,

24 saying, "What concern are we to You, Jesus *the* Nazarene? Have you come to destroy us? I know You *and* who You are—the Holy One of God!"

25 And Jesus rebuked him, saying, "Be muzzled and come out of him!"

26 And having convulsed him, the unclean spirit made a great noise and came out of him.

27 And they were all astonished, so that they debated among themselves, saying, "What is this? A new teaching with authority! He commands the unclean spirits and they obey Him!"

28 And the report of Him went out immediately everywhere into all the surrounding-country of Galilee.

The first miracle Mark relates is one of exorcism. That is significant, for Christ's ministry in general is seen as one large exorcism—as the overthrow of Satan, prince of this world (see John 12:31), and the liberation of men from his fatal grasp.

It was in **Capernaum** in Galilee, the town in which Christ had made His headquarters and home. Capernaum was at that time a bustling center of commerce, and had a large synagogue. Christ went into the synagogue, and **was teaching** there on the **Sabbath**—even as distinguished guests were invited to teach (see Acts 13:15). (The word **enter** here is in the so-called "historic present" tense. As in other places in the Gospels, the writer here uses the present tense to convey a sense of immediacy, though he actually describes past events.) Those in that synagogue were **thunderstruck at His teaching**, for He was not quoting other authorities, as **the scribes** and other teachers did. (The **scribes** were a body of men trained in interpreting the Law, mostly Pharisees, who functioned as the authoritative teachers of the people.) Rather, Jesus taught **as one having authority**—able to say, for example, "You have heard that it was said thus to men of old, but I say to you . . ." (see Matt. 5:21, 22). More than that, He taught that the prophecies of old predicting the coming of Messiah were being fulfilled even then, while His hearers were listening to Him (Luke 4:21). What proof could He offer for claiming such astonishing authority?

They were soon to discover. For there was a man there **with an unclean spirit**. At the Presence of Christ, the final appointed Judge of all, the demon panicked and **cried out, saying, "What concern are we to You, Jesus *the* Nazarene? Have you come to destroy us? I know You *and* who You are—the Holy One of God!"** That is, the demon, on seeing the Judge, thought the judgment was at hand and feared its immediate destruction. Vainly, it tried to wield the knowledge of His Name as the messianic **Holy One of God** to fend Him off—for knowledge of someone's name was thought to give power over that person. But not *this* Person! The Lord simply said sharply, **"Be muzzled and come out of him!"** and the demon was forced to come out.

The Jews were used to exorcisms. Exorcism was a well-known trade (see Matt. 12:27; Acts 19:13). In attempting to cast out a demon, the exorcist would pray and use incantations, invoking other spirits and using magical texts. But here was exorcism with a simple word of command: a mere five words in the original Greek, two verbs that ring out like cracks from a whip: "Shut up and get out!" They had never seen anything as authoritative as this, nor anything so devastatingly effective: **having convulsed him, the unclean spirit made a great noise and came out of him**. No wonder they were **all**

astonished and **debated among themselves**, arguing, discussing what it all could possibly mean. They perhaps reached no conclusion, but nonetheless, **the report of Him went out immediately everywhere into all the surrounding-country of Galilee.** Soon, all knew of the astounding exorcist and miracle-worker who spoke with authority and brought **a new teaching.**

❧ EXCURSUS
ON ACTION AND ASTONISHMENT

One of the characteristics of St. Mark's Gospel is that Jesus is presented as a vigorous man of action. Mark uses the word *immediately* (Gr. *euthus*) many times (nine times in the first chapter alone) to indicate the speed and energy which accompanied Christ's ministry. It is as if when Jesus appeared, things happened at an accelerated pace as the Kingdom of God came rushing in.

Also characteristic of St. Mark's Gospel is his emphasis on how astonishing the power of Christ was to those who saw Him. Mark uses many synonyms to describe the effect that Jesus had on people: they were "thunderstruck" (1:22; 6:2; 7:37; 10:26; 11:18); they "marveled" (5:20; 15:5, 44); they "marveled greatly" (12:17); they "were astonished" (1:27; 10:24, 32); they were "startled" (9:15; 16:5); they were "beside themselves" (2:12; 5:42; 6:51); they "were afraid" (4:41; 5:15, 33, 36; 6:50; 9:32; 10:32; 11:18). Mark ransacks the language to show how greatly Christ alarmed His generation with demonstrations of divine power.

---

§II.4   Healing in Capernaum

ॐ ॐ ॐ ॐ ॐ

29 And immediately coming out of the synagogue,
    they went into the house of Simon and Andrew,
    with James and John.

> 30 Now the mother-in-law of Simon was lying
>   down, *having* a fever, and immediately they
>   speak to Him about her.
> 31 And having come to *her*, He raised her up,
>   seizing *her* by the hand, and the fever left her,
>   and she was serving them.

But there was more to come that Sabbath. Having left the synagogue, Jesus and His disciples returned to Simon's and Andrew's
home (their new base of operations). The womenfolk present would
have provided the hospitality of the Sabbath meal. Simon's **mother-
in-law**, however, was not among them, for she **was lying down,**
having **a fever**, separated from the press of the others serving the
meal. They spoke to Him concerning her plight, and He entered the
room where she was lying. Mark relates what happened next quite
simply: Christ **seized** *her* **by the hand** (the word translated *seized*,
Gr. *krateo*, is a strong word, used also for placing someone under
arrest). The divine strength flowed into her instantly, and **the fever
left her**. Indeed, she was so completely recovered that she joined
the others in **serving them**—all the more gladly, we may imagine,
to offer her grateful love to her Benefactor and Healer. Once again,
Mark relates the story simply, to show Christ's absolute sovereignty.
Demons and disease are as nothing before His authority. He has
only to speak and to take hold, and the powers of death give way.

> ॐ ॐ ॐ ॐ ॐ
> 32 And evening having come, when the sun had
>   set, they were bringing to Him all the sick and
>   the ones demon-possessed.
> 33 And the whole city was gathered together at
>   the door.
> 34 And He healed many sick *with* various diseases
>   and cast out many demons, and did not per-
>   mit the demons to speak, because they knew
>   Him.

The result of the public exorcism in the synagogue that morning was predictable: **evening having come, when the sun had set, they were bringing to Him all the sick and the ones demon-possessed. And the whole city was gathered together at the door.** The people waited until the Sabbath ended, and then descended on Him in teeming droves. Simon, looking out of his door, perhaps first heard and then saw an amazing sight: hundreds and hundreds coming to his home, the lame limping up or being carried, the blind being led, the demon-possessed being brought by family. "Young men and virgins, old men and children" all came with hopeful eyes and nervous impatience, waiting to see the new prophet and wonder-worker, for God "had lifted up a horn of salvation for His people" (Ps. 148:12, 14). His love and His power were equal to the challenge: **He healed many sick *with* various diseases and cast out many demons.**

Like the demon in the synagogue, those demons also recognized their Judge, but He **did not permit** them **to speak** and disclose His true identity, for He did not want to be hailed then as Messiah. The popular understanding of Messiah was then too military and carnal. For the people, Messiah was a military leader, one who was to raise an army and declare war on the Romans. This was not the way to fulfill God's righteousness and bring in the Kingdom. Thus the Lord resisted being hailed as Messiah, lest this spark a fire of messianic enthusiasm, and the people try by force to make Him an earthly King (see John 6:15).

꙳ ꙳ ꙳ ꙳ ꙳

35 And having arisen very early, at night, He went out and went away to a wilderness place, and was praying there.

36 And Simon and the ones with him hunted *for* Him,

37 and they found Him, and say to Him, "Everyone is seeking You."

38 And He says to them, "Let us go elsewhere to

> the nearby villages, that I may herald there also,
> for I came out for this *purpose*."
> 39 And He came heralding into their synagogues,
> in the whole of Galilee, and casting out the
> demons.

Our Lord's popularity at Capernaum then overflowed—
everyone was seeking Him. Rather than basking in the glow, however, He arose **very early, at night,** just before the dawn, **went out**
from the city, and **went away to a wilderness place** beyond the city
limits to pray. Rather than seeking the approval of men, He sought
the Face of God. (Here is a lesson for all in such times: When our
popularity swells, let us flee the applause of the world, lest it turn
our hearts from God, and let us seek Him in solitude, for safety is in
His smile alone.) In such times, when the days were full to bursting,
the Son of God still made time for communion with God. If *He*
needed such communion, how much more do *we* need it?

Simon and his companions, however, could not understand
such humility and suspicion of worldly popularity. They **hunted**
for Him and urged Him to return to the adulation of the crowd.
But He refused. Rather, He said to them, "**Let us go elsewhere to
the nearby villages, that I may herald there also, for I came out for
this** *purpose*." The Lord even then set His face steadfastly against
the way of popularity, setting His feet on the road that would lead
ultimately to the Cross. He left Capernaum and **came heralding into
their synagogues, in the whole of Galilee,** intent only on doing the
will of the Father, establishing His Kingdom and **casting out the
demons** who were tyrannizing God's beloved People.

§II.5   Cleansing a Leper

ॐ ॐ ॐ ॐ ॐ

> 40 And a leper comes to Him, urging Him and
> kneeling down and saying to Him, "If You are
> willing, You can cleanse me."

41 And *moved with* heartfelt *love*, and stretching out His hand, He touched *him*, and says to him, "I am willing, be cleansed."

42 And immediately the leprosy went away from him and he was cleansed.

43 And having scolded him, immediately He cast him out,

44 and He says to him, "See that you say nothing to anyone, but go, show yourself to the priest and offer for your cleansing what Moses commanded, for a witness to them."

45 But having gone out, he began to herald many *things* and to spread the word, so that He could no longer openly enter into a city, but stayed outside in the wilderness places, and they were coming to Him from everywhere.

In summarizing this opening part of His Galilean ministry, Mark concludes with a story of the healing of a leper. The term "leprosy" included any number of infectious skin diseases, but all of them meant disaster for the sufferer. Having been labeled as a leper, one was doomed to be driven from common society, to face a life of isolation and poverty, far from human warmth and family, cut off from the worship of temple and synagogue. It was, in fact, a kind of living death—and a fitting image for the sin that afflicts all our race.

The man approached Christ boldly and with faith in His power. In the midst of the crowd (which we may imagine made way for him and stood well back!), he intercepted the Lord and fell on his knees before Him, in complete and utter desperation. What he wanted from Him was only too obvious. With heartrending pathos, he could only manage to say, "**If You are willing, You can cleanse me.**" His whole life and his only hope lay in the compassion of Christ. A safe place for anyone to place his hope! The Lord was *moved with* heartfelt *love*. (The word so translated is the Gr. *splagxnizomai*, derived from *splagxna*, designating one's inmost and strongest emotions. To love with the *splagxna* is to love with a love so intense it is felt in the "guts" and tightens the stomach—a powerful love indeed!)

The Lord therefore **stretched out His hand** and **He touched him.** We must not miss the significance of this touch, for one did not touch lepers. If one did, one was made ceremonially unclean, and risked physical contamination also. But the Lord's compassion and power were stronger than that living death. Instead of leprosy contaminating Him, His power rolled back the leprosy! With a mere two words (the Gr. *thelo, katharistheti*), He drove the leprosy away, even as His sovereign Word before had driven away the demons.

The man, though grateful, was too jubilant to be restrained. Mark's account of the leper's discussion with Christ is compressed and summarized in a few words, and we can be misled and perplexed at what follows. The Lord no doubt told the man to tell no one of how he had been healed, but simply to **show himself to the priest** so that the priest could pronounce him clean and restore him to society. As a good Jew, he was to offer the sacrifice that Moses had commanded (in Lev. 14:2f)—not (Mark stresses) because the Law was supreme, but simply as **a witness** to them that he had been healed.

The man, however, seems to have resisted this command to keep things quiet. He insisted on staying there in town, telling others the whole story! The Lord no doubt repeated His order; the man again resisted. The Lord therefore had to **scold** him into being quiet. The word used is the Greek *embrimaomai*—the same word used in 14:5 for the scolding of the woman who anointed Jesus at Bethany. That is, the Lord sternly warned him to do as he was told—and **cast him out** (Gr. *ekballo*, the same word used in v. 34 for the casting out of demons). That is, He forced him to leave his audience and return to his life.

It was, of course, to no avail. As soon as he left Christ, he **began to herald many *things* and to spread the word, so that He could no longer openly enter into a city.** The result was that Christ's popularity swelled even more. The crowds were so overwhelming that He could no longer **enter into a city, but stayed outside in the wilderness places**—the very situation He meant to avoid. He could not go to them. Nevertheless, *they* still came to *Him*—and from everywhere!

§II.6   Opposition from the Pharisees

Mark next relates a series of five challenges to Christ's authority by the Pharisees. The Pharisees were a lay brotherhood dedicated to a zealous keeping of the Law as interpreted through the "tradition of the elders," or oral law interpretations current in their day. They were judgmental of others who were not as strict in their keeping of the Law and were abundantly confident of their own righteousness. Not surprisingly, therefore, they mostly rejected the call of John to turn back to God in humble repentance. And having in their pride rejected Christ's Forerunner, they were set to reject Christ Himself as well.

ॐ ॐ ॐ ॐ ॐ

2 1 And when He had come into Capernaum again after *some* days, it was heard that He was in *the* house.

2 And many were gathered together, so as to no longer have room at the door, and He was speaking the Word to them.

3 And they come, bringing to Him a paralytic, taken up by four.

4 And not being able to bring *him* to Him because of the crowd, they removed the roof where He was, and when they had *made* an opening, they let down the pallet on which the paralytic was lying down.

5 And Jesus, having seen their faith, says to the paralytic, "Child, your sins are forgiven."

6 But there were some of the scribes sitting there and questioning in their hearts,

7 "Why *does* this one speak thus? He blasphemes! Who can forgive sins, but God alone?"

---

8 And immediately Jesus, having really-known in His spirit that they were questioning thus among themselves, says to them, "Why are you questioning *about* these things in your hearts?

9 "Which is easier: to say to the paralytic, 'Your sins are forgiven,' or to say, 'Arise, and take up your pallet and walk'?

10 "But that you may know that the Son of Man has authority on the earth to forgive sins"—He says to the paralytic—

11 "I say to you, rise, take up your pallet and go away to your house."

12 And he arose and immediately taking up the pallet, he went out before all, so that *they* all *were* beside themselves and *were* glorifying God, saying, "Like this we have never seen!"

After a time in the more remote areas outside the city, Christ then returned to the **house** where He was staying in **Capernaum**—probably Simon's house (see 1:29). Houses for the working man usually could hold about fifty people at a maximum. But Christ's popularity meant that many more wanted to see Him. All the multitudes **gathered together** in such numbers that there was **no longer room at the door**, but they thronged around the house, forming a wall of people, all of them listening intently to **the Word** and message of the Kingdom that He was speaking to them (see 1:15).

One group of people in particular wanted to reach him: **four** men, carrying a fifth, **a paralytic**, who was lying on a **pallet**, or a light mattress. When the crowd about the door made normal entry impossible, they did not give up. Such was their faith in Christ and their determination to find healing for their friend that they carried him up the exterior steps common to homes in those days and went up on the roof (which, like all such roofs, was flat). Those roofs were usually made of tiles and thatch, making it relatively easy for one to dig through, and this is just what they did. Digging through and making **an opening**, they let down the pallet, thus bypassing the crowds and gently easing the paralytic into the Presence of Christ.

One can imagine the astonishment of the apostles—and of Simon, seeing his roof being destroyed! What Christ saw, however, was the **faith** of the bold group, which refused to be deterred. Tenderly, He **says to the paralytic** [the words are again in the present tense, to convey immediacy], **"Child, your sins are forgiven."**

Why, some have asked, did the Lord first speak this word of forgiveness, when the obvious request was for healing? The insight of those days was that healing for the body is bound up with forgiveness for the soul, since man is a single compound of soul and body. It may not be the case in every instance that a specific sickness is caused by a specific sin; but, in general, sickness has afflicted our race because of sin and, to be completely whole, a person needs both healing and forgiveness. With His divine insight, it would seem, the Lord knew that this man particularly needed forgiveness, and the power of the Kingdom of God coming to him included this forgiveness as well as the requested healing.

His claim to be able to forgive sins, however, horrified the Pharisaical **scribes**. For Christ was claiming to have the authority to pronounce that, on the Day of Judgment, God would not require an accounting of this sin, but would then deem it forgiven. Who was Jesus, a man on earth, to speak for God in heaven and to usurp the authority to judge which was God's alone? They therefore **questioned in their hearts**, startled and scandalized, **"Why *does* this one speak thus?"**

Jesus had intimate knowledge in His inner **spirit** of the secrets of their hearts. (The word translated here **really-known** is the Greek *epiginosko*, which describes not just "knowledge" [Gr. *gnosis*], but deeper recognition [Gr. *epignosis*]. Christ therefore had complete knowledge of their inner reasonings.) He therefore challenged them as to why they rejected His authority so easily and quickly. Indeed, He asked them, **"Which is easier: to say to the paralytic, 'Your sins are forgiven,' or to say, 'Arise, and take up your pallet and walk'?"** They would have to admit that both were impossible for mere men on earth. Such men could not forgive sins—but neither could they heal a paralytic with a mere word. Christ continued the argument. **"But that you may know,"** He said, **"that the Son of Man has authority on the earth to forgive sins"**—here He turned from them to the paralytic and spoke the simple sentence, **"I say to you, rise, take up your pallet and go away to your house."**

For a moment, perhaps, the paralytic was motionless, hardly daring to move. Then he uncurled himself, stretched the limbs not used in long months and years, and stood up. With wide-eyed and open-mouthed joy, he stood erect, bent down to roll up his pallet, and obediently walked through the crowd to his house—which crowd now parted for him in astonishment. They were, in fact, **beside themselves** with amazement (Gr. *existemi*, the word used in 3:21 to describe being out of one's mind). Christ's miracle led all the crowd (but not the vanquished Pharisees) to **glorify God** for a work the likes of which they had never before seen.

This miracle set the stage for the controversy between Christ and His foes that would continue throughout the Gospel and lead ultimately to His death. The central question was: Who was Jesus of Nazareth? This miracle is given here, at the outset of the conflict, to prove the point that Christ does indeed exercise on earth all the authority of God in heaven. The Father gave to the incarnate Son all His authority to be exercised in His stead (see John 5:26, 27), since He is Himself the expression and fullness of the Father. Here is the Faith of the Church, which she would later embody in the Creed, already proclaimed and proven. Christ exercises all the authority on earth of Him who will not give His glory to another (Is. 42:8), for He is Himself One with the Father, and our true God.

ক্ট ক্ট ক্ট ক্ট ক্ট

13 And He went out again beside the sea, and all the multitude was coming to Him, and He was teaching them.

14 And passing by, He saw Levi the *son* of Alphaeus sitting at the tax-table, and He says to him, "Follow Me!" And arising, he followed Him.

15 And it came about that He was lying down in his house, and many tax collectors and sinners were co-reclining with Jesus and His disciples, for there were many, and they were following Him.

16 And the scribes of the Pharisees, seeing that He was eating with the sinners and tax collectors, said to His disciples, "*Why is it* that He eats with the tax collectors and sinners?"

17 And having heard this, Jesus says to them, "The strong ones have no need of a physician, but those who are sick. I did not come to call righteous *people*, but sinners."

The Lord again went out by the Sea of Galilee, thronged by the usual crowd, and **He was teaching them** about the Kingdom of God. He soon manifested the Kingdom He was teaching about, for, passing by a crossroad or bridge, He saw **Levi the *son* of Alphaeus sitting at the tax-table**. Such tax collectors were familiar sights. They sat at such conspicuous places, where, as customs officers, they could easily exact custom tax of those merchants traveling over road or bridge. They were heartily hated by the common folk, who, because the tax collectors served the conquering Romans and were corrupt, classified them with murderers and robbers and would have nothing to do with them.

Christ's message of the Kingdom of God was about how the Father was now calling all His children home. It was to just such sinners as Levi that Jesus came to proclaim this Kingdom, so He called the tax collector to join Him, saying, **"Follow Me!"**

Levi (later known as Matthew; see Matt. 9:9) had doubtless heard much about the Prophet of Nazareth. As a tax collector, he had taken it for granted that respectable and religious people detested him, and hardly dared to hope for anything else. But here was a religious man, a famous man, a popular Rabbi, opening His heart to him, accepting him, forgiving him, and calling him—personally and by name—to join Him. He was offered a new life, one filled with unknown adventure certainly, but also one filled with peace with God. He jumped at the chance—jumped up from his tax-table, making a complete break with his profitable past, and **arising, he followed Him.**

We can catch a glimpse of Levi's joy in the great banquet that he gave in honor of his newfound Teacher. (Even without the confirming testimony of Luke 5:29, one would assume that the big reception with many tax collectors and sinners was Levi's doing.) Levi wanted to honor his Teacher, so he hosted a huge reception. His own friends were of course there—that is, other tax collectors and notoriously immoral people (for that is the meaning of **sinners** in this context), for these were the only friends Levi had. Pious folk usually took great pains to avoid such people—and would certainly not eat with them. To eat with someone, and accept his hospitality, meant to accept *him*—and this was clearly out of the question for any pious person.

Yet Christ clearly was comfortable in such company, and did not scruple to accept these people as He had accepted Levi. As He was **lying down** and reclining at table in Levi's house (for such feasts were taken while reclining on couches, after the Roman manner), He was surrounded by **many tax collectors and sinners** who were **co-reclining** with Him, sharing the table fellowship and **following Him** as disciples and interested hearers.

The Pharisaical **scribes**, fresh from being scandalized in verse 6, are scandalized again. Any pious man would indignantly refuse to eat with such riffraff, for fear of being somehow contaminated himself! One can almost hear the boggled recoil in their voices as they hiss out to His disciples, "*Why is it* **that He eats with the tax collectors and sinners?**"

Though perhaps they said it behind the hand to His disciples, and not as a direct challenge to Himself, Jesus heard their outrage. Compassionately trying to reclaim the scribes too, He did not rebuke their judgmental attitude. Rather, He strove to help them see it from a new perspective, and gave them a parabolic image. **The strong ones** and the healthy ones **have no need of a physician**—only **those who are sick** do. The physician obviously would go to the homes of the sick and surround himself with their sickness. He does not fear to become sick himself: he is a physician and it is his job to go where sickness is. Surely they could see that? In the same way, Christ also **did not come to call righteous** *people*, **but the sinners.**

It was a parable and an image meant to shake the scribes out of their old ways of thinking. Of course Christ came to call *both* the righteous (such as Simeon in the Temple; see Luke 2:25) *and* the sinner (such as Levi). This was the normal Hebrew way of producing a dichotomy in order to make a point—as in Hosea 6:6, where God says He desires "loyalty and not sacrifice." In fact, God desired *both* loyalty *and* sacrifice. But the dichotomy forcibly underscores the point made: sacrifice is nothing without loyalty. It is the same with this parable: the point is that God's mercy especially shines in the reclamation of sinners. So the Pharisees should not stumble and reject Christ simply because He eats with notorious sinners. For in the final Banquet of the Last Day, all are welcome to come home to God's mercy and feast at His messianic table.

ॐ ॐ ॐ ॐ ॐ

18 And the disciples of John and the Pharisees came fasting, and they come and say to Him, "Why do the disciples of John and the disciples of the Pharisees fast, but Your disciples do not fast?"

19 And Jesus said to them, "Do the sons of the bridal-chamber fast while the bridegroom is with them? As long as they have the bridegroom with them, they cannot fast.

20 "But days will come when the bridegroom is taken away from them, and then they will fast in that day.

21 "No one sews a patch of unshrunk cloth on an old garment; otherwise the patch will pull away from it, the new *piece* from *the* old, and a worse split occurs.

> **22** "And no one puts new wine into old skins; otherwise the wine will tear the skins and the wine is destroyed, and the skins, but new wine for fresh skins!"

Some there, however, found such new ways too difficult for them to accept. And they had another reason for stumbling at the generosity and joy of Jesus: He was not fasting.

The pious in Israel fasted twice every week, on Mondays and Thursdays (see the Didache, an early Church document, which recalls how the Jews fasted on those days [ch. 8]). On those days, they ate nothing until the evening. It would appear that Levi's feast took place on one of these weekly fast days—and here were Jesus and His disciples ignoring the Jewish "canons"! So it was that the **disciples of John** and those influenced by the teaching and piety of the **Pharisees** came there **fasting**, refusing to eat. They came up to Jesus (no doubt as He was reclining and eating) and challenged Him directly: **"Why do the disciples of John and the disciples of the Pharisees fast, but Your disciples do not fast?"** That is, everyone else—including the Baptist with whom You had connections—is fasting today. Why don't You make *Your* disciples fast too? For them, authentic piety was inflexible piety.

Jesus did not rule out fasting. Rather, He assumed it and mandated it for His disciples (see Matt. 6:16–18). But not inflexibly. Rules must give way to love—in this case, love for Levi and his friends, whom Christ was striving to bring into the Kingdom. The old way said, "The letter of the Law is everything; there can be no exceptions to rules." The new way of the Kingdom said, "Love is everything; there must be room for exceptions to rules."

As usual, Christ sought to teach them this with parables. Think of a wedding feast, He said. In those days, the wedding feast would go on for seven days. Even though it might be a Monday or a Thursday, the regular fast days, obviously **the sons of the bridal-chamber** (the technical term for the wedding guests) could not fast **while the bridegroom was with them**! Indeed, as long as the wedding feast is being held and the groom is present, **they cannot fast**! It would be an unthinkable insult to the bridegroom and his bride. If this is the case for a mere human groom, how much more for the Son of Man! Fasting was an expression of mourning for sin, and as such was incompatible with rejoicing. Thus, at a wedding party, they must share the bridegroom's joy, even if it meant suspending their usual fasting. How much more then must they suspend fasting to share the joy of having Jesus with them!

Then the Lord speaks with a grim irony, not understood at that time—and only later understood in light of the Cross. Don't worry, He says, they will fast soon enough! **"Days will come when the bridegroom is taken away from them, and then they will fast in that day."** In terms of the parable, it simply meant, "One cannot fast until the party ends." But in light of His Cross, the Lord meant, "These days of joy and lightheartedness will end with My death—there will be plenty of time for mourning and fasting then."

It is a question of the relation of the new ways of the Kingdom and the old ways of thinking that prevailed until then. The new Kingdom requires new ways of piety and a new flexibility. One cannot inherit the Kingdom while clinging to the old inflexible ways. New cannot be combined with old.

It was like trying to combine a new **patch of unshrunk cloth** and an **old garment**. You cannot put the one on the other. The garment has already been shrunk through washing; it cannot shrink anymore. But the patch can shrink—and it will, **pulling away** from the garment it was meant to patch and making an even **worse split** and tear.

Or consider the parable of new wine. You cannot combine the new with the old there either. Old wineskins are tough and leathery, with no stretchable "give" to them. If one puts freshly fermented **new wine** into those **old skins**, the wine will expand too much for the skins and will burst them. Then the wine will be **destroyed** and lost—**and the skins** too. No one will have any benefit from the wine at all. Even the skins cannot be reused. (These lost skins are an image of the uselessness of a Judaism that tries to combine Christianity with the old legalism.) If one is to have **new wine**, one must also have **fresh** and stretchable **skins**—these are what go together. The new joy of the Kingdom demands a fresh approach and a new flexibility to inherited ways.

৵ৎ ৵ৎ ৵ৎ ৵ৎ ৵ৎ

23 And it came about that He was going through the grainfields on *one of* the Sabbaths, and His disciples began to make their way, picking the heads.

24 And the Pharisees were saying to Him, "Behold, why are they doing what is not permitted on the Sabbaths?"

25 And He says to them, "Have you never read what David did when he had need and was hungry, he and the ones with him;

26 "how he entered the House of God, in the *passage about* high priest Abiathar, and ate the Bread of the Presentation, which is not permitted to be eaten except by the priests, and gave also to the ones who were with him?"

27 And He said to them, "The Sabbath happened because of man, and not man because of the Sabbath,

28 "so the Son of Man is Lord even of the Sabbath."

The next conflict with the Pharisees was occasioned by the behavior of His disciples on the Sabbath. As they went hurriedly from place to place with little time to eat, He and His disciples were **going through the grainfields**. As they went, His disciples **picked the heads** of the grain, rubbing them in their palms and blowing away the chaff in order to eat the grain remaining in their hands as a kind of granola snack in their hunger. Such behavior was specifically allowed by the Law, which permitted the traveler to eat such food (Deut. 23:25). The Pharisees, however, with their detailed elaboration of the basic law forbidding work on the Sabbath, could only see violations of the Law and sin. As far as they were concerned, by plucking the heads of grain, the disciples were harvesting; by rubbing them in their hands, they were threshing; by blowing the chaff away, they were winnowing. God in His Law had forbidden work on the Sabbath—but it was left to the Pharisees to define work in such a way as to empty the divine Law of common sense and authentic content. By their manmade traditions they had made void the Law of God.

They could not see the great task the disciples were engaged in as they served Jesus, nor the legitimacy of their satisfying their hunger as they performed this task. All they could see was that, according to their own definitions, the Law had been broken. So, with all the passion of righteous indignation, they demanded of Jesus why He allowed His disciples to do **what was not permitted on the Sabbaths**.

Jesus replied by referring to the Scriptures. The examples of the Scriptures proved that men might do what was not technically permitted in order to meet human need. **In the *passage about* high priest Abiathar** [i.e. the latter half of the Book of 1 Samuel], **David** and **the ones with him** were hungry as they fled from Saul (1 Sam. 21). They had no choice but to eat **the Bread of the Presentation**, the twelve loaves of the Showbread which were set out in the Holy Place and which were, technically, only **permitted to be eaten** by **the priests** (Lev. 24:9). They were in genuine need and hunger—and therefore cultic details of the Law gave way before human need. It was the same here—any other considerations of Law must give way before human need. The Pharisees were concerned about honoring the Sabbath—and unconcerned about man. Yet **the Sabbath happened** and was brought into existence by God **because of man**, for the sake of his welfare and rest (see Deut. 5:12–15). Meeting human need and providing for man's salvation was the goal of the Sabbath—and of the entire Law. The Sabbath was simply a means to that end. It followed then that Christ, the messianic **Son of Man**, since He was the Lord of men, was **Lord even of the Sabbath**, with authority to declare what was and was not allowed regarding it. Since He had authority to rule over men, He could rule over the Sabbath also—and declare that His disciples' behavior was allowed.

Here was a sweeping and breathtaking claim. For the Pharisees, the Sabbath had an importance that dwarfed almost all else. What were men and their problems compared to the divine Sabbath? Yet Jesus declared Himself superior even to the Sabbath—He claimed to be its legitimate Lord. This was, in fact, tantamount to claiming the authority of God Himself.

(One final note: Verse 26, translated here as **in the** *passage about* **high priest Abiathar**, is often translated as if it were a temporal reference: "in the days of Abiathar the high priest," or "in the time of Abiathar the high priest." Such a translation is problematic—for, though Abiathar features prominently in the rest of the story of David [see 1 Sam. 22:23; 30:7], the visit to the sanctuary described actually occurred when Abiathar's father Ahimelech was high priest [1 Sam. 21:1]. The Greek of this passage is: *epi Abiathar arxiereos*. This is similar to a passage in 12:26, describing the burning bush: *epi tou batou*, which is translated "in the passage about the bush." It would appear then that the word *epi* as used here denotes the place where the story can be found, not the time it occurred. Our Lord's point is not *when* David ate the loaves, but *where* the scribes could look up the passage and read it for themselves.)

ঙ্গ ঙ্গ ঙ্গ ঙ্গ ঙ্গ

3 1   And He entered again into the synagogue, and a man was there having a withered hand.

2   And they were keeping *watch* on Him, if He would heal him on *one of* the Sabbaths, that they might accuse Him.

3   And He says to the man having the withered hand, "Arise and *come* into the midst!"

4   And He says to them, "Is it permitted on the Sabbaths to do *that which is* good or to do bad, to save a life or to kill?" But they were silent.

5   And after looking around *on* them with wrath, deeply-grieved at the hardness of their heart, He says to the man, "Stretch out the hand."

> And he stretched *it* out, and his hand was restored.
>
> 6 And going out, the Pharisees immediately gave counsel with the Herodians against Him, how they might destroy Him.

The final story of conflict with the Pharisees once again focuses on the Sabbath. Jesus **entered again into the synagogue**, probably in the town of Capernaum, and found there a man **having a withered hand**, one paralyzed and useless. He was, it would seem, well-known to all the locals—perhaps because he had made known to them his desire to be healed by Jesus. His mere presence in the synagogue was a standing invitation to Jesus to heal, and **they were keeping *watch on Him***, to see if He would indeed heal him, even though it was the Sabbath. No doubt all that crowd, including the hostile Pharisees present, had their keen eyes fixed on the Lord, waiting breathlessly to see what He would do.

They did not have to wait long. As if in answer to their unspoken challenge, He called to the man, **"Arise and *come* into the midst!"** That is, He bade the man arise and come forward to the front of the synagogue, to where the Lord no doubt was. We may imagine the man, now reluctantly the center of controversy and attention, standing beside Jesus and trying to evade the stares of malevolence from the Pharisees, who were incensed that he had not chosen to wait until after the Sabbath had passed to seek healing. The Lord stood as his defender and champion.

He did not address the man, but the crowd. Let the synagogue give a ruling on this legal question: **"Is it permitted on the Sabbaths to do *that which is* good or to do bad, to save a life or to kill?"** That is, which course of action, of the two now available to Him on this Sabbath, was the best way to honor the day—by doing a good deed, saving life and restoring to health and vitality; or by evildoing, killing, and leaving a man in his suffering? Is a good deed permitted on the Sabbath? The issue was not whether the man could or should wait. The Sabbath was now, and the man had made his wordless request. The question was: what was now the godly course of action?

Put this way, there could only be one answer. The crowd, however, **were silent**, as they either agreed with the Pharisees that it was a violation of the Sabbath and a sin before God to heal this man now, or else they disagreed with them, but did not possess the courage to voice their disagreement. (We may note here the necessity of courage in matters of conviction.) Their silence and refusal to side with the man hurt the Lord, as He was **deeply-grieved** over this **hardness of heart**. He **looked around** *on* **them**, scanning the crowd, looking to see "if there were any who understood and sought after God" (Ps. 14:2). Alas, all refused to side with the poor man, who was standing trembling beside the Lord, awaiting the outcome, fearing perhaps he would not be healed after all. The crowd had "all turned aside; there was none who did good, not even one" (Ps. 14:3). The Lord was indignant at this stony-hearted refusal, and His scanning of the faces was **with wrath**. He had had enough, and turned from striving for their enlightenment to dealing with the man waiting for His salvation. "**Stretch out the hand**" that was afflicted, He ordered him, and when he obeyed and **stretched** *it* **out** in the sight of that watching multitude, it **was restored**.

The reaction of the crowd is not recorded. The Pharisees, however, stormed out, and lost no time in giving **counsel with the Herodians against Him, how they might destroy Him.** The Herodians were the partisans of Herod the Tetrarch. In most circumstances, the Pharisees would want nothing to do with these political men, whose only concern was political peace and who cared little for the Law. They had this in common with them, however: they both wanted Jesus out of the way—the Herodians because He was perceived by them as a possible threat to the peace, and the Pharisees because they hated His supposed flouting of the Law. These two groups began talks as to how they **might destroy Him.** The shadow of the Cross had fallen early across the path of Christ.

Notes for Section II:

_____

_____

_____

Notes for Section II:

_____

_____

_____

_____

_____

_____

_____

_____

_____

_____

_____

_____

_____

_____

_____

_____

_____

_____

_____

_____

_____

_____

_____

_____

_____

_____

_____

_____

_____

_____

_____

_____

_____

_____

❧ III ❧

LATER GALILEAN MINISTRY
(3:7—6:29)

§III.1 Withdrawal with Disciples

❧ ❧ ❧ ❧ ❧

3 7 **And Jesus with His disciples withdrew to the sea, and a great multitude from Galilee followed, and from Judea,**

8 **and from Jerusalem, and from Idumea, and the other** *side* **of the Jordan, and around Tyre and Sidon, a great multitude hearing all that He was doing, came to Him.**

9 **And He said to His disciples that a boat should wait on Him because of the crowd, that they might not crush Him,**

10 **for He had healed many, so that as many as had afflictions fell on Him that** *they might* **touch Him.**

11 **And whenever the unclean spirits beheld Him, they were falling before Him and were crying out, saying,** "*It is* **You** *who* **are the Son of God!"**

12 **and He greatly rebuked them, lest they make Him manifest.**

Having given this selective portrait of Christ's early ministry in Galilee, Mark then turns to record some events from His later ministry.

As His popularity continued to increase, **Jesus with His disciples withdrew to the sea** of Galilee. That is, He left the towns and took refuge away from the crush of the synagogue. He was followed by **a great multitude**, not just **from Galilee**, but also **from Judea** in the south and **from Jerusalem** itself. People came from farther afield too—**from Idumea** further south still, and **the other** *side* **of the Jordan**, and even from completely outside the sacred borders of Israel, in pagan **Tyre and Sidon** farther up the north coast. These had heard **all that He was doing** and came to see for themselves.

Such swelling crowds created a new problem. Jesus had healed so many that **as many as had afflictions** and plagues (literally "scourges") **fell on Him**, pressing on Him in their desperate determination to **touch Him** and find healing. The Lord therefore instructed His disciples **that a boat should wait on Him** and be in constant readiness, so that He might, if necessary, escape from the crowd, that they **might not crush Him** or inadvertently trample Him.

Our Lord's authority was not recognized only by these multitudes. The **unclean spirits** who beheld Him from within those they afflicted also recognized His authority and power. When the demoniacs were brought to Him, the demons within them **cried out** in despair, "*It is* **You** *who* **are the Son of God!**" (the **You** is emphatic in the Greek), in a futile attempt to prevent their expulsion. As with the demon in the synagogue (1:23f), He **rebuked** such talk, **lest they make Him manifest**. The nature of His Messiahship would not have been understood, and He did not want it noised abroad. He healed the demoniacs, not to prove anything, but out of love for them and out of compassion for their suffering. In relating the recognition of even the demons, Mark means to contrast this with the blindness of the Pharisees related in the previous sections. The *demons* can see He is the Son of God, Mark seems to say, but the *Pharisees* cannot see it—being blinder than the demons!

§III.2 Choice of the Twelve

ॐ ॐ ॐ ॐ ॐ

13 And He ascends the mountain and calls to *Him those* whom He Himself willed, and they came to Him.

14 And He made Twelve, that they might be with Him, and that He might send them out to herald

15 and to have authority to cast out the demons.

16 And He made the Twelve: Simon (to whom He gave the name Peter),

17 and James, the *son* of Zebedee, and John the brother of James (to them He gave the name Boanerges, which is "Sons of Thunder");

18 and Andrew, and Philip, and Bartholomew, and Matthew, and Thomas, and James the *son* of Alphaeus, and Thaddaeus, and Simon the Cananean,

19 and Judas Iscariot, who also delivered Him *up*.

Our Lord had many disciples, those who followed Him to hear what He had to say, but now, in the midst of great popularity, He moves to select twelve of them for a special destiny. Like Moses ascending Mount Sinai for communion with God, Jesus **ascends the mountain** (the historic present is used to describe this dramatic moment) and spends the entire night there in prayer to God (Luke 6:12). The choice of the Twelve is therefore the fruit of this prayer. The image recalls Moses calling others to join him in his mountain-top communion with God (see Ex. 19:20–24) and thus teaches that the Twelve are called to join the Lord in His divine mission, even as Aaron was called to join Moses.

The Twelve were **made** and appointed for a specific purpose: **that they might be with Him, and that He might send them out to herald** and proclaim His mission **and to have authority to cast out the demons.** That is, they were to be His special companions, learning His words that they might convey them to others, and sharing His authority to overthrow the kingdom of Satan and establish the Kingdom of God. They were thus not mere messengers, like slaves sent to carry a message. They were also His plenipotentiaries, bearers of His full authority, apostles.

The choice of twelve is also significant. Just as the twelve sons of

Jacob were the seed of the People of Israel, so the Twelve Apostles were to be the seed and beginning of the reborn and messianic Israel, the Church. (That is why, after the defection of Judas, another had to be chosen to take his place; see Acts 1:15–26.) Our Lord was not simply taking on helpers; He was laying the foundation for the renewal of the whole People of God.

Mark then gives the list of the Twelve, drawn it would seem from an already existing list, since he refers to Levi (mentioned in 2:14) now as **Matthew**, the name by which he was later known in the Church.

Simon comes at the head of the list, since he was the leader of the apostles, with the comment that the Lord **gave** him **the name Peter**. The name **Peter**, meaning "rock," is the Greek *Petros* and translates the original Aramaic *Kephas*. It was something of a nickname, alluding to Simon's potential for rocklike fidelity (or his rocklike stubbornness?—sometimes our frailties are also our strengths). This bestowal of a second name, however, was more than the giving of a simple nickname. It had a more formal quality, more like the changing of Abram's name to Abraham (Gen. 17:5), for it spoke of a change of destiny. Jesus, in taking it on Himself to rename Simon, was exercising the authority of God over him, for only God can truly bestow new names and give new destinies.

Simon is followed by **James** and **John**, the sons of Zebedee. The Lord gave new names to them too, calling them **Boanerges**, an Aramaic word meaning **"Sons of Thunder."** (This seems to have been more of a nickname than a formal change of name and destiny, since it was not a name bestowed on each individually, but a term to denote them as a pair. James and John were still individually called James and John.) The term **Boanerges** seems to refer to their ability to thunder and react forcefully (such as when they felt insulted by Samaritan villagers and wanted to rain down fire from God on them; Luke 9:52–54). (The actual Aramaic word remains a bit uncertain. The *Boan* part surely corresponds to *beni* or "sons," but the "thunder" part of the term remains elusive to contemporary linguists—a reminder to us that we do not know all the vernacular loan-words spoken by that generation, and an incentive to our humility in approaching the text.)

Next in the list comes **Andrew** (separated here from his brother Simon by the inclusion of James and John, since James and John joined Simon in forming an inner circle of three; see 5:37).

Philip, who was an early follower of the Lord (John 1:43), comes next, followed by **Bartholomew**. Bartholomew was in all likelihood the same as the Nathanael of John's Gospel. The synoptic Gospels all mention Bartholomew and not Nathanael, while John's Gospel mentions Nathanael and not Bartholomew. Nathanael was a friend of Philip and also an early disciple (John 1:45), and was present during the Resurrection appearances of Christ to His apostles (John 21:2). It would seem that he was known by both these names.

Next come **Matthew and Thomas**, then **James the *son* of Alphaeus** and **Thaddaeus** (called "Judas the son of James" in Luke 6:16; perhaps Judas was his name and Thaddaeus his preferred nickname?).

Next comes **Simon the Cananean**. The word **Cananean** is a transliteration of the Aramaic *Qanna* or "zealous," and is translated by Luke as "the Zealot" in Luke 6:15. He was, it would seem, a former Zealot, or member of the group dedicated to the liberation of Israel by military means. His joining Jesus required as much of an inner revolution as that of Matthew, the former tax collector.

Last in the group comes **Judas Iscariot, who also delivered Him *up*** and betrayed Him. For obvious reasons, he comes last in the list. His sin of betrayal came to define him, so that he was later known simply as "Judas the traitor" (see John 18:5). Like the other apostles, Judas once also did good works. Like them, he also preached and healed (Luke 9:1, 6; see Acts 1:17), but all these accomplishments were blotted out and forgotten because of this act of betrayal. Here is a warning for all of us. None of our good works and faith will avail to save us, if we fall away from Christ at the end. Perseverance is everything.

ॐ ॐ ॐ ॐ ॐ

§III.3 Opposition and Jesus' True Family

ॐ ॐ ॐ ॐ ॐ

20 And He comes into a house, and the crowd comes together again, so that they *themselves* could not eat bread.

21 And having heard this, His family went out to seize Him, for they were saying, "He is beside Himself."

22 And the scribes from Jerusalem, having come down, were saying, "He has Beelzebul," and, "By the ruler of the demons He casts out the demons."

23 And having called them to *Himself,* He spoke to them in parables: "How can Satan cast out Satan?

24 "And if a kingdom is divided-up against itself, that kingdom is not able to stand.

25 "And if a house is divided-up against itself, that house will not be able to stand.

26 "And if Satan has arisen against himself and has been divided-up, *he* will not be able to stand, but he has an end!

27 "But no one is able, having entered the strong *one's* house, to rob his possessions unless he first binds the strong *one*, and then he will rob his house.

28 "Amen I say to you, all will be forgiven the sons of men, the sins and the blasphemies, whatever they may blaspheme,

29 "but whoever blasphemes against the Holy Spirit does not have ever-forgiveness, but is guilty of an eternal sin,"

30 for they were saying, "He has an unclean spirit."

After narrating His choice of the Twelve, Mark then narrates the growing opposition in Israel to Christ and His mission, to throw into greater relief the fact that these disciples—the Twelve and others—were Christ's true family and the true Israel.

The story begins with Christ's return to **a house**, probably the house of Simon and Andrew, which He was using for His base of operations in Capernaum. When it was learned that He had returned, such a great **crowd** came together about Him that He and His disciples **could not eat bread**—that is, they were so busy that they did not even have time to eat a meal.

It was therefore out of concern for Him and His physical and mental health that **His family** decided on an intervention. The Greek there is not the usual word for "family," but is *oi par' autou*. This is a very general term, denoting not necessarily family but any of those nearby or close to one. They knew He was the center of controversy and was saying scandalous, crazy things, such as claiming the authority to forgive sins (see 2:1f). They therefore **went out** from Nazareth to Capernaum **to seize Him**, since they thought, **"He is beside Himself"** and delusional.

This unbelief was mirrored by **the scribes from Jerusalem**, an official delegation which had come to check Him out, concerned that He was spreading heresy and false doctrine. They thought He could not possibly be of God, since He did not (according to their own legalistic understanding) keep the Sabbath. Therefore, His miracles must have a demonic source—He had **Beelzebul**, the devil, in Him, and it was by the authority of this **ruler of the demons** that He **casts out the demons**.

In answer to this challenge, **He called them to** *Himself* and strove to reassure the people, speaking **in parables** and aphorisms, as He usually did.

In His first parabolic saying, He asks rhetorically, **"How can Satan cast out Satan?"** That would be self-contradictory—and a ludicrous sight, like someone trying to pick himself up physically to throw himself out!

What they were suggesting meant that there was a kind of civil war in Satan's realm, with Jesus forming some sort of rebel force and warring against His "master" Satan. That also could not be, for everyone knew that **if a kingdom** was **divided-up against itself**, that kingdom would **not** be **able to stand**, and if a **house** or family was **divided-up against itself**, that house also would **not** be **able to stand**. Such division, civil war, and rebellion would mean the effective end of whatever was divided. If Satan has **arisen against himself and has been divided-up**, *he* **will not be able to stand, but he has an end** and will not be able to oppress men anymore. But clearly that was not the case! Satan's kingdom, alas, was obviously as strong as ever. Clearly, then, it was not divided from within. Rather, it was being violently *attacked from without*. The Lord's exorcisms were not proof that there was internal rebellion in that kingdom of evil, but rather that the Kingdom of God was invading it and overthrowing it.

Continuing His use of parables, He said that it was like a home invasion. **"No one is able,"** He pointed out, **"having entered the strong *one's* house, to rob his possessions unless he first binds the strong *one*."** A well-armed man, guarding his house and possessions, will not simply allow a robber to come in and plunder him to his heart's content! Rather, he will violently and effectively resist such robbery. If a thief wants to rob the house of a strong man, he must first tie up the strong man—only then will he be able to **rob his house**. It was the same here with Satan. Satan was strong and capable of keeping his demon-possessed prey captive and secure. Christ was only able to plunder Satan of his prey and liberate those poor demon-possessed souls because He first overpowered Satan with His divine messianic authority. His exorcisms proved that Satan was being overcome.

Christ then made a solemn pronouncement, prefacing it with His customary **"Amen I say to you"** to indicate the divine authority and certainty of His Word, as if echoing and confirming the Word of His Father. **"All will be forgiven the sons of men,"** He said, **"but whoever blasphemes against the Holy Spirit does not have ever-forgiveness, but is guilty of an eternal sin."**

That is, if one repents, errors and sins can find forgiveness with God. In the Temple, at the altar of sacrifice, one could find remission for all sins, even **blasphemies, whatever** one **may blaspheme**. But what the Pharisees were doing was different altogether, for in saying that Christ had **an unclean spirit**, they were **blaspheming against the Holy Spirit**. Here was not a matter of insulting and misjudging men, but of setting oneself against all the work that God was doing on the earth. Christ was casting out demons by the power of **the Holy Spirit**, but they were attributing this power to the devil, thus pronouncing the Holy Spirit to be **unclean**. Such a sin, if unrepented, could **not have ever-forgiveness**. No amount of sacrifice in the Temple could expiate such a sin. It was **an eternal sin**, barring one from life in the eternal age to come. In other words, willful and deliberate rejection of Jesus as demonic excluded one from eternal life. The Pharisees, in rejecting Him like this, were on dangerous ground. Let not any of His hearers follow them!

(We note in passing that this is a sin which, by its very nature, cannot be committed unknowingly by Christians. As long as one sincerely confesses that Jesus is Lord, one cannot be guilty of this sin.)

ॐ ॐ ॐ ॐ ॐ

31 And His mother and His brothers come, and standing outside, they sent to Him, calling Him.

32 And a crowd was sitting around Him, and they say to Him, "Behold, Your mother and Your brothers *are* outside, seeking You."

33 And having answered them, He says, "Who are My mother and My brothers?"

34 And having looked-around on those around Him sitting *in a* circle, He says, "Behold My mother and My brothers!

35 "Whoever does the will of God, this *one* is My brother and sister and mother!"

Also challenging His authority (though not with such determined and dangerous obstinacy as the Pharisees who were blaspheming the Holy Spirit) were His family. This group included (but was perhaps not limited to) His **mother and** His **brothers**. They came to the house in which He was teaching a more intimate gathering of disciples and stood **outside**. They **sent** a message to Him, **calling Him**. That is, they implicitly demanded that He respect the superior authority of His family, break off teaching those disciples in the house, and come with them—probably home to Nazareth. What was demanded was not a brief audience, but the cessation of His mission and ministry. They had not come to talk with Him, but to "seize Him" (v. 21).

We may ask in passing what His mother was doing with this unbelieving crowd. Certainly His brothers did not believe in Him (John 7:5), but could it be that His own mother shared this unbelief?

It is impossible to think this. The Theotokos had received a heavenly visitation from the Archangel Gabriel, telling her that her virgin-born Son would be called the Son of God (Luke 1:35). Her kinswoman Elizabeth said that her own baby leapt with joy at the Virgin's holy approach, and she pronounced her blessed among women for the sake of her Child (Luke 1:41, 42). The Mother of God had heard the news of the angelic choir of praise from the local shepherds when He was born and treasured this in her heart (Luke 2:18, 19). Is it likely that she could forget all this? No; rather, what happened was that, as a powerless and poor widow with no other children (see the Excursus "On the Brothers of the Lord," page 85), she was brought along with them to be used as a kind of "bargaining chip." The Lord's unbelieving kinsmen hoped that her presence would add persuasiveness to their demands and make Him accompany them. The Theotokos, as a widow and a woman in a man's world, had little to say about it.

Her Son, however, was not one to be seized, nor deflected from His Father's will. He did not acknowledge that He was under any such human authority, nor subject any longer to any will save the Father's only. As He sat in the house of Simon and Andrew, with a group of disciples **around Him sitting** *in a* **circle**, His eyes **looked-around** the room, taking in those who had left the loyalties of the world to follow Him. Pointing to them, He says (the historic present is used, so that we can almost see His outstretched hand), **"Behold My mother and My brothers!"** Those who came to seize Him said that He must acknowledge the rights and claims of His family and remain with them. Here, He says in reply, is My true family! I am indeed acknowledging their claims, and remaining with them! **Whoever does the will of God** the Father, **this** *one* is His child—and therefore also **My brother and sister and mother!** Christ thereby rejected the claims of the world from having any binding authority over Him. He was refusing to obey those claims and be deflected from His mission of doing **the will of God**. In this way, He set the pattern for all who would follow Him as well. They too must reject the claims of family if it came to a choice between loyalty to them and loyalty to God and His Christ. Discipleship to Jesus means being adopted into a new family.

§III.4 Parables of the Kingdom

> ꗞ ꗞ ꗞ ꗞ ꗞ
>
> **4** 1 And again He began to teach by the sea. And a large crowd gathered together to Him so that He got into a boat to sit down in the sea, and all the crowd was near the sea on the land.
>
> 2 And He was teaching them with many parables, and was saying to them in His teaching,

Our Lord's popularity and the large crowds necessitated His teaching **sitting down** in a boat, with **the crowd near the sea on the land**. Thus not only was He safe from being trampled (see 3:9, 10), but He could also use the natural acoustics of the cove. His teaching used **many parables**. The word *parable* (Gr. *parabole*) literally means something "thrown beside" another, set down for comparison. The literary form was very diverse, including not only involved allegories such as the parable of the sower (vv. 3–8), but also proverbs, similitudes, fables, and other enigmatic utterances. By using such images, Jesus was able to reach the common man, appealing to the heart.

That meant, of course, that if the hearer's heart was open to truth, he would be able to perceive the true inner meaning, whereas if the heart was not open, he would not be able to perceive it. For the Lord was teaching about the nature of the Kingdom of God, and telling them that this Kingdom was not such as they had expected—or perhaps even wanted. They had thought that the Kingdom would come cataclysmically and in political form—that when Messiah came, He would rally an army of angels and men and sweep the sinner out of the land, exalting Israel to a place of power in the world. The Kingdom would thus come to all Jews equally, regardless of the state of their heart, regardless of their response.

This, however, was not the Kingdom that Jesus was bringing. Would they be able to put their prejudices aside and hear about the true nature of that Kingdom? That is why the Lord taught them of the Kingdom in parables. The true, teachable, and humble of heart would learn; but the unbelieving and stubborn would "see and not perceive," they would "hear and not have insight" (v. 12). In this way, the word of prophesied judgment spoken of in Isaiah 6:9f would be fulfilled. For God worked in Jesus not only to reward and call the humble, but also to judge and condemn the proud, "lest they turn back and it be forgiven them" (Is. 6:10).

꙳ ꙳ ꙳ ꙳ ꙳

3   "Listen! Behold, the sower went out to sow,

4   "and it came about that while sowing, some *seed* fell beside the road, and the birds came and ate it up.

5   "And others fell on the rocky *soil* where it did not have much earth, and immediately it sprang up because it did not have depth of earth,

6   "and after the sun had risen, it was burnt, and because it did not have a root, it withered.

7   "And others fell into the thorns, and the thorns came up and choked it out and it did not give *any* fruit.

8 "And others fell into the good earth and as they rose up and grew, they gave fruit and brought thirtyfold, sixtyfold, and a hundred-fold."

9 And He was saying, "He who has ears to hear, let him hear!"

10 And when He was alone, the ones around Him, along with the Twelve, were asking Him *concerning* the parables.

11 And He was saying to them, "To you has been given the mystery of the Kingdom of God, but those outside *have* all in parables,

12 "that while seeing, they may see and not perceive, and while hearing, they may hear and not have insight, lest they turn back and it be forgiven them."

13 And He says to them, "Do you not know this parable? And how will you know all the parables?

14 "The *one* sowing sows the Word.

15 "And these are the ones beside the road where the Word is sown, and when they hear, immediately Satan comes and takes the Word that is sown in them.

16 "And these are the ones sown on the rocky *places*, who when they hear the Word, immediately receive it with joy,

17 "and they do not have a root in themselves, but are temporary; then when tribulation or persecution because of the Word happens, immediately they stumble.

18 "And others are the ones sown among the thorns; these are the ones who have heard the Word,

19 "and the worries of the age and the deceitfulness of riches and the desires for the remaining

> things enter in and choke the Word, and it
> becomes unfruitful.
> 20 "And those are the ones sown on the good earth,
> who hear the Word and accept *it* and bear fruit,
> thirtyfold, sixtyfold, and a hundredfold."

St. Mark reproduces five of the Lord's parables as examples of His teaching, beginning with the parable of the Sower. In its basic form, this parable teaches that the Kingdom of God does not come cataclysmically and equally to all in Israel. All will not be saved and enjoy the Kingdom simply because they are Jews. Rather, their experience of the Kingdom will depend on the state of their individual hearts. If they have hard and unbelieving hearts, the Kingdom's coming will not profit them. It is only the true of heart and good who will know the blessedness of the Kingdom of God.

Thus, the Lord says, the coming of the Kingdom is like a **sower** of seed going out to sow. In those days, sowers would walk along narrow paths through the fields, throwing seed from a bag onto the wide earth. Inevitably, not all of the seed sown would fall into the fertile earth and germinate; some seed would be lost. This was the same with the coming Kingdom. Just as whether or not the seed germinated depended on the state of the soil, so the experience of salvation depended on the state of the hearer's heart.

Our Lord elaborates by pointing to the different types of soil. A **sower sowed** his seed, even as Christ and His disciples by their preaching spread **the Word**. Some of this seed **fell beside the road** where **the birds came and ate it up**. That is like the experience of those who hear the Word and **immediately Satan comes and takes the Word** from their hearts, as they listen to lies about Jesus (see 3:22). Just as this seed could not germinate, so also this seed of the Kingdom cannot bear fruit in their lives.

Some other of the seeds would **fall on the rocky *soil* where it did not have much earth**. This happened when seed would fall onto rocks that had a light covering of dirt. **Immediately** the seed would **spring up** without any real roots, and **after the sun had risen, it was burnt**. That is like the experience of those who give in to their own shallowness. They have no **root in themselves** so that their faith is only **temporary**. Though they receive the Word **with joy**, when **persecution** because of the Word happens, immediately they **stumble** and fall away into apostasy. Just as seed sown on the rock could not germinate, so also these shallow enthusiasts can bear no real fruit.

Some of the seeds sown by a sower would **fall into the thorns**, where the thorns would **choke out** the seed. That is like the experience of those who allow **the worries of the age and the deceitfulness of riches and the desires for the remaining things** to **enter in** to their hearts. Wealth, which promises fulfillment but cannot grant it, comes to dominate their lives. Such priorities claim their attention and energies and they are unwilling to make space for Christ's call in their lives. Just as seed sown among thorns cannot **give *any* fruit**, so attendance to such worldly concerns also makes the Kingdom of God **unfruitful** in the lives of those hearers.

Most of the seed sown, however, would **fall into the good earth** and so germinate and **grow** and **give fruit**. The crop varied, some places bearing a crop of **thirtyfold**, some **sixtyfold**, and some even **a hundredfold**. That is like the experience of those who respond to Jesus' message, **accepting** it and becoming His true disciples. In them and in them alone, the Kingdom of God comes and bears fruit, in some more than others, depending on the extent of their dedication. Thus, the blessing of the coming Kingdom does not depend on one's being a Jew, but on one's goodhearted response to Christ.

The meaning of this parable was not immediately apparent to His disciples, and **when He was alone**, they all asked Him to explain it. Christ did not rebuke them for their slowness, but affirmed that they, as His disciples, were privileged beyond other hearers in Israel. To them was **given the mystery of the Kingdom of God**. The word translated *mystery* is the Greek *musterion*, which means not something incomprehensible but something secret, something revealed only to the inner circle of the initiated. The disciples of Jesus were such. The Church, therefore, has the key to understand the inner meaning of God's salvation, while **those outside** the Church, "the pillar and bulwark of the truth" (1 Tim. 3:15), *have* **all in parables** and insoluble puzzles.

Christ is willing to enlighten **the Twelve** and those **around Him.** Without understanding this parable, they will not be able to **know** and understand **all the parables**, for this parable is basic. He therefore teaches them, giving them the key to understand all.

ॐ ॐ ॐ ॐ ॐ

21 And He was saying to them, "Does the lamp come to be put under the measure, or under the bed? Is it not to be put on the lampstand?

22 "For there is nothing hidden but to be made manifest; nor become secret but that it should come *to be* manifest.

23 "If any has ears to hear, let him hear!"

St. Mark then relates a second parable, that of **the lamp.** The Lord asked, **Does the lamp come** into a room in order **to be put under the measure, or under the bed?** Every evening, in every Jewish home, there would be the ritual of the lamp, when a lamp would be brought into the main room to give light to all, the ancients having a horror of the dark. When the lamp arrived, the pious Jews would recite a blessing, thanking God for the light. (This ritual was retained by the Christians, who would then recite a blessing thanking God for Christ as the true Light of the world. The evening hymn *Phos Hilaron* or "Gladsome Light" comes from this practice.) It is inconceivable, the Lord said, that one would bring the lamp into the room and then cover it up with **the measure** (Gr. *modios*—a word originally meaning a peck-measure containing about nine liters, but later used to mean a container of any size). Nor would they place it **under the bed** or the dining couch, where it could not be seen. Obviously, all knew that it was **put on the lampstand** so that all the darkness could be dispelled and its light could reach all.

In the same way, Christ had **come** in order to teach and illumine all His hearers. He had not come to speak and not be heeded. They must not listen to His Word and then do nothing about it. That would be as senseless as having **the lamp come** and then not using its light, but remaining in the dark! For just as the light of the lamp reached to all in the house, so Christ's light would eventually illumine all their deeds, as they would be judged on the Last Day. There was **nothing hidden** which would not then **be made manifest**, no deed or **secret** which would not **come** *to be* **manifest** and brought into the open. Let them not ignore His message; **if any had ears to hear** His Word, **let him hear!**

ॐ ॐ ॐ ॐ ॐ

24 And He was saying to them, "See *to it* what you hear. By what measure you measure it shall be measured to you, and it will be added to you.

25 "For he who has, it will be given to him; and he who does not have, even what he has will be taken from him."

Next is related the parable of the measure. All His hearers must **See** *to it* what they **hear** and take care not to hear with hard hearts. It is like a man having a **measure**. If one brings a big measure along to be used, then one receives a correspondingly big portion of whatever is being given away and **measured to him**. If one brings a small container, then one receives correspondingly little back. In the same way, we must take care to **hear** His message with big and generous and good hearts—then we will receive from God a suitably big helping of blessing and salvation. If we listen to Him with small, narrow, and suspicious hearts, we will receive little back from God. So the generous of heart, **he who has** God's blessing now, **will be given** more in the Kingdom if he hearkens to Christ; whereas **he who does not have** now, who keeps God at bay with his hard heart, will lose **even what he has** in the final judgment.

ॐ ॐ ॐ ॐ ॐ

26 And He was saying, "Thus the Kingdom of God is like a man who casts seed on the earth,

27 "and sleeps and rises, night and day, and the seed sprouts and grows, he does not know how.

28 "The earth bears fruit by itself; first the grass, then the head, then the full grain in the head.

29 "But when the fruit permits, he immediately sends forth the sickle because the harvest has come."

The fourth parable to be related was that of the secret seed. The Lord's hearers all assumed that the Kingdom would only come with their active assistance. When Messiah came to rally His army of angels, they too must take up arms and fight! They saw the Kingdom in military and political terms, and as requiring their help. On the contrary, the Lord says to them, **the Kingdom of God is like a man who casts seed on the earth, and sleeps and rises, night and day.** A farmer gets a crop by putting seed into the earth and then passively and patiently waiting. The farmer does not help the seed grow. It grows without his assistance—and even when he is unconscious! He goes to bed and sleeps by night and rises up by day, and all by itself **the seed sprouts and grows**—how **he does not know.** Just as **the earth bears fruit by itself**, so the Kingdom will come without the military assistance of men. The Zealots' arms cannot hasten the Kingdom. It will grow at its own rate—**first the grass, then the head, then the full grain in the head.** The long-awaited judgment will come at its own time, but not until **the fruit permits.** Only when God decides the time is right will He judge and consume sinners from the earth (Ps. 104:35). Just as the farmer will only come with the sickle when **the harvest** is ripe, so too God will only **send forth the sickle** of judgment at the appointed time of the end. Let not the Zealots misunderstand the nature of the Kingdom in this age and try to alter God's timing and plan.

ॐ ॐ ॐ ॐ ॐ

30 And He was saying, "How will we liken the Kingdom of God, or by what parable will we present it?

31 "—like a mustard seed, which when sown on
   the earth, *is* smaller than all the seeds that are
   on the earth,
32 "yet when it is sown, it comes up and becomes
   greater than all the vegetables and makes large
   branches, so that the birds of the heaven are
   able to nest under its shadow."

The last parable to be related was the parable of the mustard seed. The Lord asks them the question, **"How will we liken the Kingdom of God?"** What image or **parable** would be fit to convey its nature to them? **"A mustard seed!"** the Lord says. It is of proverbial smallness, **smaller than all the seeds that are on the earth.** But despite its small size, when **it comes up** and sprouts, it **becomes greater than all the vegetables** and other plants sown in the garden. Indeed, it forms **large branches, so that the birds of the heaven** were able to **nest under its shadow.** The image was drawn from such Old Testament passages as Ezekiel 17:23, which spoke of the Kingdom of God growing tall above all the other kingdoms of men, like a tree tall enough to provide the birds with shelter.

The people needed such an image of the Kingdom and the visible reminder from the mustard seeds growing around them. The ministry of Jesus seemed to be small and insignificant. What was He and His ragtag gathering of common people, tax collectors, and sinners? He had no outward glory, no mighty army, no important political connections. *This* was the Kingdom of God which would topple earthly kingdoms and overthrow sin from the earth? Not likely! But they must remember the mustard seed. It too was small—yet would later grow to be greater than all the other garden plants. So too Jesus' own ministry and authority would later grow to fill the cosmos. Though seemingly insignificant now, He would one day sit at the right hand of God's majesty so that, at His Name, all the universe would bow.

༄ ༄ ༄ ༄ ༄

> 33 And with many similar parables He was speaking the Word to them as they were able to hear,
> 34 and He did not speak to them without a parable, but privately to *His* own disciples He was settling all.

St. Mark concludes with a statement that these five parables were not the only ones Jesus used. Rather, here was a mere selection of them. He used the parables to measure out the truth to them **as they were able to hear**, according to the openness of their heart to receive such things. But *His* **own disciples** had all His truth. **Privately** to them, **He was settling all** their perplexities and explaining all.

§III.5 Christ's Authority over All

Next are related three miracles, showing Christ's authority over the violence of nature (4:35–41), over demons (5:1–20), and even over sickness and death (5:21–43). Demonstrations of such power provoked the question, "Who then is this?" who could perform such miracles (4:41). The reader is meant to understand that the miracles themselves answered that question and revealed "the carpenter, the son of Mary" (6:3) to be the Son of the Most High God (see 5:7).

> ॐ ॐ ॐ ॐ ॐ
> 35 And He says to them on that day, when evening had come, "Let us go across to the other side."
> 36 And leaving the crowd, they take Him with *them* in the boat, as He was, and other boats were with Him.
> 37 And there arises a great storm of wind, and the waves were beating against the boat so that the boat was already filling.

38 And He *Himself* was in the stern, on the cushion, sleeping, and they rouse Him and say to
   Him, "Teacher, does it not matter to You that
   we are perishing?"
39 And being roused, He rebuked the wind and
   said to the sea, "Be silent, be muzzled!" And
   the wind ceased and a great calm happened.
40 And He said to them, "Why are you cowardly?
   Do you not have faith?"
41 And they were very afraid and were saying to
   one another, "Who then is this, that even the
   wind and the sea obey Him?"

The story begins with the drama of the historic present, as Jesus
**says to them when evening had come, "Let us go across to the
other side."** Evidently Christ was exhausted—for He was able to
sleep through a storm! There were **other boats with Him**, hemming
Him in, and it was out of a desire to escape from this crowd that He
commanded His disciples to **go across to the other side**, to the east
of the Sea of Galilee, where He could find rest—notwithstanding
that a storm seemed to be brewing.

Indeed, such storms could sweep down quite suddenly on the Sea
of Galilee, and one such storm assaulted them on the lake now. In
St. Mark's vivid narrative (in which he continues to use the historic
present), one can almost feel the boat writhing on the waves and
feel the cold water on the face. **There arises a great storm of wind**,
he says, which threw wave after wave against the little boat, filling it
up and threatening to capsize it and drown them all. Jesus, however,
was in the stern on the little **cushion** which was usually kept under
the seat for passengers. As God's beloved, He was asleep, resting in
the Father's protection (see Ps. 127:2).

His disciples, however, had no such faith in God's protection!
Though experienced fishermen and intimately familiar with this
lake and all its perils, they were terrified. **They rouse Him** (again the
historic present is used—we can almost see them shaking Him), and
they cry out against the lashing wind, **"Teacher, does it not matter**

71

to You that we are perishing?" (We note an element of exasperation and rebuke in this question, no doubt born of their terror.)

He does not immediately answer their question (and what answer could He give—that their lives *did* matter to Him?). Rather, being thoroughly **roused** and wide awake, He **rebuked the wind** and **the sea** and said, **"Be silent, be muzzled!"**—two simple words in the Greek original—*siopa, pephimoso*—and with these couple of words changes their world. **The wind ceased and a great calm happened** instantly. Rebuking the violence of nature in the same way that He rebuked the violent demons (see 1:25), He demonstrated His complete and serene authority over the sea and its untamable waves.

Having dealt with the present peril, He then turns back to deal with them—with a kind of rebuke of His own. **"Why are you cowardly?"** He asks them. (The word in Greek is *deilos*—used also of the cowards of Rev. 21:8.) **"Do you not have faith?"** That is, how could they imagine that God would let the Messiah and His chosen disciples drown in the sea?

The disciples, for their part, **were very afraid** at such an exercise of naked power. All knew that the waves of the sea were rebellious and untamable, a remnant of the primeval chaos and flood that once engulfed the world. For the Jews, the sea was no object of romantic longing—no "sea fever" for them! The sea was a place of restless evil and unpredictable threat. It was only God Himself who could tame the sea (see Job 38:8–11). Yet here was Jesus rebuking its violence almost casually, with complete confidence in His authority —and commanding the sea's instant obedience! No wonder that the disciples were cowed before such power and could not forbear to whisper among themselves (perhaps after Christ returned to His interrupted sleep), **"Who then is this, that even the wind and the sea obey Him?"**

ॐ ॐ ॐ ॐ ॐ

5 1 And they came to the other side of the sea, into the region of the Gerasenes.

2   And having come out of the boat, immediately there met Him out of the tombs a man with an unclean spirit,

3   who had a dwelling among the tombs. And no one was able to bind him any longer, not *even* with a chain,

4   for he had often been bound with fetters and chains and the chains had been torn *in pieces* by him and the fetters broken and no one was strong *enough* to subdue him.

5   And through all *the* night and day, among the tombs and in the mountains, he was crying out and bruising himself with stones.

6   And having seen Jesus from afar, he ran and worshipped Him,

7   and having cried out with a great voice, he says, "What am I to You, Jesus Son of the Most High God? I adjure You by God, do not torture me!"

8   For He was saying to him, "Come out from the man, you unclean spirit!"

9   And He was asking him, "What *is* your name?" And he says to Him, "My name *is* Legion, for we are many."

10   And he was urging Him greatly not to send them outside of the region.

11   Now there was on the mountain a great herd of pigs feeding.

12   And they urged Him, saying, "Send us into the pigs that we may enter into them."

13   And He allowed them. And having come out, the unclean spirits entered into the pigs, and the herd rushed down the slope into the sea, about two thousand *pigs*, and were drowned in the sea.

14   And the ones feeding *them* fled and reported *it* in the city and in the country. And they

> came to see the thing that had happened.
>
> 15 And they come to Jesus and observe the man who had been demon-possessed sitting, clothed and sound-minded, the one who had had the legion, and they were afraid.
>
> 16 And those who had seen it described to them how it had happened to the demon-possessed man and about the pigs.
>
> 17 And they began to urge Him to go away from their area.
>
> 18 And as He was embarking in the boat, the man who had been demon-possessed urged Him that he might be with Him.
>
> 19 And He did not let him, but says to him, "Go away to your house, to your *people*, and report to them what the Lord has done for you, and that He had mercy on you."
>
> 20 And he went away and began to herald in Decapolis what Jesus had done for him, and all marveled.

It would seem that the Lord arrived on the eastern shore during the night. Stepping ashore under the moonlight, He was in the region of **the Gerasenes**—i.e. near to what is now the town of Kersa, a mile or so to the south. He was now in a predominantly Gentile area, where He might expect some rest from the demands of His ministry in Israel.

He was, however, not to find such rest. For as soon as He had disembarked, **immediately there met Him out of the tombs a man with an unclean spirit**. This poor wretch was apparently something of a local celebrity, famous for his extreme misery and his demonically supernatural strength. He **had often been bound with fetters** on his feet and with **chains** around his arms, no doubt by his distressed family, who thereby desired to **subdue him** and take him home. But the demons within him resisted such intervention. As often as his loved ones tried to take him home, the demons drove him to **tear** *in pieces* those **chains** and break those **fetters**. Overcoming all who sought to overpower and restrain him, he would tear himself free from them and run off back to the desolation of the **tombs**, where he had made **a dwelling** for himself. There, far from love and hope, he remained in the hellish prison of his insanity, naked to the elements, **crying out** with mad misery **through all** *the* **night and day**, having none but a fellow lunatic for his company (see Matt. 8:28), and **bruising himself with stones** in a frenzy of self-destruction.

In St. Mark's narration of the events, his enthusiasm for telling the demon's helplessness before the power of Christ outstrips his concern for consecutive order. The consecutive order of events seems to be as follows.

In the eerie moonlight, the wretched demoniac saw Christ **from afar** and the spirits within him recognized their Judge. The man **ran** up to Jesus and **worshipped Him**—that is, he bowed down before Him in desperate (and perhaps wordless) supplication. The Lord, in response, said to him, **"Come out from the man, you unclean spirit!"**

The spirit then quailed before Jesus' sovereign authority (Mark loves this part and in his narrative rushes to relate it). The spirit therefore **cried out with a great voice** of fear and said, **"What am I to You, Jesus Son of the Most High God? I adjure You by God, do not torture me!"** That is, the demon recognized in Christ the final Judge of the Last Day, and feared that the final torture of Gehenna was at hand. The spirit desperately invoked the name of God, in a vain attempt to ward off Jesus' power.

The Lord continued to exercise His authority over the spirit, demanding, **"What** *is* **your name?"** for knowledge of one's name gave authority over the one named. The spirit could not resist Christ's question. **"My name** *is* **Legion,"** it confessed, **"for we are many."** Many spirits had indeed invaded the poor maniac. A Roman legion consisted of six thousand soldiers, and by taking this name, the ruling spirit within indicated that a tremendous invasion had taken place.

The spirits **urged** Christ **greatly not to send them outside of** the region, that is, into the abyss of final judgment. Rather, they requested to be allowed to leave voluntarily and enter into the great herd of pigs that was then feeding on the hillside nearby. If the Lord had forced them to leave by expelling them against their will, no doubt the cost to the demoniac would have been very great. Later on, when the Lord forcibly expelled a single demon from a boy, that demon convulsed the boy so badly that he nearly died (9:26). Perhaps it was out of compassion for the man that Christ allowed such a multitude of demons within him to leave voluntarily and enter into the pigs, lest the man be even more terribly convulsed and hurt.

Whatever His reason, the Lord did allow them to come out and enter the herd. The herd reacted unexpectedly—they stampeded in panic and rushed down the slope into the sea—all two thousand of them—and finally drowned in the sea.

The ones feeding and tending the herd were aghast. The slope was perhaps a mere forty yards from the shore and they could quickly come to investigate. Climbing down the steep bank, they would have seen their vast herd dead and floating in the lake, with the famous lunatic (and his demoniac companion, whom the Lord also included in His mercy; see Matt. 8:29f) sitting calmly by the Lord, taking from the disciples one of their extra cloaks. Astonished, the swineherds fled and reported it in the city and in the country, telling all they met about this incredible nocturnal act of power and the resulting carnage.

As the day was dawning, many from the city and the surrounding farms came to see the thing that had happened. Coming to the scene, they observed the man who had been demon-possessed sitting down calmly, clothed now for the first time in perhaps years and sound-minded, in his right mind and fully self-controlled. When they asked what had happened, it would seem the herdsmen could not be restrained from repeating their tale! For those who had seen it described to them how it had happened to the demon-possessed man and—what was perhaps more important to herdsmen charged with protecting the herd—about the pigs!

The people did not understand, we may think, about the

authority of the Jewish Messiah. What they *did* understand was that this Man had power, and could be dangerous. They were afraid of such power, and **began to urge Him to go away from their area**.

The Lord, who stayed in foreign Samaria when the Samaritans begged Him to stay (John 4:40), left when these Gentiles begged Him to leave. For Christ, the Lover of mankind and the Maker of free will, does not linger where He is unwelcome.

In that fearful crowd of foreigners, there was at least one who would cling to Him. The saved knew the Savior, and wanted to join Him. As the Lord was **embarking in the boat** and in the act of leaving, the former demoniac was overcome at the thought of being separated from his Benefactor. He seems to have rushed to Him, **urging** and begging to **be with Him** as one of His disciples, even as his countrymen had **urged** Him to leave.

The Lord, however, **did not let him**. He knew that the man's place was now with his loved ones, who had long yearned for his healing and his return. The Lord therefore tells him (Mark again uses the historic present), **"Go away to your house, to your *people*."** He was to report to them **what the Lord** God of Israel **had done** for him, and how **He had mercy** on him. Significantly, the man went away as commanded and reported **what Jesus had done** for him. Though told to declare the works of God, he in fact declared and **heralded** to all in the surrounding **Decapolis** the works of Jesus. By saying this, St. Mark means the reader to understand how Jesus exercises all the power and authority of God on earth, as His true and divine Messiah.

---

৯৯ ৯৯ ৯৯ ৯৯ ৯৯

21 And Jesus having crossed over again in the boat to the other *side*, a great crowd gathered about Him; and He was by the sea.

22 And one of the synagogue-rulers by *the* name *of* Jairus comes up and having seen Him, falls at His feet,

23 and greatly urges Him, saying, "My *little*

daughter is at the end; come and put *Your* hand on her, that she may be saved and live."

24 And He went with him, and a large crowd was following Him and crushing together on Him.

25 And a woman was there who had had a flow of blood for twelve years,

26 and had suffered much under many physicians, and had spent all she had and had not benefited, but rather had *come* to *be* worse.

27 Having heard about Jesus, and having come behind *Him* in the crowd, she touched His garment.

28 For she said, "If I even touch His garments, I will be saved."

29 And immediately the fountain of her blood was dried up, and she knew in *her* body that she was cured of her scourge.

30 And immediately Jesus, really-knowing in Himself that the power from Him had gone forth, turned back in the crowd and said, "Who touched My garments?"

31 And His disciples said to Him, "You see the crowd crushing together on You, and You say, 'Who touched Me?'"

32 And He looked around to see the one who had done this.

33 Now the woman was afraid and trembling, knowing what had happened to her; she came and fell before Him and told Him all the truth.

34 And He said to her, "Daughter, your faith has saved you; go in peace and be healthy, *relieved* from your scourge."

35 While He was speaking, they come from *the house of* the synagogue-ruler, saying, "Your daughter has died; why still harass the Teacher?"

36 But Jesus, having overheard the word spoken, says to the synagogue-ruler, "Do not be afraid, only believe."

37 And He did not allow anyone to follow along after Him, except Peter and James and John the brother of James.

38 And they come into the house of the synagogue-ruler; and He observes an uproar, and weeping and much wailing.

39 And having entered in, He says to them, "Why make an uproar and weep? The child has not died, but is sleeping."

40 And they laughed at Him. But casting them all out, He takes along the child's father and mother and those with Him, and goes in where the child was.

41 And seizing the hand of the child, He says to her, "Talitha, kum!" (which is, being translated, "*Young* girl, I say to you, arise!"

42 And immediately the *young* girl rose and walked, for she was twelve years *of age*. And immediately they were beside themselves in a great ecstasy *of amazement*.

43 And He strictly gave orders to them that no one should know this; and He said to give her *something* to eat.

In this last of the series of three miracles showing Christ's authority, the Lord demonstrates His power over sickness and even death. Having returned from the region of the Gerasenes to the western side of the lake (probably near Capernaum), He was mobbed again by **a great crowd** as He was teaching **by the sea** of Galilee. It was there that **one of the synagogue-rulers by** *the* **name** *of* Jairus came through the crowd to find Him. Synagogue-rulers were lay officials of the local synagogue. As the co-equal head with the other rulers of the synagogue and the one whose task it was to take care of the building itself and arrange for the conduct of the services, he was a man of some importance and wealth.

He was also a father, and one who was almost beside himself with distress. He had a twelve-year-old daughter who, when he left her, was **at the end** and was dying. No doubt he ran from his house to where Jesus was as soon as he heard that He had returned. Every second seemed to count as he forced his way through the crowd to find the Lord. In the parallel account in Matthew's Gospel, he is reported as saying that she had "just died" (Matt. 9:18); he no doubt breathlessly blubbered out a confused account of both her state when he left her and his worst fears for the present. Suppressing a rising sense of urgency and panic, he **greatly urged** and entreated the Lord to come and **put** His **hand on her, that she may be saved and live.** The Lord then **went with him** along with the **large crowd** that **was following Him and crushing together on Him.** This huge multitude started laboriously to make its way through town to the house of the desperate man.

There was, however, in that crowd someone almost as desperate as the ruler of the synagogue—**a woman** of the town **who had had a flow of blood for twelve years.** That is, she had an internal hemorrhage. Her desperation was due not only to the fact that she **had suffered much under many physicians, and had spent all she had and had not benefited, but rather had** *come* **to** *be* **worse.** Her desperation was also due to the fact that she was considered unclean because of the flow, and could not have any physical contact with other people without rendering them unclean as well. Her condition was not only one of physical sickness, but also one of social and spiritual isolation. She could not attend synagogue nor worship God in the Temple. The pious would avoid her touch, and she could not enter a crowd without spreading contagion. How then could she come to Jesus, since He was always surrounded by a crowd?

In her desperation, she decided on a course of action: she would enter the crowd without telling anyone and come to Jesus secretly. When everyone else was also jostling and pressing on Him, something unavoidable in such a crowd, she would quickly reach out and grab His outer garment (probably by the fringes that pious Jews wore on the corners of their robes, in obedience to Num. 15:39). Jesus would, she thought, be none the wiser that she had touched Him, and thus she would be spared the rebuke she thought would be inevitable if He knew that an unclean woman had touched Him. For her part, she would be **saved** and delivered from her afflicting **scourge**, for she knew that even the garments of holy men could convey their power (see Acts 19:12).

In accordance with this plan, she moved through the multitude of jostling men and women, came up **behind** *Him* **in the crowd** and quickly **touched His garment.** She received immediate healing and **knew in** *her* **body that she was cured,** perhaps feeling a surge of healing warmth. Jesus, she thought, would continue on, unaware of her, and she could gratefully slip home.

The Son of God, however, was not unaware. **Really-knowing** (Gr. *epiginosko*) that **the power from Him had gone forth** by the will of the Father, He stopped in His tracks and **turned back in the crowd** with the seemingly inane question, **"Who touched Me?"** (We may imagine the effect of this apparently perverse delay and question on the father of the dying girl, for whom every second was precious.) The woman, no doubt, also stopped dead in her tracks, her heart sinking, a fear of being furiously rebuked growing within her. In Old Testament times, when Gehazi sought to deceive the prophet Elisha, he earned not only a stunning rebuke but the curse of God, when the leprosy of the recently healed Naaman clung to him (2 Kings 5:25–27). Would the prophet of Nazareth curse her too—perhaps bringing her scourge back on her permanently? No wonder she **was afraid and trembling!**

The crowd was also perplexed at the question. In the long pause that followed the question, His disciples sought to end the impasse by calling their Master to some sort of sense. They asked Him, perhaps with gentle exasperation, **"You see the crowd crushing together on You, and You say, 'Who touched Me?'"** But the Lord was immovable—both psychologically and physically!—and **looked around to see the one who had done this.** There was nothing for it—the woman knew she had been found out. She came before Him with pounding heart and **told Him all the truth.** But instead of finding the expected rebuke, she found the mercy of God. Jesus addressed her tenderly as **daughter** and told her, "**Your faith has saved you; go in peace and be healthy,** *relieved* **from your scourge.**" He was quite unconcerned about any possible contagion of uncleanness (even as He had been unconcerned about the contagion of leprosy; see 1:41). His power was stronger than sickness and contagion, and these dark forces gave way before His sovereign authority.

The delay, while it meant salvation for the woman, proved disaster for the father of the dying girl. Confirming his worst fears, **while He was speaking** to the woman, messengers came **from** *the house of* the **synagogue-ruler**, pushing their way through the crowd to bring their sad and dreaded message. "**Your daughter has died,**" they said to the father as he was wringing his hands in anguish and wordlessly urging the Lord to haste. "**Why still harass the Teacher?**" There was nothing left, they thought, but to return to the house of death and bury the young girl. Indeed, the professional mourners, expecting her imminent death, had been waiting at the house from before his departure. He would find them wailing her death when he returned.

As the Lord watched the anguished father begin to fall apart, He spoke His word of comfort, bringing comfort such as only God can give. "**Do not be afraid,**" He told him, "**only believe.**"

The Lord continued the trek to the father's house, the father in an agony, balanced between faith and despair. When the Lord came to the house, He **observes** the expected **uproar** (St. Mark uses the historic present, as if to allow us onsite participation in the events that follow). The custom of that day was for even a poor man to provide two flute-players and one professional mourner to wail for the death of such a loved one. The rich synagogue-ruler must have had many more there, so that there was indeed **weeping and much wailing.**

The Lord **entered in** to the house where the dead child lay and began His work. At the door, He encountered the professional mourners, engaged in their sad flute-playing and wailing, each note falling like a blow on the heart of the father. Compassionately, the Lord denied such work was needed. "**Why make an uproar and**

weep?" He said to them. "**The child has not died, but is sleeping.**"
With the proud contempt of those who are confident in their own
wisdom, **they laughed at Him**, knowing she was truly dead. The
Lord, however, took decisive action and **cast them all out.** He allowed only **the child's father and mother** and His own inner circle
of **those with Him** (that is, **Peter, James, and John the brother of
James**) to accompany Him—the father and mother because of their
relation to the child, His disciples as witnesses of His work. Entering
the room where the child was lying dead, and **seizing the hand of
the child** with His life-giving grip, **He says to her, "Talitha, kum!"**
The words are translated as "*Young* **girl, I say to you, arise!**" but
St. Mark records the actual Aramaic words, which had so burned
their way into the heart of St. Peter the eyewitness that he could
still hear them in his mind years later. With these two simple and
casual words, Christ rolled back the presence of death itself, as One
having the very authority of God.

Immediately the *young* **girl rose** in obedience to that word **and
walked**—so completely was she restored and full of youthful energy.
And not only full of energy, but hungry! Her parents were **beside
themselves in a great ecstasy** *of amazement* (a difficult phrase to
translate; in Gr. *exestesan ekstasei megale*). The Lord knew that report
of such a miracle going out would make it even more difficult for
Him to enter a city (see 1:45), so **He strictly gave orders to them that
no one should know this.** St. Mark, with a human and somewhat
humorous touch, adds the mundane detail that He also said that
they should **give** the hungry girl *something* **to eat!** The parents were
lost in their own ecstatic and tearful joy; the Lord was in tune with
the young girl. No doubt the first thing she said was, "I'm hungry!"
and the Lord, ever the lover of children, was concerned that she
be fed.

All of these miracles (stilling the storm, casting out the "Legion,"
healing the sick woman, and raising the dead child) revealed the
Lord's authority as the divine Son of God. They form the back-
drop for the next story St. Mark relates, that of His rejection at
Nazareth—which prefigures the final rejection by all Israel at the
Cross.

ॐ ॐ ॐ ॐ ॐ

§III.6 Christ's Rejection at Nazareth

ॐ ॐ ॐ ॐ ॐ

6 1 And He went out from there and comes into His hometown; and His disciples follow Him.

2 And when *the* Sabbath came, He began to teach in the synagogue; and many listening were thunderstruck, saying, "Where did this one *get* these things, and what *is* the wisdom given to Him, and such works of power as these which happen through His hands?

3 "Is not this the carpenter, the son of Mary, and brother of James and Joses and Judas and Simon; and are not His sisters here with us?" And they stumbled at Him.

From His base at Capernaum, the Lord went south to His **hometown** of Nazareth, accompanied by His disciples. On the next **Sabbath**, He **began to teach in the synagogue** as was His custom, speaking authoritatively of the Kingdom of God and His central place in inaugurating it. From the parallel passage in Luke 4:16–30, we know that He was commenting on the messianic passage in Isaiah 61:1–2 and telling his hearers how that promised Kingdom was coming on them even as He spoke.

The **many listening** to Him that day **were thunderstruck** at the thought that He, whom they had known all their lives and who came from common stock like them, could possibly be the Messiah. Indeed, He was by trade a simple **carpenter** like His father before Him! His family was well-known in town—the very ordinary **James and Joses and Judas and Simon**, and **His sisters** too. They were mystified that He now taught with such authority, and they asked themselves, **"Where did this one *get* these things, and what *is* the wisdom given to Him?"** Obviously, they thought, Jesus could not be the Messiah—what was the source then of His self-confident words and such miraculous **works of power** as He was performing? There is a hint in their question that the source of these might be demonic, as the Pharisees were suggesting (3:22). Thus **they stumbled at Him**, taking offense that such a One should claim such things for Himself. Their disrespect for Him is seen in their calling Him **the son of Mary**. Even when a man's father had died (as Joseph His foster-father had apparently done), it was still the invariable custom to refer to a man as "so-and-so the son of (father's name)." To call a man the son of his mother was to imply that one did not know who the father was—i.e. that he was illegitimate. It would appear that the Lord's Virgin Birth and Mary's being found to be pregnant before her marriage to Joseph (see Matt. 1:18ff) had given rise to ugly rumors.

❧ EXCURSUS
ON THE BROTHERS OF THE LORD

Mention of the "brothers of the Lord," named as "James, Joses" (in Matthew's Gospel, "Joseph," an obvious variant for Mark's "Joses"), "Judas and Simon," and of His "sisters," have prompted many to ask the precise relationship of these kinsmen to Jesus. In particular, were they the children of Mary the Theotokos, or not? If not, whose children were they?

Mere use of the term "brother" (Gr. *adelphos*) is of little help one way or the other. The word has the same elasticity of meaning in Greek as in Hebrew, where it means any blood-relative. (Thus Lot is referred to in Genesis 14:14 as Abraham's "brother," even though he was in fact his nephew.) The term *adelphos* can mean the child of the same mother; it can equally well mean simply a near blood-relative.

What is more relevant is that two of the names of the Lord's "brothers" show up again in the Gospels. In Mark 15:40, James and Joses are again mentioned as children of "Mary," just as Matthew 27:56 mentions James and Joseph. The question is: Who are these James and Joses/Joseph?

In 15:40, St. Mark speaks of "Mary the mother of James the Little and Joses" as if these two men were already known. Obviously, they are the same men he previously mentioned in our present passage of 6:3. If these are not the same men, then we must conclude that St. Mark mentions James and Joses in chapter 6 and then *a completely different James and Joses* in chapter 15. It is apparent that the mention in chapter 15 is meant to refer back to the men already introduced in chapter 6, and that they are in fact the same men.

It seems also undeniable (with all due respect to such exegetes as St. John Chrysostom) that the "Mary" mentioned in 15:40 as "the mother of James the Little and Joses" *cannot be* Mary the Theotokos and Mother of Jesus. It seems inconceivable that the Theotokos would be identified at the Cross as "the mother of James the Little and Joses" and not as "the mother of Jesus," whose Passion was then being related.

This episode of the women at the Cross may be looked at more closely. In Mark's Gospel (15:40), the women there present were: (1) Mary Magdalene; (2) Mary the mother of James and Joses; and (3) Salome. In Matthew's Gospel (27:56), they are listed as: (1) Mary Magdalene; (2) Mary the mother of James and Joseph; and (3) the mother of the sons of Zebedee. In John's Gospel (19:25), they are listed as: (1) Jesus' Mother; (2) His Mother's sister, Mary wife of Clopas; and (3) Mary Magdalene. (This assumes that "His Mother's sister" and "Mary wife of Clopas" are the same person; otherwise we would have the odd situation of "His Mother's sister" being left nameless and another person, "Mary wife of Clopas," mentioned, who was otherwise unknown. It seems clear that "Mary wife of Clopas" *was* "His Mother's sister.")

I would suggest that "Mary mother of James and Joses" (in Mark's list) is the same person as "His Mother's sister, Mary wife of Clopas" (in John's list). Some historical confirmation of this surmise comes from Eusebius's work,

History of the Church (3.33). In this work, Eusebius quotes the previous historical work of Hegesippus, who, as Eusebius said, "belonged to the first generation after the apostles." Hegesippus affirmed that Clopas was the brother of St. Joseph, the Lord's foster-father, and was therefore the uncle of the Lord. If this assertion is true, it would mean that "Mary wife of Clopas" (John 19:25) was the Lord's aunt, and was the Theotokos' "sister" in that she was actually her sister-in-law. This would fit the Gospel accounts perfectly. It means that the "brothers" of the Lord were actually His first cousins—as St. Jerome said, many centuries ago.

There were other surmises in the early Church also. The popularity in the East of the apocryphal work *The Proto-Gospel of James*, which proposed that the Lord's "brothers" were actually children of Joseph by a previous marriage, meant that many Orthodox accepted this surmise as the true one. However, I would prefer St. Jerome's position. For otherwise we must accept that the "James and Joses" mentioned in 6:3 are completely different from the James and Joses mentioned again in 15:40, and it seems clear that St. Mark means us to identify these men as one and the same pair. All this does not mean, however, that the Eastern tradition of Joseph having children from a previous marriage is untrue, for Christ could have both stepbrothers and cousins. It would suggest, though, that the "brothers" mentioned here in Mark 6:3 are to be identified with those cousins.

ॐ ॐ ॐ ॐ ॐ

4   And Jesus said to them, "A prophet is not dishonored except in his hometown and among his relatives and in his house."

5   And He could do no work of power there except that He laid His hands on a few infirm and healed them.

6   And He marveled at their unbelief.

The Lord discounts their lack of acceptance as irrelevant and without significance. He ironically and wryly observes that a true prophet is always honored—except, of course, in **his hometown and among his relatives and in his house!** It is only among those closest to him that the true prophet finds **dishonor**—a reference to the fact that the prophets of old were consistently rejected by Israel. Thus, the Lord's rejection by His hometown does not somehow tarnish or diminish His credibility. Their rejection of Him was consistent with Israel's rejection of all their prophets—and a sign that Israel would be judged (see Luke 4:24–27).

Nazareth did not take our Lord's response very well—in fact, the parallel passage in Luke's Gospel says that they rose up to throw Him out of town and down the nearby cliff (Luke 4:29)! Nazareth as a whole rejected His claims and authority, so that **He could do no work of power there**, finding none worthy or receptive. There were **a few infirm** people who believed in Him and on these He **laid His hands** and **healed them**. But the city as a whole rejected Him, so that **He marveled at their unbelief**. This is one of the two instances in the Gospels where Christ was said to **marvel** and be amazed (the other being at the Gentile centurion's faith in Matt. 8:10). What the Son of God found truly amazing was faith among the Gentiles (where one would not expect to find it) and the lack of it in Israel (where one would expect to find it). He had done so many wondrous works among the chosen and covenant People. Their rejection of Him in the face of it was perverse and inexplicable.

§III.7 Mission of the Twelve

ॐ ॐ ॐ ॐ ॐ

6b And He was going around the villages in a circuit *and* teaching.

7 And He calls *to Him* the Twelve and began to send them out two *by* two, and He was giving them authority over the unclean spirits;

8 and He ordered them that they should take

> nothing for *the* road, except only a staff, not bread, not a bag, not copper-*coins* for the belt,
>
> 9 but to be shod with sandals. And (He said) "Do not be clothed with two shirts."
>
> 10 And He said to them, "Wherever you go into a house, remain there until you go out from there.
>
> 11 "And whatever place does not welcome you or hear you, as you go out from there, shake out the dust under your feet for a witness against them."
>
> 12 And they going out, they heralded that *all* should repent.
>
> 13 And they were casting out many demons and were anointing with oil many infirm and healing them.

It was about this time that the Lord **was going around the villages in a circuit *and* teaching.** That is, He made a circuit through Galilee, going from place to place with His message. The rejection that He was experiencing and the haste to bring the message to all Israel before His Passion led Him to enlist the Twelve in a special mission. Instead of simply accompanying Him, they were to go out themselves, **two *by* two,** as His ambassadors and apostles. (The verb **send,** Gr. *apostello*, is related to the word for "apostle," Gr. *apostolos*).

As His own representatives, they shared His sovereign **authority over the unclean spirits,** so that their word also might have persuasive power. There would be as little excuse before God to reject *their* Word as there was to reject *His*!

They were to go immediately, as they were, with no added preparations, relying entirely on such welcome and hospitality as they should receive. Thus they were to **take nothing for *the* road.** They might retain the **staff** they may have had in their hand as He spoke, but they were not to procure another if they did not have one (see Matt. 10:9, 10, "do not acquire a staff"). They should not store up a provision of **bread,** nor carry a beggar's **bag** to take money while on the road, nor take along even **copper-*coins* for the belt**—copper being the smallest of coins. They were to travel with simply the **sandals** on their feet. And (He made a point of saying), they should **not be clothed with two shirts**. That is, they should not wear the extra shirt customary for those camping outdoors. They were to depend on the indoor welcome they would receive.

They were to enter a town and find lodging in whatever **house** and family first heeded their message and welcomed them. They were not to seek better or more prestigious lodging, exchanging their first place for a better, richer one. Rather, they were to **remain there** in the first house until they left that city. Their comfort was irrelevant; what mattered was the message and the mission!

If no one in the **place** and town would **welcome** them or **hear** them, they were to leave that city to the judgment of God, denouncing it to God as if it were pagan—for indeed a Jew cannot reject Jesus the Messiah and still retain covenant status as a blessed Jew. Just as pious Jews wiped the pagan dust from their feet as they crossed the border and reentered Israel, so the apostles were to **shake out the dust under** their **feet** when they left that Christ-rejecting town, **for a witness against them**. God would see and judge that town on the Last Day!

The apostles obeyed their orders. They went out two by two and **heralded** that Israel **should repent**. In confirmation of their Word, as undeniable proof to all, **they were casting out many demons and were anointing with oil many infirm and healing them**. There would be no excuse to reject their message.

§III.8 Herod's Reaction and the Death of John

ॐ ॐ ॐ ॐ ॐ

14 And King Herod heard, for His Name had become manifest; and they said, "John the Baptizer has been raised from *the* dead, and that is why the acts of power are at work in Him."

15 But others said, "*It* is Elijah." And others said,

> "*It* is a prophet, like one of the *old* prophets."
> 16 But when Herod heard, he said, "John, whom
> I beheaded, has been raised!"

The Lord's wider fame, promoted by the mission of the Twelve, came even to the court of **King Herod**. (While not actually a king, but rather a tetrarch, with authority over a fourth part of Roman Palestine, Herod was popularly known as "king," and it is this popular usage which is reflected here.)

Herod (son of the famous Herod the Great, who slew the children of Bethlehem) evidently did not know much of Jesus before this, for he was apparently unaware that John and Jesus were contemporaries. Rather, he did not hear of Jesus until after he had had John put to death, and so could be misled into thinking that Jesus was John **raised** from the dead. Certainly **the acts of power** and miracles he had heard of Jesus performing pointed to someone who had been to the land of the dead and had miraculously returned from there, armed with supernatural powers which were **at work in Him**.

There were many estimates of who Jesus was and what was His significance. Some said He was **Elijah**, whose return was literally expected as the fulfillment of the prophecy of Malachi 4:5–6. Elijah had performed miracles when he first walked the earth, and some felt the miracles done by Christ proved that He must be him. Others suggested that He was **a prophet**, newly raised up by God **like one of the *old* prophets** of ancient time. Certainly His word was with power, as theirs was.

Those in Herod's court favored the explanation that Jesus was John raised from the dead, and Herod tended to this view as well, haunted as he was by his guilty conscience. For Herod, it was not simply "John" returned, but **John, whom I beheaded**. Herod had the Baptizer executed with the greatest reluctance, for in some small corner of his mind he knew that John was a holy man and that the sin of slaying him would come back to haunt him. In the reports of a new and popular wonder-worker in the land, it must have seemed to the guilty tyrant that John had come back indeed!

ॐ ॐ ॐ ॐ ॐ

17 For Herod himself had sent and seized John and bound him in prison for the sake of Herodias, the wife of his brother Philip, because he had married her.

18 For John said to Herod, "It is not permitted for you to have your brother's wife."

19 And Herodias had a grudge against him and wanted to kill him and could not;

20 for Herod feared John, knowing that he was a righteous and holy man, and kept him *safe*. And when he heard him, he was very perplexed, yet he heard him gladly.

21 And an opportune day came when Herod on his birthday gave a supper for his great *men* and generals and the leading *men* of Galilee;

22 and when the daughter of Herodias herself came in and danced, she pleased Herod and those reclining with him; and the king said to the *young* girl, "Ask me whatever you want and I will give it to you."

23 And he swore to her, "Whatever you ask me, I will give you, up to half of my kingdom."

24 And having gone out, she said to her mother, "What shall I ask for?" And she said, "The head of John the Baptizer."

25 And immediately she came in eagerly to the king and asked, saying, "I want you at once to give me, on a plate—the head of John the Baptizer!"

26 And the king became very grieved, but because of his oaths and the ones reclining with him, he did not want to nullify *his word* to her.

27 And immediately the king sent an executioner and commanded that he bring his head. And

> he went and beheaded him in the prison,
>
> 28 and brought his head on a plate, and gave it to the *young* girl; and the *young* girl gave it to her mother.
>
> 29 And when his disciples heard, they came and took his corpse and put it in a tomb.

Mention of Herod's guilty conscience gives Mark the opportunity to relate the story of John's execution. John came as a prophet to call all Israel to repentance for their sins (1:4), and he did not shrink from rebuking even Herod himself. This was not a question of John meddling in politics. Israel knew no constitutional separation of Church and State. Israel was a theocracy, and the sins of the king could bring divine judgment on the whole land (see God's judgment on Israel for King David's sins; 2 Sam. 24:10–13). So it was that **John said to Herod, "It is not permitted for you to have your brother's wife."** This was indeed forbidden by God's law (Lev. 18:16). Herod had no intention of repenting (he was, in fact, a very irreligious man). More than that, he feared that John's public denunciation might give a signal for a public uprising and rebellion.

So it was that he **seized John and bound him in prison**, probably in the dungeon at Machaerus. He held him there as a kind of political prisoner. His wife **Herodias had a grudge against** John, and would doubtless have liked to have him killed outright. Herod was reluctant to do this, however. Not only would such a martyrdom inflame the masses even more, but he **feared John, knowing that he was a righteous and holy man**; he feared that God would in some way avenge the unjust murder of one of His own. So it was that he **kept him** *safe* in prison. He often came to hear him, being drawn almost against his will by the evident holiness of the strange prophet. He was **perplexed**, at a loss as to what to make of him, though **he heard him gladly** and willingly enough. Perhaps he even toyed with the thought of having him released as a grand political gesture of clemency. The scheming malevolence of Herodias, however, did not sleep.

So it was that **an opportune day came** when she could have her hated nemesis killed. **Herod on his birthday gave a supper**, a great banquet, for all his supporters and those whose favor he longed to gain. (We note in passing that the celebration of birthdays was a pagan custom, not a Jewish one.) All the important people were there, **his great *men* and generals and the leading *men* of Galilee.** At some point in the boisterous proceedings, as he reclined at table with all his guests, **the daughter of Herodias herself came in and danced,** and **she pleased Herod and those reclining with him.** The dance was no doubt one of the lascivious, erotic dances such as were done only by prostitutes in the pagan Hellenistic world. Its performance by the princess caused a sensation. (It is possible that Herod had been lusting after the princess, and that Herodias, aware of that, arranged the whole thing.) Anyway, the king, no doubt flushed with wine, stood up and made a grand promise, probably as a public exhibition of his great generosity. After the style of King Ahasuerus in Esther 5:3, Herod offered the young girl any gift she would care to name. (The limit of **up to half of my kingdom** is hyperbolic.) He was no doubt expecting her to ask for gold or garments or perhaps a favorite property.

The girl instantly left the room to consult with her mother, asking her hurriedly, **"What shall I ask for?"** The moment of Herodias' triumph had come. **"The head of John the Baptizer,"** was her cold and deliberate reply.

The young girl (perhaps about sixteen years of age) returned to the assembled guests as quickly as she departed, coming in **eagerly** and with haste. She evidently shared her mother's coldness of heart and sick morbidity. Enjoying her moment in the spotlight, she made the most of the drama, and made as if requesting a certain dish be brought her as the next course in the lavish banquet. One can almost hear her slow and deliberate request, and see her quick eyes scanning the crowd, relishing the moment. **"I want you at once to give me,"** she said, in slow, deliberate words, **"on a plate—"**—one can imagine the dramatic pause that followed—**"the head of John the Baptizer!"** These last words (they come as the end of the sentence in the Greek) were uttered like the punchline to a joke, the surprising, dramatic, and horrifying climax of the request.

The king was no doubt properly surprised and horrified, as much perhaps at the request as at the grim and jesting manner in which it was made. He **became very grieved**, his eyes widening, his jaw dropping, his face contorting in an agony of regret. But **because of his oaths and the ones reclining with him, he did not want to nullify *his word* to her**. The oaths were made expressly to impress his guests with his royal generosity, as a kind of drunken object lesson and display of his power. He could not afford politically to be seen publicly reneging on his word and oath. What other political promises might prove disposable?

So it was that **immediately the king sent an executioner and commanded that he bring his head**. The executioner fulfilled his task, and the head of John was duly brought to the assembled guests (after what was perhaps an exceedingly awkward pause, unsuccessfully filled by more music and wine). The head was given **to the *young* girl; and the *young* girl** in turn **gave it to her mother**.

Thus John the Baptizer met his inglorious end through the scheming of an adulterous wife and her lascivious daughter, and the weakness of a drunken ruler, illustrating vividly the fate of holiness in this age. John's disciples, however, **came and took his corpse and put it in a tomb**, allowed this final act of devotion by King Herod in an attempt to assuage his guilty conscience. (Later tradition reports that John's head was also recovered—perhaps by Chuza, Herod's steward; see Luke 8:3.) John's death is related here as a kind of foreshadowing of the Passion of Christ.

Notes for Section III:

_____

_____

_____

_____

_____

_____

_____

_____

_____

Notes for Section III:

_____

_____

_____

_____

_____

_____

_____

_____

_____

_____

_____

_____

_____

_____

_____

_____

_____

_____

_____

_____

_____

_____

_____

_____

_____

_____

_____

_____

_____

_____

_____

❧ IV ❧

WITHDRAWAL BEYOND GALILEE
(6:30—8:30)

§IV.1 Bread in the Wilderness

> ❧ ❧ ❧ ❧ ❧
>
> **6** 30 **And the apostles came together to Jesus; and they reported to Him all they had done and taught.**
>
> 31 **And He says to them, "Come away by yourselves to a wilderness place and rest a little." (For there were many coming and going, and they did not have an opportunity to eat.)**
>
> 32 **And they went away in the boat to a wilderness place by themselves.**

After the exertions of their mission, **the apostles came together to Jesus**, probably at their home base in Capernaum, and **reported to Him all they had done and taught**, relating their varied adventures. Though exciting, it was also exhausting, and they desperately needed a chance to rest and revive their energy. Their present location, in the midst of the town, made that impossible, **for there were many coming and going**, seeking healing and help, so that **they did not** even **have an opportunity** to stop and take time out **to eat**.

So it was that the Lord **says to them** (the historic present is again used, to convey the dramatic urgency of their need), **"Come away by yourselves to a wilderness place and rest a little."** The wilderness features prominently in Mark's Gospel. John the Baptizer came to the wilderness for his ministry; Christ was tempted in the wilderness, and He frequented lonely "wilderness places" (see 1:35,

45) for prayer and teaching. Such concern for the wilderness is not accidental. Mark means the discerning reader to see an echo of Israel's sojourn in the wilderness. As Israel spent time in the wilderness after leaving Egypt and found grace there with God (Jer. 31:2), so Israel again finds Christ in the wilderness, and with Him, the grace of God.

ॐ ॐ ॐ ॐ ॐ

33 And many saw them going, and recognized them, and they ran-together there on foot from all the cities and preceded them.

34 And having come out, He saw a great crowd and He had heartfelt *love* for them, for they were like sheep that did not have a shepherd, and He began to teach them many *things*.

35 And when it was already a late hour, His disciples came up to Him and said, "This is a wilderness place and *it is* already a late hour;

36 "dismiss them, *that they may* go into the surrounding farms and villages and buy themselves something to eat."

37 But He answered and said to them, "You *yourselves* give them something to eat!" And they say to Him, "Shall we go away and buy two hundred denarii *worth of* bread and give them *something* to eat?"

38 And He says to them, "How many breads do you have? Go *and* see!" And when they knew, they say, "Five, and two fish."

39 And He commanded them all to recline party *by* party on the green grass.

40 And they reclined in grouping *by* grouping of hundreds and of fifties.

41 And having taken the five breads and the two fish, and having looked up to heaven, He

---

> blessed and broke the breads and gave *them*
> to the disciples to set before them, and He
> divided-up the two fish *among them* all.
> 42 And they all ate, *even* to the full.
> 43 And they picked up twelve full baskets of bro-
> ken *pieces* and also from the fish.
> 44 And those who ate were five thousand men.

The hoped-for time of rest was not to be. **Many** from the villages **saw them going** to the desert place just outside the city of Bethsaida, across the northern end of the lake of Galilee (see Luke 9:10). They **recognized** them and **ran-together there on foot from all the cities and preceded them** to their foreseen destination. (If they indeed set out from Capernaum, the distance involved would be no more than about four miles.)

Any other man might have been expected to be disappointed and vexed. But not the Shepherd of Israel, who "leads Joseph like a flock" (Ps. 80:1). Rather, He **had heartfelt *love* for them**. The word here translated *had heartfelt love* is the Greek *splagxnizomai*, cognate with the word *splagxna* or "innards." The "innards" were metaphorically the seat of feeling and emotion, and the word here means that Christ's great heart was wrung with compassion for the people, **for they were like sheep that did not have a shepherd**. That is, He saw that they were downcast, confused, hurt, and entirely at the mercy of hard men. Despite Herod (the political shepherd and ruler of Israel), despite the work of the priests of Jerusalem, and despite the lay work of the Pharisees, the people were still leaderless and abandoned. Even as Joshua of old was appointed to lead the flock of God (Num. 27:17, 18), so this new Joshua was the God-appointed Shepherd of the flock (for "Jesus" and "Joshua" are the same name in the Hebrew).

Thus, despite His own exhaustion, **He began to teach them**. And not just a few simple, perfunctory lessons, to quickly satisfy them enough so He could make His escape. Rather, He began to teach them **many *things***, generously spending the whole day with them into the waning evening.

The apostles realized that a crisis was mounting. The crowd contained five thousand men, plus women and children, for a possible total of at least fifteen thousand people. The population of all of Capernaum itself was only about two thousand five hundred. Evening was coming, and with it the problem of where to find food for such an immense crowd. The apostles **came up to Him** and wondered aloud what they were to do in the face of the impending crisis, since it was indeed **a wilderness place** with no resources for food and it was **already a late hour**. Some said that the Lord should **dismiss them** and send them away to **the surrounding farms and villages** where they might **buy themselves something to eat**, for they would have to scatter far and wide to find such a large amount of food.

The Lord at length responded to their alarm. First He tested them, asking them what *they* thought should be done (see John 6:5, 6), and then suggesting that *they* could feed the multitude themselves. To their astonishment, He directed, "**You** *yourselves* **give them something to eat!**" It was, of course, an invitation for them to put their faith in His messianic power. God fed His people of old in the wilderness. Surely He could do the same through His Messiah!

Sadly (and characteristically of the apostles at this time in their life), they failed to perceive His power. Rather, they responded with incredulity, "**Shall we go away and buy two hundred denarii** *worth of* **bread and give them** *something* **to eat?**" Two hundred denarii was two hundred days' wages for the working man. They had that total in their purse (which is why that amount was mentioned), but even that could not provide everyone with even a little bite (see John 6:7).

Ignoring their failure of faith, Christ moved to meet the need of the multitude. **He says to them** [we note the historic present again in this exchange], "**How many breads** [or loaves] **do you have?**" They counted up all their resources (taken from a little boy who generously volunteered the food he had probably brought for his family; John 6:9), and found it to be **five** barley loaves, **and two fish**. (We learn from the parallel account in John's Gospel that these **fish** were not large fishes, but small pickled fish, like sardines. The Greek for the fish in John 6:9 is *opsarion*, meaning "a tidbit, something eaten with bread.")

It was not very much, and altogether insignificant for the task of feeding at least fifteen thousand people, assuming that each of the **five thousand men** (Gr. *aner*) had at least a wife and one child with him (see Matt. 14:21). Nonetheless, the Lord with untroubled sovereignty **commanded them all to recline** as for a feast, **on the green grass**. (The mention of the **green** grass is perhaps to echo the care of the divine Shepherd in Psalm 23:1, 2, who makes His own "to lie down in green pastures.") Mark uses the phrase **party** *by* **party**, the Greek word being *sumposion*, or "banquet party." That is, they were to arrange themselves in smaller party groups, as if sitting at separate tables, ready for the food to arrive. And indeed they did so, reclining **in grouping** *by* **grouping of hundreds and of fifties**. Like Israel encamped by military hundreds and fifties in the wilderness (see Ex. 18:21), so God's people again encamped in the wilderness, awaiting the divine bread of God. Mark, the interpreter of Peter, adds the eyewitness touch that they looked like so many **groupings**—the Greek word here being *prasia*, meaning "garden-plot, garden-bed." Like so many neat groupings in a garden, so were the people reclining huddled together on the green grass in the wilderness.

The Lord took **the five breads and the two fish** to recite the customary Jewish blessing before a meal. Jewish custom dictated that the one reciting the blessing look down at the food to be blessed, but Christ **looked up to heaven**, for here was no ordinary blessing, but the miraculous power of the heavenly Father. He recited the blessing (doubtless the standard prayer, "Blessed are You, O Lord our God, King of the world, who brings forth bread from the earth") and **broke the breads and gave** *them* **to the disciples** to distribute and **set before** the assembled multitude. He continued to give them bread and fish until all were fed *even* **to the full**.

The word here translated *even to the full* is the Greek *chortazo*, translated in Revelation 19:21 as "to gorge." This was not a light snack, but a full feast! In fact there was so much food that **they picked up twelve full baskets of broken** *pieces* **and also from the fish**. The *baskets* were the Greek *kophinos*, the little wicker carrying-basket that the pious Jew customarily carried about with him as part of his daily attire. Each of the Twelve was able to stuff his **basket** full of the leftover pieces. As the divine Shepherd of Israel, Christ was able to "open His hand and satisfy the desire of every living thing" (Ps. 145:16). In stark contrast to the drunken banquet of King Herod (v. 21), the glorious banquet of Israel's *true* King brought the Presence and blessing of God, revealing Jesus as the True Bread that came down from heaven to give life to the world (John 6:33–35). The feast in the wilderness was an image of messianic abundance and an unmistakable sign that Jesus was indeed the Christ.

§IV.2   Walking on the Sea

ॐ ॐ ॐ ॐ ॐ

45 And immediately He compelled His disciples to embark in the boat and precede *Him* to the other side, to Bethsaida, while He Himself was dismissing the crowd.

46 And after taking leave of them, He departed to the mountain to pray.

47 And when evening had come the boat was in *the* middle of the sea, and He *Himself* was alone on the land.

48 And seeing them tormented at the rowing (for the wind was against them), about the fourth watch of the night, He comes to them, walking on the sea; and He wanted to come alongside them.

49 But when they saw Him walking on the sea, they supposed, "It is a phantom!" and they cried out,

50 for they all saw Him and were shaken. But immediately He spoke to them and says to them, "Have courage; I *myself* am *here*; do not be afraid!"

> 51 And He got into the boat with them, and the wind ceased; and they were greatly beside themselves,
> 52 for they did not have insight about the breads, but their hearts were hardened.

The suddenness with which the Lord **immediately compelled His disciples to embark in the boat** becomes clearer when the parallel account in John's Gospel is read. There we discover that the miracle of the loaves ignited a fever of messianic enthusiasm, and that the people were intending to come and take Jesus by force to make Him king (John 6:15). It was to avert this disastrous riot and the debacle that would inevitably follow that He strove to pacify and **dismiss** the tumultuous **crowd**. In the confusion and chaos of that hour, the Lord quickly sent His disciples away, lest they be swept up in the fray or otherwise compromised. They were to **precede *Him* to the other side** of the lake, back to the western side, to **Bethsaida** near Capernaum. (This was a different Bethsaida from that on the northeastern side, called Bethsaida-Julias to differentiate it from its western namesake.) When Jesus had finally **taken leave** of the crowd, He **departed to the mountain to pray.**

He remained praying until somewhat after three A.M. It was then that He knew that His disciples needed Him. For what should have been an easy journey across the Sea of Galilee had become a nightmare—all the more so after that extraordinary day. The disciples had come to the eastern Bethsaida wilderness in the first place to find some much-needed rest, for prior to that they did not have time even to eat (v. 31). The events of that day denied them their anticipated rest, as their Lord beheld the multitudes harassed like sheep without a shepherd, and spent the whole day teaching and healing them (see Matt. 14:14). Then came the climax when the Lord multiplied the loaves—and ignited the riot of messianic enthusiasm, from which they barely escaped. And now, when it seemed their nerves could stand no more, came the storm of **wind** which was **against them** and frustrated all their exhausted efforts to reach the shore, so that they were **tormented** in their **rowing**. (The word translated *tormented* is the Gr. *basanizo*; its noun form *basanos*, "torment," is used in Luke 16:23 for the torment of the fire of Hades.)

In their hour of distress, then, their Lord came to them, **about the fourth watch of the night** (that is, between three and six A.M.), **walking on the sea.** His intention was evidently **to come alongside them** (Gr. *parerchomai*; see its use in Luke 12:37 for the master who "comes alongside" the reclining slaves to serve them). That is, He intended to come close to comfort, encourage, and rescue them.

In the dark and clouded night, however, the disciples did not recognize the shape moving eerily across the waves as their Lord. The sea was, for them and for all Jews, a place of restless evil. Demons were thought to haunt the sea. In their sleep-deprived state, with their nerves already stretched to the breaking point and beyond, it seemed that this could only be such a figure of haunting evil, and they **were shaken** to the core. **They supposed, "It is a phantom!"** and **cried out** with hideous fear.

The Savior was quick to calm them. **Immediately,** His familiar voice rang out across the wind and the waves, as **He says to them** [the historic present is used, to heighten the drama], **"Have courage; I *myself* am *here*, do not be afraid!"**

When at length He got into the boat with them (Matthew relates Peter's abortive attempt to join the Lord on the water, failing only because of his momentary doubt; see Matt. 14:28–31), **the wind ceased** and a great calm settled on the lake. This was the final miracle in a day too full of miracles, and the disciples **were greatly beside themselves** with astonishment (Gr. *lian en eautois existanto*). His mere Presence was enough to tame the untamable wind and sea.

St. Mark adds the comment that they were astonished at His authority and power only because **they did not have insight about the breads, but their hearts were hardened.** That is, the disciples at this point still mirrored faithless Israel. They had as yet gained no insight from Christ's multiplication of the loaves and how it pointed to Him as the Messiah. His power was still a source of amazement to them.

ৡ৾ ৡ৾ ৡ৾ ৡ৾ ৡ৾

53 And when they had crossed over onto the land, they came to Gennesaret, and moored *there*.

54 And when they got out of the boat, immediately they recognized Him,

55 and ran-about all that region and began to carry-about the ailing on their pallets, to where they heard He was.

56 And wherever He entered villages or into cities or into farms, they put the infirm in the marketplaces and urged Him that they might touch even the fringe of His garment; and as many as touched Him were saved.

This blindness is reflected in the general populace as well. When Jesus and His disciples **crossed over** the lake and **came to Gennesaret** on the west side of the Sea of Galilee, **immediately** the people **recognized Him**. That is, they identified Him as the famous wonder-worker, even as they failed to recognize His true significance. For them, He was simply the healer, someone to be used. They **ran-about all that region** and brought their **ailing** to Him **on their pallets**, converging on the place **where they heard He was**. He was immensely popular: **wherever He entered villages or into cities or into farms, they put the infirm in the marketplaces and urged Him that they might touch even the fringe of His garment.** Their faith was not misplaced. In God's mercy, **as many as touched Him**, even the fringe of His outer garment, **were saved** and healed. Nonetheless, we may detect a subtle echo of lonely sadness in the narration. Jesus was supremely alone even in the midst of such crowds. All came running to use Him and find healing, but none seemed to open their hearts to His mission, nor to understand the true nature of His Kingdom.

ৡ৾ ৡ৾ ৡ৾ ৡ৾ ৡ৾

§IV.3 Conflict with the Pharisees over Ritual Uncleanness

ॐ ॐ ॐ ॐ ॐ

7 1   And there came to Him the Pharisees and some
of the scribes who had come from Jerusalem,

2   and saw that some of His disciples ate the
breads with common hands, that is, unwashed.

3   (For the Pharisees and all the Jews do not eat
unless they wash the hands with the fist, seizing
on the Tradition of the Elders,

4   and when they come from the marketplace,
they do not eat unless they sprinkle themselves,
and there are many other *things* which they have
received to seize *on*—the dipping of cups and
pots and copper-*vessels*.)

5   And the Pharisees and the scribes ask Him,
"Why do Your disciples not walk according to
the Tradition of the Elders, but eat the bread
with common hands?"

St. Mark next describes a conflict with the Pharisees and a delegation of scribes from Jerusalem. The scribes had doubtless been sent to
check Jesus out, to investigate the rumors of heresy (see 3:22). What
they instantly noticed was that He and His disciples disregarded the
customary ritual handwashing before meals.

This handwashing had little to do with hygiene. Rather, it was
entirely a matter of religious ceremony. The Law mandated that
priests wash their hands before offering sacrifice (Ex. 30:19); the
Pharisaical custom (which was increasing in popularity) was for *all
the people* to wash their hands before eating any food (whether sacrificial food or not), in order to wash away any ceremonial defilement
they may have contracted **from the marketplace**. This washing or
sprinkling consisted of washing the hands **with the fist**—that is,
by pouring water down the joined and upraised hands and then by
rubbing one hand with the other (the fist). This practice was **seized**

on and firmly held by them (the word used, the Gr. *krateo*, is the same word used in 14:46, where it means "to seize and hold onto"). It was considered by the scribes to be a part of the oral law going back to Moses himself, the so-called **Tradition of the Elders**. It included, St. Mark tells us, a multitude of other details as well—including such minutiae as **the dipping of cups and pots and copper-*vessels***. One can detect a certain impatience in Mark's cataloging of such apparent trivialities.

For scribal piety, however, such things were of immense importance. To omit the washing (and thus disregard the whole **Tradition of the Elders**) was to eat one's bread **with common hands**—that is, with hands that were ceremonially unpurified and thus defiled. It meant that one became impure and defiled in the sight of heaven, ineligible for contact with the Holy God. They were scandalized that the Lord and His disciples could willfully reject such a tradition and **walk** through life with such obvious impiety.

ॐ ॐ ॐ ॐ ॐ

6 And He said to them, "Well did Isaiah prophesy of you hypocrites, as it is written, 'This people honors Me with the lips, but their heart is removed far from Me;

7 " 'They venerate Me uselessly, teaching *as* teachings *the* commands of men.'

8 "Leaving the commandment of God, you seize on the tradition of men."

The Lord, however, did not deign to defend Himself against such a charge, or to answer the scribes in such a way as to give the impression that He was answerable to them and their scribal interpretations. Rather, He lashed out, denouncing the whole system of oral law of which these washing regulations were a part.

For Him, such hypocritical regulations were a part of the externalism and impiety condemned by **Isaiah** long ago. He **prophesied** accurately and **well** of these modern-day scribes! They were to be included in his denunciations, since they persevered in the sins he denounced. The passage in Isaiah 29:13 (quoting from the Septuagint version, rather than the Hebrew) speaks of the **people** posing as pious before God, when **their heart** was truly **removed far** from Him and from what He really required. Thus they **venerated** Him **uselessly**, substituting *the* **commands of men** for the **teaching** and response He truly wanted. This, the Lord says, is what the Pharisees and the scribes were doing with their oral tradition and their legalistic and detailed elaborations of the Law. Though they intended merely to apply the Law, they were in fact overthrowing its true and original intention. The result of it all was that they **left the commandment of God** and **seized on** instead the mere **tradition of men**. No wonder they were denounced by the Prophet Isaiah—for they had replaced the divine Law of God with their own merely human substitute!

ॐ ॐ ॐ ॐ ॐ

9   And He said to them, "You nullify well the commandment of God in order to make your tradition stand!

10 "For Moses said, 'Honor your father and your mother,' and 'He who speaks-evil of father or mother, let him die the death';

11 "but you *yourselves* say, 'If a man says to the father or the mother, "Korban [that is, 'a gift'] be anything of mine from which you might have been benefited",'

12 "*then* you no longer permit him to do anything for the father or the mother,

13 "*thereby* voiding the Word of God by your tradition which you have delivered, and you do many things similar to that."

With withering sarcasm, the Lord commended them for **well** and effectively overthrowing **the commandment of God**—in order to **make** their precious **tradition stand**. (The word *well*, Gr. *kalos*, is the same word used in v. 6—as if to say, "Isaiah prophesied so effectively about you, because you so effectively nullify God's Word!")

And the Lord did not merely make this charge against their oral tradition, but proved it by a common example—that of the practice of **korban** (Heb. for "an offering or gift"). In the legal niceties of that time, one could take something out of the common reckoning simply by pronouncing that it was **korban** or **a gift** to God, dedicated to Him. Originally the idea of making a thing *korban* was simply that it was intended as a gift for sacrifice and could only be used for that (see Lev. 2:1 LXX). By our Lord's time, it was accepted that one could pronounce the formula, "*Korban* to you be this item of property," and thereby make it off-limits to that person. The item of property was not actually promised or given to the Temple, nor was it off-limits to the person owning it and pronouncing the ban, who could still use the item—it was only off-limits to the person against whom the vow of *korban* was pronounced.

Thus, in this example of how the oral law could actually work *against* the Law of Moses, by the scribal understanding of *korban*, one was actually bound by the formula even if it meant hardship to one's parents.

For the Law of **Moses** was obviously concerned with giving honor and help to one's parents. The Law commanded one to **honor** one's **father and mother** (Ex. 20:12) and even said that **he who speaks-evil of father or mother** by invoking a curse on them should **die the death** and be executed (Ex. 21:17). Yet the scribal interpretations were in clear contrast and opposition to that. Denouncing them to their face (the **you** is emphatic in the Greek), the Lord pointed out that their interpretations ruled that if a man pronounced the **korban** formula about any item of property **from which** his father or mother **might have been benefited**, that man was, as far as the scribes were concerned, *positively forbidden* to help them. He might not use that item to help, even if he changed his mind. Thus, the final result of the scribal oral law, in this instance, was actually not to apply **the Word of God**, but rather to **void** it! And this, the Lord said, was not an isolated and atypical example of how their oral law worked. Rather, they did **many things similar to that**. Their vaunted **tradition** of the Elders actually worked in contradiction to the divine Word it pretended to honor. No wonder He and His disciples did not walk according to it!

ॐ ॐ ॐ ॐ ॐ

14 And after He called to Himself the crowd again, He said to them, "Hear Me, all of you, and have insight:

15 There is nothing outside the man which *by* going into him is able to defile him, but the things which come out of the man are the things which defile the man.

16 "If any has ears to hear, let him hear!"

17 And when He entered into a house *away* from the crowd, His disciples asked Him *about* the parable.

18 And He says to them, "Are you *yourselves* thus uninsightful also? Do you not understand that everything outside going into the man is not able to defile him;

19 "because it does not go into his heart, but into the belly, and goes out into the latrine?" (Thus *He* cleansed all foods.)

20 And He said, "That which comes out of the man, that is what defiles the man.

21 "For from within, out of the heart of men, the wicked questionings come out—fornications, thefts, murders, adulteries,

22 "*acts of* greediness, *acts of* evil, *along with* deceit, sensuality, an evil eye, reviling, arrogance, and senselessness.

23 "All these evil things come out from within and defile the man."

After dealing with the accusations of the Pharisees and the scribes, the Lord then goes on to deal with the original issue of ritual uncleanness. He gives this teaching to **the crowd** of listening disciples and followers, which He **called to Himself** for this purpose, and not to His accusers, for He would not give the impression that He was in any way accountable to the scribal delegation.

To His followers, He gave the solemn pronouncement that eating food with unwashed hands could not bring ritual uncleanness. Indeed, in a new and radical pronouncement, He declared that **there is nothing outside the man** at all—no food eaten whatsoever—which, taken into his body, is **able to defile him** (Gr. *koinoo*, literally, "to render common," uncleansed, impure). The scribes were exactly wrong. It is not what *goes into* a man that defiles him. On the contrary, it is what **comes out** of him that **defiles** him!

The disciples, though joining their Lord in rejecting the scribal oral law, still did not understand the reason behind the saying, or what His parabolic saying meant. So, **when He entered into a house** *away* **from the crowd, His disciples asked Him** *about* **the parable.**

The Lord explained the meaning of the parable to His disciples: **everything outside** and external to man **is not able to defile him**, for true defilement before God is a matter of the heart and will. External things, such as food eaten with unwashed hands, **does not go into** man's **heart**, but rather merely **into the belly**, and from there **goes out** again when it is eliminated. It thus simply passes through him, remaining external to the heart. Such food **going in** cannot defile; rather it is **the wicked questionings**, doubts and rebellions of man—all those things that **come out** of him which truly defile him before God. For these **evil things** come out from the inner **heart of men**, and it is therefore these which defile and render him ineligible to approach the holy God.

The word translated *questionings* is the Greek *dialogismos*, sometimes rendered "doubts" (such as in Luke 24:38). Here it embodies all man's rebellious resistance to God's will. Ever since the Enemy first cast doubt on God's goodness, saying, "Has God indeed said, 'You shall not eat from any tree of the garden'?" (Gen. 3:1), man has doubted God and turned aside to his own wicked plans. These include all the acts that darken our world—**fornications, thefts, murders, adulteries,** *acts of* **greediness,** *acts of* evil, *along with* **deceit, sensuality, an evil eye** [i.e. stinginess], **reviling, arrogance, and senselessness.** The list is not meant to be exhaustive, but it adequately describes the wretched condition of the world. All these things, embodied in actions, first of all live in the human heart, and it is these things, proceeding from the heart, which truly defile a man before God.

To the Lord's answer, St. Mark adds a parenthetical comment at the end of verse 19. The Lord had said that food eaten with unwashed hands, being merely **outside** of man's heart, **is not able to defile him.** Mark adds his own conclusion, which follows inevitably from this teaching. If that is so, he says, then *all* food is clean. Not merely bread eaten with unwashed hands, but also such previously forbidden foods as pork—for these foods also are external to man; they also **do not go into his heart, but** merely **into the belly.** The implication of this teaching of Christ (important for Mark's day, in a Church consisting of Gentiles as well as Jews) was that in saying this, *He* **cleansed all foods** and declared that no food was unclean in itself. This implication was not seen and appreciated in its Jewish context at the time Christ said it. Nonetheless, the implication was truly drawn, and was a valid and important application of His teaching in a later and different situation.

§IV.4 Healing for a Gentile

The incomprehension of those in Israel sets the scene for the faith of the Gentile. By this juxtaposition, St. Mark shows how what truly matters is not race, but humble faith.

ॐ ॐ ॐ ॐ ॐ

24 And from there He arose and went away to
the district of Tyre. And having entered into a
house, He wanted no one to know, and *even so*
He could not escape notice.

---

25 But immediately a woman heard about Him, whose *little*-daughter had an unclean spirit, *and* came and fell-down at His feet.

26 Now the woman was a Greek, a Syrophoenician by race. And she asked Him to cast the demon out of her daughter.

27 And He said to her, "Permit first the children to eat-to-the-full, for it is not good to take the children's bread and cast it to the *little* dogs."

28 But she answered and says to Him, "Lord, even the *little* dogs under the table eat from the children's crumbs."

29 And He said to her, "Because of this word, go your way; the demon has gone out from your daughter."

30 And going back to her house, she found the child thrown on the bed, the demon having gone out.

This event must be read within the more general context of the frenetic pace Christ and His disciples had been keeping. The disciples were desperate for rest, not even having time to eat (6:31). They were starving, as it were, for a time of stillness, a lull in their ceaseless work. Their previous attempts to find that rest within Israel's borders had been frustrated (see 6:33, 34), so Jesus took them to the very limits of those borders, to the **district of Tyre**. There He hoped His spiritual children could find their needed repose.

This hope was frustrated too. **He wanted no one to know** that He **entered into a house**, thinking to throw the cloak of anonymity about them in the outskirts of foreign territory. But even so, **He could not escape notice.** He was known by those who came from this territory (see 3:8), and it was this fame that caused Him to be noticed and identified now.

In particular, a **woman**, who was **a Greek** (that is, a Gentile), **a Syrophoenician by race** (that is, belonging to that part of Phoenicia under the administration of Syria), got word that He was nearby.

She was in great need and distress, for her *little*-daughter had an unclean spirit. (We may surmise too that she had been widowed or abandoned by the child's father, since it was unusual for a married woman to make such connections in public.) Learning that the Jewish wonder-worker was at hand, she ran after them, crying out, "Have mercy on me, O Lord, Son of David," insisting that He accompany her to her home in Tyre to heal her daughter, who was cruelly demon-possessed (see Matt. 15:22).

The apostles had little time for such requests from a Gentile—and a Gentile woman at that. They entreated the Lord to give her an audience and send her away. They assumed, we may think, that the Lord would not grant her request and make the exhausting journey into Tyre. That would mean even more work—for the etiquette and social customs of the day did not permit a quick visit. To grant her request would have meant spending some days in Tyre, healing not only the woman's daughter, but also all the multitude of Gentiles who would surely throng them to seek healing for themselves too. The disciples simply wanted Jesus to tell her to go away. The Lord, however, would not see her at all, for He was not sent at that time to go among the Gentiles, but only to the lost sheep of the house of Israel (see Matt. 15:23, 24).

The woman, however, was insistent. She pushed past the disciples and came and fell-down at His feet in a desperate prostration, saying, "Lord, help me!" (see Matt. 15:25). The Lord was still reluctant to deprive His spiritual children and disciples of their rest to go with her on a mission to pagan Tyre. "Permit first the children to eat-to-the-full," He gently responded, "for it is not good to take the children's bread and cast it to the *little* dogs." That is, it would be as inappropriate for Him to take their anticipated rest away from the disciples in order to meet her need as it would be to take food prepared for the children and instead throw it on the floor for the little lapdogs to eat.

The woman did not argue with the Lord. She had absolute faith in His power to heal. If He would not go with her, let Him simply give the word and heal her daughter from a distance! The children's meal did not need to be interrupted and preempted. While the children ate in peace, **the *little* dogs under the table** could **eat from the children's crumbs** which they let drop on the floor. They could continue to rest there, and He could but speak the word.

The Lord was impressed by such faith (see Matt. 15:28). Because of her faithful response and **word**, He told her to return home; she would find **the demon** had **gone out** from her daughter. Hurrying **back to her house**, she found it was as He said. **The demon** had indeed **gone out** from her, leaving her **thrown on the bed** after its forcible expulsion. The child was exhausted, but in peace. The faith of the Gentile woman was enough to prevail on the Jewish Messiah.

§IV.5   Healing in Decapolis

ॐ ॐ ॐ ॐ ॐ

31 And having come out again from the district of Tyre, He came through Sidon to the Sea of Galilee, in the middle of the district of Decapolis.

32 And they bring to Him one who was deaf and spoke-with-difficulty, and they urge Him to put His hand on him.

33 And having taken him from the crowd by himself, He put His fingers into his ears, and having spit, He touched his tongue,

34 and looking up to heaven, He groaned, and says to him, "Ephphatha!" (that is, "Be opened-up!").

35 And his ears were opened and the bond of his tongue was loosed and he spoke correctly.

36 And He ordered them to tell no one, but the more He ordered them, the more abundantly they *themselves* heralded *it*.

37 And they were thunderstruck beyond measure, saying, "He has done all things well; He even makes the deaf hear and the dumb speak."

After the Lord **came out again from the district of Tyre** where He had healed the daughter of the Syrophoenician woman, He first traveled north to **Sidon** and then returned again to the eastern side of **the Sea of Galilee,** to the predominantly Gentile **district of Decapolis,** thereby avoiding Galilee altogether, along with the exhausting resumption of work which would await them there.

When He arrived in Decapolis, **they bring to him one who was deaf and spoke-with-difficulty,** entreating Him to **put His hand on him** to heal him. (The historic present tense is again used in this passage, allowing us to focus on the drama more intensely.)

The word translated *spoke-with-difficulty* is the Greek *mogilalos.* It is the word used in Isaiah 35:6 (LXX), where it is translated "stammerer." It would seem from verse 35 that the man was, in the literal sense, tongue-tied. Whatever the exact cause of his inability to speak, he presented a heart-wrenching sight.

The Lord wanted to deal with the man one-on-one, perhaps because the nature of his afflictions meant that he had been ignored and shunted to one side for so long. His deafness and dumbness had taught him to be passive, and the Lord was now calling him back to active converse and life with his fellowmen. So it was that He **took him** away **from the crowd** to a place **by himself,** where He could deal with him without the visual distractions of the pressing crowd.

To restore his hearing, **He put His fingers** into the deaf man's **ears.** Then He **spit** onto His finger and **touched** the man's **tongue** with it. To our contemporary society (where spitting has only contemptible connotations), this may seem odd. But for the ancients, saliva was thought to have curative powers (as indeed it does to some degree). This touching of his tongue with the saliva, therefore, was a kind of natural anointing.

The Lord then **looked up to heaven,** drawing on the Father's power, and **groaned** or sighed (Gr. *stenazo,* the same word used in 2 Cor. 5:2 for our lamenting our earthly condition). This audible expression of emotion was perhaps motivated by our Lord's sorrow for the man's affliction. As it says in the Prayer for the Blessing of Water at Baptism, "You could not bear to behold mankind oppressed by the devil." He then utters a single Aramaic word (related by St.

Mark in the historic present): "**Ephphatha!**" That is, the entire man was to be **opened-up** to the power of God (Gr. *dianoigo*, a more intensive verb than the simple *anoigo*, "to open").

This simple and sovereign word of command was enough to heal all the man's afflictions. **His ears were opened** [Gr. *anoigo*] **and the bond of his tongue was loosed** so that he was able to speak **correctly**, without any stammering or distortion (the Greek word for *correctly* is *orthos*; see its use in Luke 10:28). The Lord did not want this healing trumpeted about everywhere, lest He be regarded as a mere wonder-worker. He therefore **ordered them to tell no one**. But to no avail, for they continued to **herald** His miracles everywhere. And little wonder—for **they were thunderstruck beyond measure** and astounded at His healing prowess. He had **done all things well** (see the acclaim due to God's creative works in Gen. 1:31 LXX). Indeed, He even made **the deaf hear and the dumb speak** (see Is. 35:5, 6), undoing all the works of the devil and restoring life and joy to the children of men.

§IV.6   Bread in Decapolis

ॐ ॐ ॐ ॐ ॐ

8 1 In those days, when again there was a great crowd and they had nothing to eat, He called to *Himself* His disciples and says to them,

2 "I have heartfelt *love* for the crowd, for they have remained with Me now three days, and have nothing to eat;

3 "and if I dismiss them fasting to *their* houses, they will faint on the way, and some of them have come from a distance."

4 And His disciples answered Him, "How will anyone be able to feed these *to the full* with bread here in *the* wilderness?"

5 And He asked them, "How many breads have you?" And they said, "Seven."

6 And He orders the crowd to recline on the earth, and taking the seven breads, having given thanks, He broke *them* and gave to His disciples to set before *them*, and they set *them* before the crowd.

7 And they had a few little-fish, and having blessed them, He ordered these also to be set before *them*.

8 And they ate *even* to the full, and there was an abundance of *leftover* broken *pieces*, seven hampers *of them*.

9 And there were about four thousand *there*, and He dismissed them.

10 And immediately He embarked into the boat with His disciples and came into the area of Dalmanutha.

This second multiplication of the loaves occurs in the mixed Jewish-Gentile area of Decapolis. Those around Him were untiringly devoted to Him and sat listening to His word for **three days** with **nothing to eat** (doubtless counting the days by Jewish reckoning, whereby each part of a day is counted for one day; the total time may have been 50 hours or so). Faced with such devotion and need, the Lord **had heartfelt *love*** for them. The word translated here *have heartfelt love* is once again the Greek *splagxnizomai*, used in 6:34, indicating a deep emotional reaction to their need. Because of this love, Christ was reluctant to simply **dismiss them fasting to *their* houses**, for some had come to be with Him **from a distance** and would **faint on the way** back home. His observation of the crowd's need was an invitation to the disciples to profit by the lesson learned the last time He multiplied the loaves.

Not surprisingly, given their present hardness of heart (6:52), they showed that they had not profited by it at all. **"How will anyone be able to feed these *to the full* with bread here in *the* wilderness?"** The Lord, with His characteristic patience for our frailty, does not rebuke them. He simply asks them **how many breads** and loaves

they have. On being told they have **seven**, He **orders the crowd**
[the historic present is again used] **to recline on the earth**, as if in
anticipation of a feast.

The Lord then **gave thanks** (again, the customary Jewish blessing; see 6:41), **broke** the loaves and **gave** them **to His disciples to
set before** the crowd. He did the same with the **few little-fish** (the
word in Greek is *ixthudion*, the diminutive for "fish," indicating
perhaps small pickled fish such as were eaten as tidbits).

The miracle is narrated with the usual restrained economy of
words. St. Mark simply says that all **ate** *even* **to the full**. Once again,
the word translated *even to the full* is the Greek *chortazo*, sometimes
translated "to gorge." And not only did the **four thousand** eat until
they were full—quite a large meal for each one, one imagines, after
fasting for three days—but once again there was **an abundance of**
leftover **broken** *pieces.* The disciples were able to fill **seven hampers**
full of the leftover pieces. The word translated here *hampers* is not
the same word translated "baskets" in 6:43. The word used here is
the Greek *spuris*. These baskets were large indeed, for St. Paul relates
that he was let down through an opening in the city wall in such a
hamper (Acts 9:25). The Lord provided a great feast indeed to fill
seven hampers full of the leftovers! Only then did He **dismiss** the
crowd, sending them away full, and leave with His disciples for **the
area of Dalmanutha**. (The location of this **Dalmanutha** is unknown,
but some believe it to be near the city of Magdala, on the west side
of the Sea of Galilee.)

In looking back on the words St. Mark chooses to relate the
miracle, one cannot but be struck by its distinctly eucharistic tone.
When the Church came to relate the Lord's example during the
eucharistic prayer (or "anaphora" as it came to be called), it would
quickly learn to quote the words of St. Paul describing the Last Supper. In this classic text (1 Cor. 11:24f), it is related that Christ "took
bread, and when He had given thanks [Gr. *eucharisto*], He broke
it and gave it to them, and said, 'This is My Body which is broken
for you; do this in remembrance of Me.'" Even in the days of St.
Mark, his original Church audience would instantly have recalled
this eucharistic parallel and thought of the weekly Eucharist, which

was the center of their own lives. It would seem that this was Mark's intention, especially since he not only uses the Greek word for *give thanks* in verse 6 (*eucharisto*), but also reproduces the eucharistic action of thanksgiving, breaking, and giving to the disciples (see 14:22). It is especially stressed that the food was given to the crowd *through His apostles*. Mark seems to be making a parallel with the Eucharist, in which the people are fed by Christ *through His clergy*. The purpose of the parallel is to show his Church audience how Christ is even now in their midst, miraculously sustaining them even as He did His devoted followers of old. He **had heartfelt** *love* for them then, and He continues now to have that same **heartfelt** *love* for us too, nourishing us with His eucharistic Presence.

§IV.7   The Pharisees' Blindness and the Disciples' Blindness

ॐ ॐ ॐ ॐ ॐ

11 And the Pharisees came out and began to debate with Him, seeking from Him a sign from heaven, to test Him.

12 And groaning *deeply* in His spirit, He says, "Why does this generation seek a sign? Amen I say to you, *may God do so to Me* if a sign will be given to this generation!"

13 And having left them, He again embarked and went away to the other side.

St. Mark next relates two incidents, revealing the blindness both of the Pharisees and of His own disciples. **The Pharisees** were concluding that He was a demonic deceiver, one who cast out demons with the help of Satan (3:22). They **came out** to confront Him publicly and **began to debate with Him** about the true source of His power. They demanded that He produce **a sign from heaven**—that is, that God speak with an audible voice from heaven, identifying Jesus as His true Prophet. *This* they would accept as proof of His divine mission—but nothing less! This was to **test Him**, even as faithless Israel tested God in the desert after they came out of Egypt (Ps. 95:9).

Even as God forbade Israel to test Him (Deut. 6:16), so also Jesus now refused to submit to such a test. For this desire did not spring from a sincere love of truth, but rather from a wanton faithless heart that insisted on having God only on their own terms. It was this very attitude which would lead to their final rejection of Jesus and bring on the divine judgment and destruction in AD 70. Out of grief for the judgment their hard heart would bring, Jesus **groaned** *deeply* from His inmost **spirit**. (The word translated *groan deeply* is the Gr. *anastenazo*, used in a Greek version of Susanna verse 22, where Susanna groans, lamenting her inevitable doom.) With a grief that rent His heart, He lamented, **"Why does this generation seek a sign?"** Why did it insist on refusing to believe and on tempting God, to its own inevitable destruction? With great solemnity, Jesus witnessed to God's truth, saying, **"Amen I say to you"**—His characteristic utterance, preceding important truth which He heard from the Father. And what He solemnly witnessed to was this: that no **sign** such as they demanded would ever **be given to this generation**. (The form of the assertion is that of an oath, which characteristically began, "May God do so to me and more also if ___"; see 2 Kings 6:31. Using such a strong verbal form made it clear that they would never be given the requested sign.)

After His categorical refusal to acquiesce to their wicked desire, the Lord **left them**, and **embarked** in the boat, going away **to the other side**. This departure has more than merely geographical significance. It signifies as well His repudiation of them in their faithlessness. Even as God refused to abide in the midst of faithless Israel (see Ezek. 11:23), so Christ **left them** to be rid of their presence.

ᘔᖇ ᘔᖇ ᘔᖇ ᘔᖇ ᘔᖇ

14 And they had forgotten to take breads, and did not have more than one bread in the boat with them.

15 And He ordered them, saying, "See *to it*! Watch

out for the leaven of the Pharisees and the leaven of Herod!"

16 And they began to question among themselves, that they had no bread.

17 And Jesus, knowing this, says to them, "Why do you question that you have no bread? Do you not yet understand or have insight? Do you have a hardened heart?

18 "Having eyes, do you not see? And having ears, do you not hear? And do you not remember,

19 "when I broke the five breads for the five thousand, how many baskets full of broken *pieces* did you take up?" They say to Him, "Twelve."

20 "And when *I broke* the seven for the four thousand, how many hampers full of broken *pieces* did you take up?" And they say to Him, "Seven."

21 And He says, saying to them, "Do you not yet have insight?"

Faced with such faithlessness, the Lord was concerned that His disciples should not be infected with such hypocrisy (see Luke 12:1). As they traveled across the lake, He **ordered them** (Gr. *diastello*, a strong word; Christ was emphatic that they should not fall prey to the disease that afflicted His foes) that they **watch out for the leaven of the Pharisees and the leaven of Herod.**

The pairing of the Pharisees with the partisans of King Herod was unusual. These two groups usually had little in common. Indeed, all that united them now was their common opposition to Jesus (see 3:6.) Herod's men may have joined the Pharisees in their demand for a sign. If Dalmanutha (v. 10) was near Tiberius, there certainly would have been many of Herod's men around, for Tiberius was Herod's capital.

In telling His disciples to beware **the leaven** of His foes, Jesus was of course warning them to beware their teaching and attitude. Though claiming to be pious and motivated only by a desire to do

God's will, they were hypocritical and were actually determined to do only their own will. The disciples were to avoid such hypocrisy at all costs.

That the Lord was speaking of His foes' teaching was the more obvious in the original Aramaic, where the words for "teaching" (Aramaic *amirah*) and for "leaven" (Aramaic *hamirah*) are homonyms—words spelled differently but alike in their pronunciation. The disciples, however, could not understand His meaning. They did not understand that He spoke parabolically, but thought that He was speaking of literal **leaven**. They more easily believed that Jesus was talking about actual bread because they **had forgotten to take breads** with them in their hurry to depart, so that that they had no more than **one** loaf of **bread in the boat with them**. Each no doubt blamed the others, and in their frustration and mutual recrimination, they assumed that the Lord's words referred to this omission.

The Lord was weary of such lack of insight and of their utter failure once again to discern His power (see 6:52). Did they really imagine that He was so intensely concerned about the fact that they **had no bread**, as if they would now go hungry? Did they imagine Him to be powerless to feed them with one loaf? After all they had seen Him do, did they **not yet understand or have insight** into who He was and what He could do? They all had eyes—did they **not see?** They all had ears—did they **not hear?** So it was that He once again patiently strove to teach His slow children.

He asked them to **remember** their own experiences. When He **broke the five breads for the five thousand**, He asked them, **how many baskets full of broken *pieces* did** they **take up?** They remembered well such a glorious day, and the excitement with which they collected the leftover fragments and filled every one of their baskets. They responded, **"Twelve."** And when He broke **the seven** loaves for **the four thousand, how many hampers full of broken *pieces* did** they **take up** at that time? They well remembered that also: **"Seven."** So, He concludes, if they can remember such miracles as clearly and easily as that, how was it that they did **not yet have insight** into His power, and know that He could easily multiply one bread to feed a mere dozen men? Obviously His concern was not with their stomachs, but with their hearts! Let them indeed **watch out** for the dangerous leaven! They should know that He was not warning them against eating *food* from the Pharisees, but against absorbing their *teaching*.

❧ EXCURSUS
ON THE BLINDNESS OF THE DISCIPLES

St. Mark is very blunt about the failings and the blindness of the disciples, far more so than the other synoptic Gospels of Matthew and Luke. Thus he mentions that the disciples did not understand the parables of Christ (4:13); they had "no faith" (4:40; see Matt. 8:26's "*little* faith"); they cried out for fear when He walked on the water "because their hearts were hardened" (6:51, 52); they were without understanding of true cleanness (7:18); they failed to understand what was the true leaven because their hearts were hardened (8:17, 18); they did not understand the Passion (9:32); they argued over greatness (9:33); they indignantly rebuked the approach of the children (10:13); they were astonished at the dangers of wealth (10:24); they were afraid to go to Jerusalem (10:32); they all fell away at the end (14:27).

Why such a negative portrayal of the disciples? Granted that this was all historically true, why make a point of reporting it? It would seem that Mark meant to show that the blindness of the disciples was a reflection of the widespread blindness of Israel. And what was the reason for this blindness? How could Israel not recognize its own Messiah when He came? Here we come to the heart of the matter.

St. Mark portrays Jesus as the Christ who voluntarily veiled His true messianic glory. Only for a moment, at the Transfiguration, was the veil removed so as to let the inner apostolic circle see His true splendor. Throughout the rest of His public ministry, He walked among the people in

---

humility. The demons could see Him as He was (consider their constant terror at His approach; 1:24), but mere men could not. This veiling of His glory meant that most men—including the disciples—could not recognize Him as the Messiah. That revelation came only slowly to the disciples, and only to a few in Israel.

St. Mark focuses on the frailties of the disciples as a way of showing how Jesus could come as the true Christ and still not be recognized by Israel.

§IV.8   Gradual Healing of a Blind Man

The healing of the blind man in stages is narrated at this point to embody the blindness of the disciples, who also are only gradually enlightened as to who Jesus really is. Like the blind man from Bethsaida, the disciples also are blind to Jesus' true messianic significance.

ॐ ॐ ॐ ॐ ॐ

22 And they come to Bethsaida. And they bring to Him a blind *man*, and urge Him to touch him.

23 And taking hold of the hand of the blind *man*, He brought him outside of the village; and having spit into his eyes, and putting *His* hands on him, He asked him, "Do you see anything?"

24 And having looked-up, he said, "I see the men, but I perceive them as trees, walking."

25 Then again He put *His* hands on his eyes, and he looked-*hard* and was restored, and looked-at everything shiningly *clearly*.

26 And He sent him out to *his* house, saying, "Do not go into the village."

When the Lord came to **Bethsaida** (a town on the northeastern side of the sea of Galilee), **a blind** *man* was led to the Lord, amid the people's urgent entreaties that He **touch him** to heal him.

Perhaps all wanted to witness a sensational miracle, being motivated as much by the desire to see wonders as by their compassion for the blind man himself. Jesus, however, as usual wanted to avoid such publicity, and desired only to relieve the long suffering of the afflicted man. As if leading a helpless child, He took **hold of the hand of the blind** *man* and led him all the way **outside the village**, far from wondering and hungry eyes. Once again He used saliva as a form of natural anointing, since all knew its proverbial curative powers and thus the use of saliva would have helped the man's faith. Having put the spit **into his eyes** and then **putting** *His* **hands on him** to heal him, He then **asked him, "Do you see anything?"**

In the verses that follow, it is instructive to follow the Greek verbs. When St. Mark narrates the Lord's question, **"Do you see anything?"** he uses the word *blepo*, the normal word for physical seeing. In response, the afflicted man then **looked-up**—the Greek word being *anablepo*. That is, he looked all around, with a kind of wild excitement. As he looked, he was able to see men walking around him (the disciples moving about?), and he said, **"I see** [Gr. *blepo*] **the men, but I perceive** [Gr. *orao*] **them as trees, walking."** That is, he could see his surroundings, but had no depth perception, nor ability to synthesize shapes. His brain took a moment to adjust to the flood of visual data now flowing into it.

The Lord **again put** *His* **hands on his eyes** to complete the second stage of his healing. The man then **looked-*hard*.** The Greek word used here is *diablepo*, meaning "to look intently, to stare, to open the eyes wide." As he stared and struggled to focus, his sight was then **restored**, as his brain finally was able to complete its recalibration and synthesize all the information it was receiving. He then **looked-at everything shiningly** *clearly* and distinctly. The Greek word here is *emblepo*. The word may simply be a synonym for *blepo*, but more likely it means "to look at, to fix one's gaze on." It is the word used in 14:67 for the intent stare the servant girl gave to Peter during the Lord's trial. That is, after the man stared and adjusted his focus, he was able at last to behold things with perfect clarity, to contemplate them with complete radiant resolution.

The man was jubilant. The Lord, however, was still concerned that He not be mobbed, nor regarded as a mere wonder-worker. He sent the man to his home, with the warning that he was not even to **go into the village** to share the news with those left behind (v. 23). Let him rather enjoy the gift of sight on his own.

§IV.9 The Disciples See That Jesus Is the Messiah

The gradual healing and physical enlightenment of the blind man leads to the account of the spiritual enlightenment of the disciples. After their blindness of heart and lack of insight into His true significance (see v. 21), their leader Peter finally confesses Him to be the true and long-awaited Messiah. This confession forms the climax of this portion of Mark's account. Having elicited this confession, Jesus immediately begins the long road to the Cross.

ॐ ॐ ॐ ॐ ॐ

27 And Jesus and His disciples went out to the villages of Caesarea Philippi, and on the way He asked His disciples, saying to them, "Who do the men say that I am?"

28 And they told Him, saying, "John the Baptizer; and others, Elijah; others, one of the prophets."

29 And He *Himself* asked them, "But who do you *yourselves* say that I am?" Peter answers and says to Him, "You *Yourself* are the Christ."

30 And He warned them to tell no one about Him.

After these events, **Jesus and His disciples went out to the villages** around **Caesarea Philippi.** Caesarea Philippi was far to the north, about twenty-five miles north of Bethsaida. It was a Hellenistic city, being a focus for the worship of Pan. In taking His disciples to such a remote location, Jesus was assured of being far from any tumultuous crowd that might be susceptible to a fever of messianism (see John 6:15). It was in this location that Jesus wanted to elicit from His disciples the confession that He was indeed the Messiah. He had been praying (see Luke 9:18) and knew the time was ripe for such a revelation.

Thus He begins by **asking** them about **who the men** of Israel said that He was. In asking this, He was inviting them to share the opinions they had learned while on their missionary journeys (related in 6:7f) and also whatever whispered gossip and surmises they had picked up.

The disciples were delighted to relate the ignorance of the masses. Some of the people, they perhaps said with a laugh, thought that He was **John the Baptizer** (the view favored by Herod's partisans). There were **others** who thought that He was **Elijah**, come down from heaven to signal the imminence of the Kingdom. Still **others** suggested He might be **one of the prophets** of old, somehow risen from the dead—perhaps Jeremiah, the defender of Israel in times of trouble (see 2 Macc. 15:13–16).

Amidst such lighthearted ridicule of the popular opinions, Christ casts His own challenge to them, chilling their easy pride and putting them to the test. Such were the opinions of ordinary **men**—but the disciples themselves, what about *them*? With this question, He brings to an end the easy conversational mood in which they were discussing this, as **He** *Himself* asks for their own verdict (the *He* is emphatic in the Greek).

As if summoning them to rise above the crowd, He asks, **"But who do you** *yourselves* **say that I am?"** In the Greek, the *you* is emphatic as well; the Lord was turning their attention away from others and back onto themselves. Ordinary men might have this or that opinion. But they were not ordinary men, but were called to be His own disciples and share His own secrets (see 4:34). What about them? Who did *they* say that He was?

Peter, the spokesman for the group, gave his own answer: **"You** *Yourself* [the *You* in the Greek is again emphatic] **are the Christ."** St. Mark relates the confession with his usual economy of words, but the brevity belies its importance. Though it is a mere four words in the Greek, here was the momentous fruit of all Jesus' work with the Twelve. All His praying, striving, miracles, and patient teaching had led to this confession—the faith on which His Church was to be built. He must still teach them what kind of Messiah He was—a Messiah who would die in agony and apparent defeat (see vv. 31f). But the foundation of faith had been laid.

For us today, such a confession seems too self-evident to be so momentous. But that is because our understanding of messiahship has already been shaped by Peter's confession and the Church's faith. In Israel at that time, the Messiah was popularly thought to be a military figure—one who would come on the clouds with heavenly glory, to smite the enemies of God and shed the blood of Roman occupiers and exalt Israel to international prominence. To see in the humble and peaceful Nazarene the glorious Messiah of God and Deliverer of Israel was indeed a momentous revelation. Merely human insight and guesswork could not reveal this—but only God in heaven (see Matt. 16:17).

Notes for Section IV:

_____

_____

_____

_____

_____

_____

_____

_____

_____

_____

_____

_____

_____

_____

_____

Notes for Section IV:

❦ V ❧

JOURNEY TO JERUSALEM
(8:31—10:62)

§V.1   First Passion Prediction—
Peter Rebuked and the Cost of Discipleship

The journey to Jerusalem is marked by three separate predictions of the Passion (8:31f; 9:31f; 10:32). Each one of these predictions is followed by a lapse on the part of the apostles, indicating that, though they confess that He is Messiah, they still have little comprehension of what this messiahship involves. Thus Peter rebukes Him when He teaches that He is to die and is rebuked in turn (8:32, 33); all of the Twelve argue over worldly greatness and are rebuked for their pride (9:34, 35); and John and James try to secure the first places in the Kingdom through favoritism and are rebuked for their presumption (10:35f). The journey to Jerusalem is characterized and punctuated by these hard lessons.

❧ ❧ ❧ ❧ ❧

8 31 And He began to teach them that it was necessary for the Son of Man to suffer many things and be rejected by the elders and the chief-priests and the scribes, and be killed, and after three days rise again.

32 And He said the word boldly. And Peter took Him aside and began to rebuke Him.

33 But having turned around and having seen His disciples, He rebuked Peter, and says, "Go away after Me, Satan! For you are not minding the things of God, but the things of men."

Having elicited a confession of faith in Him as Messiah, Jesus next begins the task of teaching them what kind of Messiah He is. That is, contrary to Israel's popular expectation, the Messiah is not simply a figure of heroic triumph. Rather, because it was pre-ordained by God and prophesied in the Scriptures, **it was necessary** for the Messiah **to suffer many** *things* **and be rejected by the elders and the chief-priests and the scribes, and be killed,** and only after this defeat to **rise again.** The Lord was explaining this **word** of teaching **boldly** and plainly to the disciples, to steel them for the storm which would break against them at His Passion.

Peter, however, was aghast. Not only did such things fly in the face of popular Jewish expectation, but they were also a dagger through his heart, because he loved his Lord and could not bear the thought of Him suffering humiliation and crucifixion. **Peter** therefore **took Him aside and began to rebuke Him.** This rebuke was not so much a scolding as it was a cry of pain and horror that shrank from such a terrible possibility (see Matt. 16:22).

Despite His love for His chief apostle, the Lord knew how fatal was the attitude expressed now by Peter. This was the same attitude that rested in the hearts of the crowd when they tried to take Him by force and make Him King (John 6:15); the same attitude that insisted on bending the will of God to the purposes of men; the same attitude that refused to submit in humility and repentance to the divine judgment, but insisted on worldly victory. It was the attitude which would eventually result in the crowd's disowning Him when they saw that He would not bring them military victory over the Romans (15:11–14). It minded **the things of men** and cared only for human agendas, not **the things of God** and His purposes. Peter, in giving himself to such worldly attitudes, had become an adversary, a **Satan** (for the word *satan* is Hebrew for "adversary"), and a stumbling-block for the Lord.

Thus, because the Lord loved Peter and His disciples, He took care that they did not fall into the snare of a worldly mindset that opposed the purposes of God. Jesus **turned around** to look back on **His disciples,** from whom Peter had taken Him aside. Seeing that they were observing Him and gauging His reaction to Peter's rebuke, **He rebuked Peter** in turn, saying to him, "**Go away after Me, Satan! For you are not minding the things of God, but of men.**"

The phrase translated *Go away after Me* is the Greek *Upage opiso mou*. The words *opiso mou* denote walking behind, and are used again in verse 34, where the Lord describes His disciple as the one who "follows after Me" (*opiso mou akolouthein*). The Lord is telling Peter that he has become His adversary by embodying these attitudes. Rather than presume to be His teacher, Peter must again take the role of His disciple; he must **go away** from *in front* of Him to take his appropriate place *behind* Him, coming **after Me.**

ॐ ॐ ॐ ॐ ॐ

34 And He called to *Him* the crowd with His disciples, and said to them, "If anyone wants to follow after Me, let him *completely* deny himself and take his cross and follow Me.

35 "For whoever wants to save his life will lose it, but whoever loses his life for the sake of Me and the Gospel will save it.

36 "For what does it profit a man to gain the whole world, and to *experience* loss of his life?

37 "For what will a man give in return for his life?

38 "For whoever is *thoroughly*-ashamed of Me and My words in this adulterous and sinful generation, the Son of Man will also be *thoroughly*-ashamed of him when He comes in the glory of His Father with the holy angels."

9 1 And He said to them, "Amen I say to you, there are some of those standing here who will not taste death until they see the Kingdom of God having come in power."

After this stunning rebuke, the Lord then turned His attention to the **crowd**. Summoning them at the next opportunity, He spoke to them **with His disciples** as well, generalizing the saving lesson He had given to Peter.

It is crucial for them not to shrink from death, preferring worldly comfort, honor, and temporal life to suffering for the will of God. Peter had reacted with horror to the thought of dying on a cross—as indeed all sensible people did. Crucifixion was the worst death imaginable in those days, and one reserved by the Romans for slaves and notorious criminals. It took the condemned days to die, as he hung suspended between earth and heaven, exposed to hunger and thirst and the mocking of men. The one so condemned was first scourged to the point of having his back laid open. Then he would take up the horizontal cross-beam on which he was to be nailed or tied and would carry it to the place of execution. There he would be nailed to it and left to die. The condemned wretch suffered excruciating pain and thirst and died shrieking out his curses on his executioners. It is significant that crucifixion did not become popular as a Christian artistic subject until after it had ceased to be popularly used. It was too obscene a sight.

The Lord knew what was in the hearts of His hearers. Like all people, they wanted comfort and ease, honor and long life—and wanted only the kind of Messiah who would bring them these things. A Messiah who would Himself die in the pain of defeat was not for them.

Like Peter, they needed to have their whole attitude rearranged. Jesus therefore taught them about the nature of the Kingdom that was coming, about the kind of Messiah He was and about their own discipleship as followers of that kind of Messiah. **If anyone wants to follow** Him and inherit the Kingdom He was bringing, that person must *completely* **deny himself** (not just "deny," Gr. *arneomai*, but "completely and totally deny," *aparneomai*). Like a condemned man **taking his cross** and walking to his execution and thus caring nothing any more for what went on in this world, so also the one who wants to be His disciple must renounce this life with all its comforts, and be prepared to bear anything for the sake of God. It is natural to shrink from this suffering and to **want to save** one's **life**. But such compromises with the truth are not the way of true

safety. If one refuses to follow Him and leaves His service to save
his own skin, that one will not succeed in saving his life, but will
lose it.

Here is the divine paradox. If one clutches and clings to his
safety and comfort, refusing to follow Jesus because of the suffering
involved, then one will lose one's life at the Judgment Seat of God.
But if one **loses his life**, sacrificing comfort, riches, and honor for
the sake of Him and His **Gospel** message, being willing even to die
for Him—then one will **save** his life at the final Judgment, inherit-
ing the true and lasting life in the age to come.

Here is the challenge of being a follower of truth in an age
devoted to compromise and lies. Here is the difficulty of discipleship. It is hard to be His disciple. Yet it is the only sensible way. **For
what does it profit a man to gain** even **the whole world**, with all
its honor, health, and riches, if he then *experiences* the **loss** of his
own **life**? In this short parabolic saying, the Lord asks His hearers
to evaluate this bargain: If a man were offered the whole world in
exchange for being killed, how sensible was that? Who would take
such an offer? For **what will a man give in return for his life?** Obviously, one would keep one's life, even if it meant forgoing the offer of
receiving the world. In the same way, Christ says, one should follow
Him and inherit life in the age to come, even if it means forgoing
all the pleasures and comforts of this world.

Now, such things seem difficult. It is hard to forgo the world
for the sake of future life when the present rewards beckon so in-
sistently. But soon this present, with its apparent ambiguities, will
pass away. **The Son of Man** will one day **come in the glory of His
Father with** all the splendor of God's fearful and **holy angels**. Then
all will stand trembling before that final Tribunal and be judged for
their earthly choices.

In **this adulterous and sinful** age, it might seem easy and obvious to renounce Jesus—to be *thoroughly*-**ashamed of** Him (Gr.
epaisxunomai; a more intensive verb than "to be ashamed," *aisxuno*).
It is easy to reject His Gospel **words** about bringing in the Kingdom
and to deny Him as if He were a deceiver (see 3:22). But if one
gives in to such cowardice and chooses earthly life over heavenly

truth, then **the Son of Man will also be** *thoroughly*-**ashamed** of that coward, and deny Him at the Judgment. That day may seem far off. Indeed, *too* far off, so that one may be tempted to think it will never come with its consequences for our cowardice. But a foretaste of Christ's future glory could soon be glimpsed, as a confirmation to them of His messianic majesty to come. The Lord solemnly vowed to them (with His characteristic **"Amen I say to you"**), that **some of those standing** there would **not taste death** until they saw that glory—the glory of **the Kingdom of God having come in power**. Some in that crowd of listeners would experience for themselves the truth of His words.

§V.2   The Transfiguration

ॐ ॐ ॐ ॐ ॐ

2   And six days later Jesus takes with Him Peter and James and John and brings them up to a high mountain by themselves alone. And He was transfigured before them,

3   and His garments became glistening and very white, such as no bleacher on earth is able to whiten them.

4   And there appeared to them Elijah, with Moses, and they were speaking with Jesus.

5   And Peter answered and says to Jesus, "Rabbi, it is good *for* us to be here, and let us make three tents, one for You, and one for Moses and one for Elijah."

6   For he did not know what to answer, for they became frightened.

7   Then a cloud occurred, overshadowing them, and a Voice occurred from out of the cloud, "This is My beloved Son; hear Him!"

8   And suddenly, having looked around, they no longer saw any one with them, but Jesus alone.

The chronology of the Transfiguration is difficult to determine with accuracy. Comparing this account with those of the other Synoptic Gospels, it would appear that the event took place after nightfall one week after the Lord's prediction of it in the previous verse, perhaps after midnight. This was reckoned by St. Mark as **six days later** (not counting the time after nightfall as another day, but as still a part of the previous day), perhaps to make it conform to the glory of Moses on Mount Sinai. According to Exodus 24:16, Moses was called up to have communion with God in His glory after the cloud of His Presence had settled on the mountaintop for six days. It would seem that St. Mark meant his Jewish hearers to make the connection between Moses and Christ.

(If the event did happen after midnight, that would explain the variant reckoning of Luke 9:28. St. Luke seems to have reckoned the day Christ uttered the prediction and the day of the post-midnight event as one day each, and so he said that the event took place after "eight days." There need not be any real discrepancy between this and St. Mark's computation of it as occurring after "six days." If Christ uttered His prediction (say) on Monday afternoon and the event happened very early the following Monday morning (say two A.M.), then the perceived contradiction is removed. St. Mark would count Monday to Tuesday as one day and the event as happening late Sunday night for a total reckoning of six days, while St. Luke would count each Monday to be one day and the event as happening early Monday for a total reckoning of "eight days.")

Whatever the reckoning, when Christ ascended the mountain, He **takes with Him Peter and James and John** (the verb is in the historic present, giving us the feeling that we also are among this select group). The **high mountain** He ascended is unnamed, though later tradition made it Mount Tabor in the north, between Nazareth and the Sea of Galilee. Tabor certainly fits the bill, rising 1300 feet above the plain below and commanding a view all around. From the Lukan parallel (Luke 9:28), we learn that He ascended the mountain to find solitude to pray. Doubtless He prayed long into the night, and it was while He continued His vigil of communion with God that His disciples slept. Something awoke them (perhaps the unexpected answering voices of Moses and Elijah?) and they saw to their astonishment that **He was transfigured before them**.

The Jews expected the Messiah to be a figure of heavenly glory and dazzling splendor. Those who suspected that Jesus was the designated Messiah were no doubt puzzled by His ordinary appearance. If He were indeed the Messiah, where was His glory, His angelic attendants, His awesome brightness? He appeared to all men in the dress of a simple field preacher, a humble carpenter and rabbi.

This stumbling block was removed before the watching eyes of the inner apostolic circle as they beheld Him in His own true messianic glory. As He walked among men, His glory had been veiled to their sight—though apparently not veiled to the horrified eyes of the demons (see 1:24)! Now, for the apostles' sakes, this veil was temporarily removed, and in a vision they saw the Lord of Glory as He truly was. Words fail St. Mark in his description of that blinding brilliance, which made even **His garments** to be **glistening and very white**, and he can only offer the homely testimony that **no bleacher** or launderer **on earth** would have been able to **whiten them** like that. Here was the glory of the Second Coming, when "the Kingdom of God" would "come in power" (9:1). The glory Jesus would openly manifest then was secretly revealed now to His disciples, confirming to them that He was indeed the true Messiah. As the Kontakion for the Feast of Transfiguration says, because of this prior revelation of glory, when the apostles would later "behold Him crucified, they would understand that His suffering was voluntary, and would proclaim to the world that He was truly the Radiance of the Father" and the Christ of God.

But it was not merely that Jesus was transfigured and manifested the glory proper to Him as the Christ. **There appeared to them** as well **Elijah, with Moses** (perhaps identified as such by the disciples as they listened to the conversation of Elijah and Moses). And Jesus did not prostrate Himself before these ancient worthies (as anyone else might have). Rather, He stood erect, almost casually **speaking with** them. (From St. Luke's account, we learn that they spoke of His exodus, His death; Luke 9:31.) It is Peter who breaks the apostles' stupefied silence. He addresses Jesus honorifically as **Rabbi**, and affirms **it is good *for* us to be here**. That is, it was fortunate they could see this vision and share the moment. For as Elijah and Moses were departing, Peter desired to prolong and repeat the time of glory, and offered to **make three tents**—one each for Jesus and **for Moses** and **for Elijah**. As a good Jew, he remembered how God's glory had appeared to this same Moses through the tent of meeting (Ex. 33:9), and he sought some way to preserve this manifested radiance. Perhaps after these tents were made, Jesus could return here, and Elijah and Moses could return also, each to his appointed tent! It was, of course, an inane response, and St. Mark almost apologizes for it, saying **he did not know what to answer, for they became frightened.** The vision, coming in the dead of night, shook them to their very core. They felt not only fear (Gr. *phobos*), but terror (Gr. *ekphobos*, a more intensive word). Little wonder that Peter's response was off the mark!

There was more fear to come. As Peter was chattering, **a cloud occurred, overshadowing them**, even as the cloud of the Divine Presence overshadowed the Tabernacle and Temple of old (Ex. 40:35; 1 Kings 8:10). Luke relates that, not unnaturally, they were afraid as they entered the cloud (Luke 9:34). Then, **a Voice occurred from out of the cloud**, the very Voice whose command created the cosmos out of nothing, whose sound even to that day could break the majestic and immovable cedars of Lebanon (Gen. 1:3; Ps. 29:4, 5). And the Voice spoke to them, pointing to Jesus, designating Him as the true Messiah, focusing their attention on Him alone: **"This is My beloved Son; hear Him!"** Perhaps in terror they had shut their eyes and prayed for mercy. But no sooner had the terrifying Voice sounded than all that atmosphere vanished instantly. They **looked around** wildly and **no longer saw** anyone. **Jesus alone** was there with them on the mountain, looking just as He had before. Perhaps He told them to go back to sleep, and we may imagine it was a long time before they could drop off to slumber as before. When they awoke in the morning to begin their descent and return to their companions, the shattering vision was still fresh in their hearts.

What did it all mean? Why was it Elijah and Moses who appeared with Jesus, and not some other ancient prophets? What did their sudden departure mean, leaving the Lord alone with His disciples? To men steeped in the Old Testament, the answers were plain enough. Elijah was the greatest of prophets, the only one whose return, as such, was anticipated (see Mal. 4:5). Moses was the great lawgiver. Together they embodied the Law and the Prophets, the entire Old Testament dispensation. As they spoke with Jesus, it was a living illustration of how all the Scriptures of old pointed to Him. It was not, as some then might have thought, that Jesus was but one more prophet among many, the next in a long line of prophets. He was not subordinate to Moses, nor inferior to any of the previous prophets—even the greatest of them, Elijah. Rather, it was *they* who were subordinate to *Him*. He did not continue their tradition, as if He were a mere man. He was the Divine Messiah, and they witnessed to Him. All of Israel's sacred history, in fact, was but a preparation for His ministry and work. Peter, in suggesting that three co-equal tents be built, was failing to appreciate this fact. Jesus was not simply one among the three, as if Moses and Elijah were His co-equal colleagues. Rather, as but the preparation for Him, they were destined to fade. And fade they did, leaving Jesus alone. That is, the Old Testament was to give place to the New Testament; the Law and the Prophets were to give place to Christ. As the Voice of the Father told Peter, all were to **hear Him** and focus on Him alone. The old dispensation was drawing to its close.

§V.3   Descent from the Mountain and Healing of a Demoniac Child

ॐ ॐ ॐ ॐ ॐ

9 And as they were coming down from the mountain, He ordered them not to describe to anyone what they had seen, until the Son of Man should rise from the dead.

10 And they seized the word to themselves, debating with one another what was "the rising from the dead."

11 And they asked Him, saying, "Why do the scribes say that Elijah must come first?"

12 And He said to them, "Elijah indeed comes first to restore all things. And how is it written of the Son of Man that He should suffer many things and be disdained?

13 "But I say to you, that Elijah has also come, and they did to him whatever they wanted, just as it is written of him."

The next morning, their hearts were full of the vision, and they were eager to tell everyone of this dramatic confirmation of Jesus' messianic status and glory. But He forbade it. He **ordered them not to describe to anyone what they had seen.** That is, fearing a further outbreak of messianic enthusiasm among the populace should they learn of the vision (see John 6:15), He commanded them to keep it a secret **until the Son of Man should rise from the dead.**

The apostles obeyed the injunction, and did not spread their news. They did, however, **seize** on **the word** among themselves, holding an intense debate. For they longed to tell the glorious secret, and began to **debate with one another what was "the rising from the dead."** It would be after this rising that they could tell everyone—but what was this **rising?**

As Jews, they knew what the final rising of the dead was to be. It was to be the end, the Last Day, when God would raise up all who had ever lived and make them stand before His terrible Judgment Seat to receive their eternal reward and sentence. But Jesus seemed to mean something else—something imminent and historical, something in this life, after which they could tell everyone what they had seen. He couldn't have meant, they reasoned, the final resurrection of all, for after that event the present age would be over, and there would be no point in telling anyone anything.

It almost seemed as if He were going to die! But that could not be. Their vision of Elijah had brought to their minds afresh the thought of the expected messianic redemption. In the usual teaching of **the scribes** about this redemption, **Elijah** the prophet would return to earth—perhaps on his fiery chariot—and **restore all things**. That is, they expected a general restoration, a time of life and blessing and universal righteousness. In this restored end-times utopia, what place was there for death?

The Lord deals with their misguided understanding of the return of Elijah. It was true, **He said to them**, that **Elijah indeed comes first to restore all things**. This had been prophesied in Malachi 4:5 and it would take place. But the Messiah must still die—or how else could it be **written of the Son of Man that He should suffer many things and be disdained** and rejected? The Scriptures also prophesied His suffering and rejection (e.g. Is. 53), and this must be fulfilled as well.

But Elijah had already come, and **they did to him whatever they wanted, just as it is written of him**. That is, just as Elijah of old suffered persecution at the hands of King Ahab, so the modern Elijah suffered at the hands of a king. Jesus was, of course, speaking of John the Baptizer suffering at the hands of King Herod. It was John who was the fulfillment of the Elijah prophecy. Elijah himself was not to return, supernaturally reappearing from heaven. Rather, the Forerunner of the end-times was one who was to come in the spirit and power of Elijah, doing again his holy prophetic work (see Luke 1:17). And as the modern Elijah had suffered as it was written of him, so would the Son of Man also suffer in fulfillment of the Scriptures. Though He was the true and transfigured Messiah, Jesus was to die.

༄ ༄ ༄ ༄ ༄

14 And when they came to the disciples, they saw a large crowd around them, and scribes debating with them.

15 And immediately all the crowd, having seen Him, were startled and ran up to greet Him.

16 And He asked them, "What are you debating with them?"

17 And one of the crowd answered Him, "Teacher,

> I brought to You my son, who has a mute spirit,
> 18 "and whenever it catches him, it dashes him down and he foams and grinds *his* teeth and withers up. And I told Your disciples, that they might cast it out, and they were not strong enough."
> 19 And He answers them and says, "O faithless generation, how long will I be with you? How long will I bear with you? Bring him to Me!"

When Christ, with Peter, James, and John, **came to the disciples**, it was to demonstrate how His messianic glory was to be manifested in this present age—not by an open demonstration of His transfigured brilliance (this was reserved for the age to come), but rather by overcoming the powers of darkness. And even *this* manifestation of glory presupposed faith on the part of those receiving it.

When they returned from their mountaintop experience the next morning, therefore, **they saw a large crowd** gathered around the rest of the disciples, consisting largely of Christ's adversaries the **scribes**, who were **debating** with them. The disciples were on the defensive. It appeared that they had been challenged to heal a poor afflicted boy, and had been unable. Their scribal opponents seized on this failure as an opportunity to deny Christ's power and mission.

It was doubtless this noisy and heated debate about the absent Jesus that caused the crowd to be **startled** when someone caught sight of Him approaching. To revile His authority when He was absent was one thing; to challenge it when He was present was another! The whole crowd therefore **ran up to greet Him**, in expectation that He would resolve the debate.

The Lord, it would seem, turned first to His own disciples, as to those who were directly answerable to Him. (This assumes the question of v. 16 is addressed to the disciples and not to the crowd, for the main focus at this point is on the disciples; see v. 15.) They were obviously in distress, having been confounded by their failure, and He wants to know the reason they were so upset. (Compare His similar question to them in v. 33.)

The disciples, however, were not allowed to answer. Before one of their number could confess to their failure, the father of the afflicted boy, being **one of the crowd**, jumped in to answer the question. Addressing Him deferentially as **Teacher**, he relates that he **brought** to Jesus his **son**, who had a **mute spirit** (that is, one which rendered the boy dumb). It was a heartrending and severe case. **Whenever it catches** the boy, the father related, **it dashes him down** to the ground so that **he foams** at the mouth and **grinds** *his* **teeth** and finally **withers up** (that is, goes rigid). He **told** Christ's **disciples** about the case, **that they might cast it out**. It was all to no avail. They **were not strong enough** to effect the cure. It was utterly hopeless. What was at stake (as well as the recovery of the boy) was the authority and status of Jesus. In bringing the boy to His disciples, the father was in fact bringing him to Jesus Himself (note v. 17: "**I brought** him **to You**"). The disciples' failure seemed to reflect on the Master's authenticity.

The Lord, however, is not in the least disconcerted. He knows the problem is not that He has insufficient power, but that they are a **faithless generation**. With the wearied resignation of the God who has long endured the faithlessness of the children of Israel (see Jer. 2:5), He rhetorically asks **how long** will He **be with** them and **bear with** them. After so many miracles, have they not yet learned to trust His power? His disciples might have failed, but He would not. In answer to the father's declaration of apparent hopelessness, He simply says, "**Bring him to Me!**" He will resolve everything.

ॐ ॐ ॐ ॐ ॐ

20 And they brought him to Him. And when he saw Him, immediately the spirit convulsed him, and falling on the ground, he rolled about and foamed.

21 And He asked his father, "How long has this

> been happening to him?" And he said, "From childhood.
> 22 "And it has often cast him both into fire and into water to destroy him. But if You can do anything, have heartfelt *love* for us—help us!"

In response, the friends of the father went to fetch the afflicted boy and **brought him** to Jesus. The demon within the lad, however, was not to go without a fight. Seeing its Judge, the spirit panicked and came out of hiding, manifesting itself in the sight of all. As the boy approached Jesus, the demon within **saw Him** and **immediately convulsed** the boy, so that he **fell on the ground** and **rolled about and foamed** at the mouth, as on other occasions. The Lord felt pity for the family, and **asked his father, "How long has this been happening to him?"** Jesus asked the father, we may think, not because He needed this information to heal the boy, but because His heart went out in compassion to him. Touched by their suffering, Christ asked how long they had endured this. Like a man answering the questions of a physician, the man responded, **"From childhood,"** adding the detail that it also **cast him both into fire and into water to destroy him.** That is, it was sometimes even worse than this! And then, watching his beloved son rolling about in degrading agony, his poor heart burst with grief, and he cried out, **"If You can do anything, have heartfelt *love* for us—help us!"** (The word translated here *have heartfelt love*, for the sake of consistency with 1:41; 6:34; 8:2, is the Gr. *splagxnizomai*, which could be more idiomatically rendered, "Have pity on us!")

> ॐ ॐ ॐ ॐ ॐ
> 23 And Jesus said to him, "If you can! All things are possible to him who believes."
> 24 Immediately the father of the child cried out and said, "I believe! Help my unbelief!"
> 25 And when Jesus saw that a crowd was running together, He rebuked the unclean spirit, saying

to it, "You mute and deaf spirit, I *Myself* command you, come out of him and enter him no more."

26 And after crying out and convulsing greatly, it came out; and he became like *one* dead, so that most said, "He has died."

27 But Jesus, having seized his hand, raised him and he stood up.

28 And when He had come into *the* house, His disciples asked Him privately, "Why were we *ourselves* not able to cast it out?"

29 And He said to them, "This kind cannot come out by anything but prayer *and fasting*."

The Lord reacts strenuously to such a lack of faith. In verse 19, He already reacted to the father's lack of faith by deploring the "faithless generation" of which he was a part. Here He again responds to the lack of faith implied by the father's request that Christ help "if" He was able, by throwing back the responsibility on him. "**If you can!**" He says, repeating the father's words with a kind of exasperation. The question is not whether Jesus can heal; it is rather whether the father can have faith—for **all things are possible to him who believes**. Faith in Jesus is the issue and the key to the boy's healing.

The boy's father was desperate. He knew and deplored the weakness of his faith, but still reached out to Jesus as his only hope. With a cry born of the urgency of a drowning man, he **cried out and said, "I believe! Help my unbelief!"** That is, he did believe as best he could. His doubt was not a rejection of Jesus' power, but a frantic seeking after elusive certainty. May the Lord accept what faith he had and pardon its weakness!

By this time **a crowd was running together**, no doubt drawn by the continued and pathetic convulsions of the boy writhing on the ground. As always, Jesus desired to keep His miracles as secret as He could, lest they ignite the ever-present possibility of messianic fever. He quickly **rebuked the unclean spirit**, addressing it as a **mute**

and deaf spirit. He stressed His own sovereign power. His disciples might have failed, but this was the Master Himself speaking to it now. "**I** *Myself* **command you**," He said (the **I** is emphatic in the Greek), as He told the demon to depart and "**enter him no more**."

The spirit was indeed stubborn, being (as we later learn) so great a demon as only to be driven out by prolonged and concentrated prayer. This stubbornness is seen in the effects on the boy as it left: the demon caused the boy to **cry out** and **convulsed** him **greatly** so that **he became like** *one* **dead**. The child lay unmoving on the ground, hardly breathing. Indeed, so great was the damage inflicted by the departing demon that **most said, "He has died."**

The Lord, however, was not deceived into thinking the child dead, for He knew His power over the demons. He **seized his hand** with the strong grip of love and **raised him** so that **he stood up** all by himself, no longer prostrated by the forces of darkness, but tall and erect in his new life.

The effect of the exorcism on the father and the crowd is not recorded, but we may easily imagine the overwhelmed relief and gratitude of the father, how he embraced his son with joy, and with tears kissed the hand of His Benefactor. The scribes, for their part, were again confounded. They had smugly rejoiced in the disciples' inability to cast out the demon as evidence that Christ's supposed authority over demons was exaggerated after all, but once again they found Jesus' power to be serene and absolute.

The disciples, we may imagine, were tempered in their exultation, and could hardly wait to be alone with the Master to ask Him the question that burned in their hearts. "**Why were we** *ourselves* **not able to cast it out?**" they plaintively asked when at last they **had come into** *the* **house** and could speak **privately**. The Lord did not rebuke them for their lack of faith. They had cast out demons before (see 6:13), but this spirit was different. A greater and more powerful demon than the others (even as archangels are greater than angels?), **this kind** could not be cast out **by anything but** concentrated **prayer**. (The accompanying *fasting*, though not mentioned in the best manuscripts, is perhaps presupposed as a part of such prayer.) The Lord, in constant and unbroken reliance on the Father's power, as the incarnate Son, could cast it out with His mere Word. The disciples, however, must seek God's special intervention for such difficult cases as this.

§V.4   Second Passion Prediction—
Disciples Rebuked for Fighting over First Place

ॐ ॐ ॐ ॐ ॐ

30 And from there they went out and proceeded through Galilee, and He was not willing that anyone should know,

31 for He was teaching His disciples and saying to them, "The Son of Man is to be delivered *up* into the hands of men, and they will kill Him, and when He has been killed, after three days He will rise."

32 But they did not understand the word, and they were afraid to ask Him.

The second prediction of the Passion takes place after **they went out** from there and **proceeded through Galilee**. Unlike previous tours through Galilee, which were characterized by public preaching and rallying as many people as possible to come and hear the Word, this journey was a quiet one. His aim was not to preach to as many as He could, but simply to pass through the territory on the way to Jerusalem. Thus, **He was not willing that anyone should know** of His route. He did not publicize His journeys, as He had before (see Luke 10:1). His focus was now primarily on His own intimate disciples. Having elicited a confession of faith, He must now teach and prepare them for what lay ahead. So it was that He said to them that **the Son of Man** was to be **delivered *up* into the hands of men** to be killed and to **rise** again **after three days**.

But just as before (see 8:32), **they did not understand** His **word**. Their minds were still filled with expectations of glory. As good Jews, they expected Messiah to triumph heroically. Defeat and death were, they felt, incompatible with messianic office. Doubtless they felt that He must be somehow speaking in another parable. Their fear of looking stupid in front of the others (for each was reluctant to be the first to admit incomprehension), combined with natural reluctance to speak openly of such an obscene horror, kept them from questioning Him further. **They were afraid to ask Him** to elaborate, and remained in their ignorance.

ॐ ॐ ॐ ॐ ॐ

33 And they came into Capernaum, and when He was in the house, He asked them, "What were you asking on the way?"

34 But they were silent, for on the way they had asked one another who was greatest.

35 And having sat, He called the Twelve and says to them, "If anyone wants to be *the* first, he shall be *the* last of all, and servant of all."

36 And having taken a child, He stood him in *the* middle of them, and having taken him in His arms, He said to them,

37 "Whoever welcomes one such child in My Name welcomes Me; and whoever welcomes Me does not welcome Me, but the One who sent Me."

As they journeyed from the foot of the mount of Transfiguration to Capernaum, and as the disciples thought of the glory of the coming Kingdom, they thought of their own places in it. A heated debate arose as to **who was greatest** among them, and which ones would have the chief seats in the restored political kingdom of Israel, which was, they felt, surely imminent.

The Lord, it would seem, was walking ahead of them, just out of earshot. Nonetheless, He knew well enough what they were arguing about. So, when **they came** home to **Capernaum** and were safely and privately **in the house** they used as their base there, **He asked them** what it was that they were **asking** and debating **on the way**. (We note in passing the compassion and sensitivity of Christ—for He waited until they were alone to expose their weakness, thus allowing them to save face and preserve their public dignity.)

When He asked them what it was they had been discussing so passionately, He received no answer, as **they were silent**. We can almost see the disciples, as each one looked down at his feet, ashamed to confess his lapse from humility.

Continuing His exquisite sensitivity and compassion, Christ does not insist that they openly confess what He already knows; nor does He single any one of them out for special reproach. (Not even Peter, who, we may imagine, as first among the Twelve, had the most to say!) Rather, He simply **sat** down, in the customary posture of a teacher about to speak, and **called the Twelve** to receive the lesson. (In the ancient world, teachers sat to teach—compare the bishop's chair as symbolic of his teaching office.)

The lesson was this: "**If anyone wants to be** *the* **first, he shall be** *the* **last of all, and servant of all.**" That is, the true path to being *the* first in the Kingdom was humility. God would choose as first and as honored leader the one who served as if he were *the* **last of all** and the **servant of all**. Wanting to be honored in the Kingdom was understandable and good—but self-exaltation was not the path toward it! Rather, humble service to one's fellows was the criterion on which God would reward those with the first and best places in His Kingdom.

In order to further demonstrate this, Jesus **took a child** (possibly one of Peter's own children or relatives?) and **stood him in** *the* **middle of them** beside Himself, as a silent model of the required humility and servanthood. (The demonstration was all the more obvious to them, since the word for "child" and "servant" was the same in Aramaic.) A servant had no status in those days, no grounds for self-exaltation or self-promotion. Similarly, a child had no social status. (As St. Paul would later say, the child, even though future master and heir, had no more status than a slave; see Gal. 4:1.) Christ therefore was commending to His disciples that they resign themselves to having no status in the world and to being utterly marginalized, just as servants and children were.

Yet, though they had no status in the eyes of the world and were considered as **last of all**, they were still precious in the Kingdom and in the eyes of God. To demonstrate this, He **took** the child up **in His arms** (a single Greek word, *enagkalizomai*—literally, to wrap one's bent arms around) and hugged the child close, thereby identifying the little one with Himself. To **welcome one such child in My Name**, He affirmed, would be to **welcome** Christ Himself—and also, to welcome God, who **sent** Him in the first place. Those whom Christ chose thus stood at the end of a holy chain of authority—to receive Him was to receive the Father, and to receive any whom Christ sent and acknowledged as His own was to receive Him. Thus—a staggering conclusion!—to receive even **one such child**, even one entirely without status or rank in the world, was to receive God Himself.

What did this mean to the disciples and their futile fighting over rank and first place? That in rejecting their fellow-disciple as too humble and as unworthy of greatness in the Kingdom, they were thereby rejecting Christ and God. *He* had called those disciples as His own, even if others thought them unworthy of such status. How dare they reject as unworthy those whom He had welcomed? The ones coveting the first places might reject their rivals as unworthy of status—but even so, these rivals could not have less status than a child! And the Lord affirmed that even such a humble one as a child was invested with honorable status if he was His chosen disciple. Therefore let their quarreling over preeminence cease!

ॐ ॐ ॐ ॐ ॐ

38 John said to Him, "Teacher, we saw someone casting out demons in Your Name, and we forbade him because he was not following us."

39 But Jesus said, "Do not forbid him, for there is no one who will do a *work* of power in My Name and be able soon after to speak evil of Me.

40 "For whoever is not against us is for us.

41 "For whoever *gives* you a cup of water to drink because you *bear* the Name of Christ, amen I say to you, he will *certainly* not lose his reward.

42 "And whoever causes one of these little ones who believe to stumble, it would be good for him rather to have a millstone *turned by* a donkey hung around his neck and be cast into the sea."

In response to the Lord's rebuke, **John** tries to deflect His attention to what he considers the failings of others—in this case, **someone** who was using Jesus' Name to **cast out demons**, even though he was **not** formally **following** Him (that is, he had not been baptized as His disciple; see John 4:2). John considered this unauthorized use of Jesus' Name unacceptable. The Twelve had been charged by Jesus to invoke His Name in order to exorcise (see 6:7), but this man had received no such authority. The tense of the verb **forbade** (the imperfect, *ekoluomen*) would seem to indicate that the disciples were not finally successful in their attempt. They had repeatedly argued with the well-meaning exorcist to desist, but to no avail. John was by implication asking Jesus to step in and officially forbid such unauthorized usage of His Name. In this the disciples seemed to be motivated by a jealousy for their own privileged status. (There is here a subtle touch of irony: John finds fault with one for performing successful exorcisms immediately after he and his fellow-disciples were unable to perform one.)

The Lord, however, was not perturbed by the behavior of the exorcist. He directed John **not** to **forbid him**, saying wryly that **no one who** did a miracle (literally, *work* of power, Gr. *dunamis*) in His Name would be likely to **speak evil** of Him anytime **soon**. (This last, we may think, was said with something of a smile, being such a colossal understatement!) In refusing to oppose the exorcist, Christ was delivering a gentle rebuke to the apostles' prideful concern for their own status. Instead of being so jealous of their privilege, they should rather rejoice in goodwill wherever they found it. Indeed, in a day when people were drawn into two polarized camps regarding Jesus, **whoever** was **not against** them was therefore **for** them. The unknown exorcist had not sided with the Pharisees, who were **against** Him and denounced Him as a deceiver. The apostles must therefore welcome whatever testimony to Him the exorcist gave (implicit in his use of Jesus' Name for working miracles), and count his work as **for** their own. He was serving their cause in his own way, and would be rewarded for it by God.

More than this, whatever service *anyone* gave them **because** they bore **the Name of Christ** would be rewarded, even the smallest. If all the hospitality one could afford was **a cup of water**—the offering of the poorest and most destitute—that one would *certainly* **not lose his reward.** The certainty that the donor would **not lose his reward** is indicated by Christ prefacing His promise with His customary oath, **"amen I say to you,"** and by the strong negative in the Greek (*ou me*), translated here as *certainly* **not.** The Lord wanted His disciples to be sure that every single act of support and encouragement they received would be abundantly compensated by God in the age to come. The disciples must therefore not disdain any such acts of service (such as those rendered by the exorcist of v. 38), for God would honor them.

Furthermore, if a man opposed such **little ones** who humbly identified themselves with Him (through their using His Name for exorcism or giving a mere cup of water), and thereby caused them **to stumble** and turn from Him, woe to that man! If one's pride and opposition caused any to lose faith, **it would be good for him rather to have a millstone** *turned by* **a donkey hung around his neck and be cast into the sea.** (The **millstone** *turned by* a donkey was the large millstone used to grind flour for bread, and was very heavy—heavy enough indeed to quickly drown one!) One must at all costs avoid causing the faithful to fall away, for this would be met by God's severest wrath on the Last Day. The most dramatic doom imaginable on earth—being drowned in the sea—would be preferable to the fate reserved by God for those who caused Christ's supporters to defect from Him.

ॐ ॐ ॐ ॐ ॐ

43 "And if your hand causes you to stumble, cut it off! It is good for you to enter Life crippled, than having the two hands, to go away into Gehenna, into the unquenchable fire.*

45 "And if your foot causes you to stumble, cut it off! It is good for you to enter into Life lame, than having the two feet, to be cast into Gehenna.*

47 "And if your eye causes you to stumble, cast it out! It is good for you to enter into the Kingdom of God one-eyed, than having two eyes to be cast into Gehenna,

48 "where their worm does not die and the fire is not quenched.

(*The best manuscripts omit verses 44 and 46, which repeat verse 48 for the sake of parallelism.)

The Lord then counsels them to cut such jealous pride from their hearts, be it ever so dear to them and ever so much a part of them. For **if** their **hand** caused them **to stumble** and sin so that they would be sent **away into Gehenna** of **unquenchable fire**, would they not **cut it off** to save themselves? Indeed, for it would be **good** for them **to enter** the **Life** of the age to come **crippled** with only one hand, **than having the two hands, to go away** into Hell. (One can imagine the disciples looking at their hands as He spoke these words.) Just so should they cast out jealous pride from their inner life.

Or their **foot**—even though it was indispensable to this life—if it **caused** them **to stumble** and fall from God, would they not **cut it off** too? For it would be better for them **to enter into** the **Life** to come being **lame** and limping **than having the two feet** they treasured **to be cast into Gehenna**.

Or even their precious **eye**—if that caused them to sin, they would **cast it out** from their body too! For it were better to **enter** into the Kingdom of God one-eyed, than having two eyes to be cast into Gehenna. For the fiery experience of **Gehenna** (the contemporary term for Hell, derived from the ever-burning garbage dump near Jerusalem in the Valley of Hinnom, or *ge hinnom* in the Hebrew) would be eternal. The suffering of having but one hand, one foot, or one eye would endure for this life, but the judgment of God would never end. Just as the **worm** did **not die** in that place and the **fire** was **not quenched** (a citation from Is. 66:24; see Sirach 7:17), so the punishment meted out by God would not cease either. Let them fear such judgment and avoid the sin of jealous pride that provoked it! Better to endure the loss of something precious now (their hand, foot, or eye—or pride!), than experience the loss of their total self in Hell.

(It should be stressed that Christ is speaking parabolically here, and is not actually counseling self-mutilation as a remedy for temptation to sin. His point is not that the thief should cut off his hand, nor the lustful man gouge out his eye. Rather, by these metaphors He teaches that one should deal with one's sins with such ruthlessness and determination. It is jealous pride that must be cut off, not one's physical limbs.)

ॐ ॐ ॐ ॐ ॐ

49 For everyone will be salted with fire.
50 The salt *is* good, but if the salt becomes unsalty, with what will you season it again? Have salt among yourselves and be at peace with one another.

Our Lord concludes His rebuke of their pride and striving over first place (see v. 34) with a parabolic saying about salt. Salt was used in those days for a variety of purposes, including offering as a part of the Temple sacrifices (Lev. 2:13). Such salt made the sacrifice acceptable to God, since it was an image of covenant loyalty. (In those days, when one pledged loyalty by eating with another, one would share salt as part of the meal, so that salt became a symbol of unbreakable loyalty; see Num. 18:19. To this day, visiting bishops are met with gifts of bread and salt.)

Building on this image, Jesus says that **everyone** of His disciples **will be salted with** the **fire** of the Holy Spirit. That is, those in the world might quarrel and betray one another, but His disciples were called to be different from the world. By retaining within themselves the fire of the Spirit, they would remain faithful and loyal to one another. As Temple sacrifices were acceptable to God only when salted, so they too would be acceptable to Him when **salted** with the Spirit's **fire**, which would preserve them in peace. That **salt** was **good**—but only if it remained salty. If it **became unsalty**, it was useless, for **with what** could one **season it again?** Salt which had became unsalty could not be restored, and was fit only to be thrown out. It would be the same with them if they lost the saltiness of the Spirit and quarreled like mere men of the world. If they would not be rejected by God, let them **have salt** among themselves and **be at peace.** Let their quarreling cease and let them have done with jealously fighting with those who supported Him.

(We note in passing that the unity of the Church, therefore, finds its daily support in this charismatic experience of the Spirit. That unity is indeed a divinely given and irrevocable gift, so that the Church cannot cease to be one. Nonetheless, in our daily lives we preserve this unity between one another in our parishes as we remain on fire with the Spirit. It is only as we allow this divine Fire to grow cold within us that we transgress the unity and love between us and our brothers; see Eph. 4:3.)

§V.5   Conflict with Pharisees over Divorce

ॐ ॐ ॐ ॐ ॐ

10 1   And having arisen from there, He goes to the area of Judea and beyond the Jordan; and crowds gather together to Him again, and, as was His custom, He taught them.

2   And Pharisees came up to Him, and asked Him

> whether it was permitted for a man to dismiss a wife, testing Him.
>
> 3 And He answered and said to them, "What did Moses command you?"
>
> 4 And they said, "Moses allowed *us* to write a booklet of divorce and to dismiss *her*."
>
> 5 But Jesus said to them, "For your hardness of heart he wrote to you this commandment.
>
> 6 "But from *the* beginning of creation, 'He made them male and female.
>
> 7 "'For this reason a man will leave behind his father and mother,
>
> 8 "'and the two will be one flesh.' So they are no longer two, but one flesh.
>
> 9 "What therefore God has yoked-together, do not let man separate."

After **having arisen** from where He had sat to teach His apostles in Capernaum (see 9:35), Christ headed south **to the area of Judea**, going through Perea in the territory **beyond the Jordan**. This was the jurisdiction of King Herod and was a dangerous place for Him politically. It was this place therefore that Christ's foes chose for **testing Him** after He stopped to teach the **crowds** that had **gathered together to Him**. Perhaps they hoped to provoke Him into making some statement about divorce that they could use in denouncing Him to Herod, whose own divorce and remarriage had been so politically controversial. Opposition to that divorce and remarriage had proved John the Baptizer's undoing (see 6:17f), and they hoped that it might prove to be Jesus' undoing too. (We are reminded how the Pharisees were allied with Herod's men in their common opposition to Christ; see 3:6.)

After He taught the crowds, a delegation of **Pharisees came up to Him**, ostensibly to be instructed on a point of the Law. They began by asking **whether it was permitted** in the Law **for a man to dismiss a wife**.

This question seems only to have been their opening gambit, for everyone knew that divorce was permitted. Deuteronomy 24:1–3 allowed that a man might divorce his wife if he found some cause for shame in her. The only question on which there was any disagreement was the issue of what was meant by "a cause of shame." Some Jewish interpreters (e.g. those following a teacher named Hillel) said that the phrase meant any act that displeases the husband, so that they allowed divorce for any reason at all. Other Jewish interpreters (e.g. those following Shammai) said the phrase meant evidence of prior sexual unchastity, so that they allowed divorce only for unfaithfulness. (The more liberal interpretation of Hillel, not surprisingly, was the more popular.) The Pharisees began by asking Christ if the Law permitted divorce, no doubt intending to draw their net tighter as the debate continued.

The Lord responded with a question of His own: **"What did Moses command you?"** In all His teaching, He preferred to return to the heart and original intent of the Law. Their response was cautious and guarded: **"Moses allowed *us* to write a booklet of divorce and to dismiss *her*."** One should note a subtle change, for they did not answer the question that they were asked. Jesus asked for the positive command of the Law—what Moses actually **commanded**. They responded not with what was positively commanded, but with what was by concession **allowed**.

The Lord did not dispute that this was allowed, but He did call attention to the historically conditioned nature of the concession. This **commandment** did not express the heart and original divine intent for marriage. Rather, it was only allowed for their **hardness of heart**. Like the laws regulating war and slavery, this law presupposed an already existing evil, and was concerned to minimize the harm.

The positive Mosaic teaching on marriage (to which Jesus first alluded in v. 3) lay elsewhere, in the opening chapters of the Law. God's will regarding marriage and divorce could be deduced from what was written about *the* **beginning of creation** in Genesis 1—2. There it was written that God **made** the human species as a duality, containing both **male and female** (Gen. 1:27). They were created not to be two self-contained autonomous beings, who might form a union as it suited them and dissolve the alliance if they willed. Rather, they belonged together, as a single unit. As it said in Genesis 2:24, **for this reason a man will leave behind his father and mother, and the two will be one flesh.** That is, marriage was not a mere legal contract (which might be terminated by a piece of paper, a **booklet of divorce**). It was the creation of a single new organism. The husband and wife together were **no longer two** different organisms, but now formed **one flesh. God** Himself had made the two into one, when He **yoked-together** the pair through their sexual union (Gr. *suzeugnumi*, cognate with the word *zeugos*, yoke). If God Himself had created this new reality, mere **man** should **not separate** them and thus undo His work.

This meant that divorce was *never* God's will. Both the interpretive schools of Hillel and Shammai erred in not going far enough and in not penetrating to the heart of the Law. Up until then, divorce had been allowed. But it was always a tragedy. And now that the Kingdom was at hand, it was God's will to overcome tragedy—what was once allowed for one's **hardness of heart** was allowed to the children of the Kingdom no longer. There was to be, if possible, a return to the ideal intent of the Law and to the original paradigm of creation.

ॐ ॐ ॐ ॐ ॐ

10 And in the house the disciples asked Him again about this.

11 And He says to them, "Whoever dismisses his wife and marries another commits adultery against her,

12 "and if she *herself* dismisses her husband and marries another, she commits adultery."

The disciples, listening to this exchange, were privately aghast at the radical nature of their Master's teaching, and when they were safely **in the house** in which they were staying, they **asked Him again about this.** They were hoping, perhaps, that His precepts had been parabolic somehow, and that they had misunderstood Him!

They had, they discovered, understood Him perfectly, and He meant what He said. He repeated it again in the form of two blunt statements, so that there could be no doubt about the upshot. **Whoever dismisses his wife and marries another commits adultery against her.** (We note in passing an advance over rabbinic teaching: adultery was normally considered as an offense against the aggrieved *husband* of the adulterous wife, but Christ here describes it as an offense against the abandoned *wife*.) That is, because the two were one flesh, for a man to divorce his wife in order to marry another woman was the same as if he committed adultery, since the bond joining him to his wife remained. The certificate of divorce he gave the first wife did not dissolve their union; it remained intact nonetheless, making the union with the second wife a kind of adultery.

And it was the same with the wife. **If she *herself* dismisses her husband and marries another** (that is, through abandoning him, as Herodias did with her first husband when she married his brother Herod; technically, women did not have the legal right to divorce in Israel), **she** also **commits adultery.** The bond uniting the two as one flesh remained for both. The disciples had not misunderstood their Lord's intention. His married disciples were not to divorce one another if they wanted to remain true to God's perfect will.

(Note: A few remarks of a pastoral nature must be added. As St. Paul would later illustrate in 1 Corinthians 7:12–16, Christ's teaching here presupposes that the husband and wife are both pious Christians. The question of what to do in a religiously mixed marriage, when only one partner is a devout Christian, is not here addressed. Though it remains true that divorce is never God's perfect will, but always involves the sundering of an essential union and the tearing apart of one flesh, it sometimes must occur nonetheless. The Orthodox Church has always lamented divorce as a fall from the norms of the Kingdom, and has always reluctantly allowed it nonetheless, restoring the broken ones to the Church's communion after a period of penance.)

§V.6 Disciples Rebuked over Christ's Blessing of Children

ॐ ॐ ॐ ॐ ॐ

13 And they were bringing children to Him that He might touch them, but the disciples rebuked them.

14 But having seen *this*, Jesus was indignant and said to them, "Let the children come to Me; do not forbid them, for to such belongs the Kingdom of God.

15 "Amen I say to you, whoever does not welcome the Kingdom of God as a child will never enter into it."

16 And He took them in His arms and *called down* a blessing *on* them, putting *His* hands on them.

St. Mark next relates a story about children, though without a precise chronological marker of when it occurred. A number of people from the crowd **were bringing children** to Jesus, **that He might touch them.** That is, they (the mothers of the children, most likely) were bringing their young children to Jesus as they would bring them to any famous rabbi, that He might lay hands on them and bless them. It was hoped that this would have good effects on their future lives.

The disciples, however, **rebuked them**, forbidding them to see the Master and telling them firmly (and probably repeatedly, striving to overcome the will of a group of determined mothers!) to go away. What was their motivation in this? It would seem likely that this event occurred at the end of a long and exhausting day of teaching. Perhaps Jesus was resting or even dozing, and they were motivated by a desire to protect Him from interruption. Children had no social status in those days, and the request of the delegation that Jesus come out and touch their children seemed to the disciples to be trivial and unworthy. Should they rouse their exhausted Master for *this*?

Jesus, who it seemed was resting nearby, heard the scene. (One can imagine the loudness of the mothers' protests when they were refused.) When He came and had **seen** for Himself what they wanted and how they were refused, He **was indignant** at His own disciples. He insisted that they **let the children come** to Him. They should have by all means disturbed Him for this and should not have **forbidden them**! For, contrary to what the world thought of children's status, they had great status in the eyes of God. Indeed, **to such belongs the Kingdom of God**. If God Himself had honored the children by giving to them—and to others like them—His Kingdom, who were the apostles to stand in His way by dishonoring and refusing them? It was a stunning rebuke, for He had publicly contradicted His male disciples in favor of women and children. He then **took** the children up one by one **in His arms and** *called down* a blessing *on* them (Gr. *kateulogeo*, a more intensive verb than *eulogeo*, "to bless"), as He **put** *His* **hands on them**. It doubtless took some time to bless all the children, since He took each one up into His arms individually. But to Him this was important work, for He was blessing those to whom His Father had given the Kingdom.

What did Christ mean when He said that the Kingdom of God belonged to them and to those like them? What was it about the children that made them suitable as heirs of the Kingdom? With our sentimental view of childhood, it is possible to miss the meaning and to become dewy-eyed talking about the innocence of children. But what was characteristic of children and was here commended was their free and open reception of Jesus and His love. They had no status on which they could rely, no claims they could press as they sought to be blessed. Unlike the proud Pharisees, who relied on their own righteousness and pressed before God their claim to receive the Kingdom based on their own accumulated merits, the children came with open hearts and open hands. They received the Kingdom as a gift, knowing they could not possibly earn it. They came to Jesus, trusting in His love, and expecting to be blessed simply because He was loving. This is how the Kingdom must be received by anyone, if it is to be received at all. As the Lord said, affirming it with His customary and emphatic **Amen I say to you**, the one who **does not welcome the Kingdom of God as a child,** with complete trust and humility, **will never enter into it** at all. Pharisaical pride and self-righteousness will exclude anyone from the Kingdom.

§V.7   The Rich Young Man and the Kingdom of God

ॐ ॐ ॐ ॐ ॐ

17 And as He was setting out on *the* way, one ran up to Him and knelt before Him, and asked Him, "Good Teacher, what shall I do to inherit eternal life?"

18 And Jesus said to him, "Why do you call Me good? No one *is* good but God alone.

19 "You know the commandments, 'Do not murder, do not commit adultery, do not steal, do not bear false witness, do not defraud, honor your father and mother.'"

20 And he said to Him, "Teacher, all these things I have kept from my youth."

21 And looking at him, Jesus loved him, and said to him, "One thing you *yourself* lack; go and sell as much as you have, and give to the poor, and you will have treasure in heaven; and come, follow Me."

22 But his face darkened at the word, and he went away sorrowful, for he was one who had many properties.

After the story of the simplicity of the children, St. Mark narrates the story of the rich young man as its counterpoint. The children may only have been concerned to freely receive Christ's love and Kingdom, but the young man was concerned to do something to earn it.

The rich man was by no means only concerned with riches. This is shown by the manner in which he approached the illustrious

Teacher: as Christ was **setting out on *the* way** and beginning His next journey, the man **ran up to Him**, in haste to catch Him. He was not simply coming to Jesus to ask a casual religious question that interested him. He felt his life was empty and that he had reached a crisis point. Deep in his young heart, he knew himself to be at a crossroads and needed before anything else to find resolution to the issue that tormented him every waking hour. That was why he **ran up to Him** with the haste of a common laborer, leaving his dignity behind in the dust, and **knelt before Him** in abject humility. With great emotion, he poured out the question that was always before his eyes: **"What shall I do to inherit eternal life?"** There was a great and aching void in his heart that told him he was far from God, and he was afraid. What could he **do**, what great exploit could he accomplish, what mighty work or mitzvah could he perform to **inherit eternal life** in the age to come and find peace in this one? In the emotion of the moment, he lavished a compliment on Jesus which was unheard of in his day, addressing Him as **Good Teacher**.

The Lord responded first of all to this unparalleled compliment and extravagant flattery. It revealed that the man had too easy and superficial a conception of goodness. Jesus answers with a question of His own: **"Why do you call Me good?"** In responding like this, Jesus is not denying that He is good. The focus of the question is not on Jesus, and the thought of whether or not He is good; the focus is on the man's conception of goodness, and whether or not it is superficial. (This is apparent in Matthew's reporting of the Lord's response. In Matthew 19:17, Jesus is reported as saying, "Why are you asking Me about what is good?") The Lord would have him know that true goodness is transcendent and otherworldly. **"No one *is* good but God alone."** That is, only God is absolutely good. If the young man is to find his way, he must recognize this. He doubtless thought of himself as a good man, one who came to ask the way of another good man. Christ stops him from pursuing this false trail at the outset. Only by recognizing the transcendence of true goodness and his own spiritual poverty can he hope to know the truth.

Then the Lord answers his question, calling him back to what

God had revealed. "**You know the commandments,**" the Lord told him, quoting a selection from the Law (see Ex. 20:12–16). Let him keep these, loving God by loving man made in His image. If he would do this, he would enter into life (see Matt. 19:17). God had already revealed the way home to His People. If they would love Him, and their neighbor, all would be well (Luke 10:28). The young man need only heed the Law that he already knew.

As expected in one so fervent, the man had already done this. "**Teacher,**" he continued (we note that he has dropped the **good** from his address; see v. 17), "**all these things I have kept from my youth.**" That is, he had always striven to keep the Law, ever since given the responsibility at his *bar mitzvah*, or coming of age. Yet he still felt that he lacked something, and still was tormented by a void that weighed daily on his heart (see Matt. 19:20).

The Lord did not contradict this answer, nor tell him that he was mistaken and that his perception of having kept the Law was an illusion. He had kept the Law as best he could. Christ recognized, however, that there was **one thing** which he himself (the **you** is emphatic in the Greek) still **lacked.** The void he felt was a sign that God was calling him to perfection, to Christian discipleship, to the Kingdom of God as it was breaking in then and there through Jesus' ministry. His keeping of the Law was enough to make him inherit life in the age to come. But God was calling him to an experience of that life right now, as a disciple of Christ. Jesus **looked at him** intently (the Greek word is *emblepo*, used in 8:25 to indicate a focused staring) and then **loved him.** That is, He kissed him, as rabbis did their promising disciples, thereby accepting and calling him to discipleship. He then told him that he need do only **one thing** more to fill up the void in his heart and find the peace to which God was calling him. Let him **go and sell as much** as he had, and **give** it all **to the poor** and **have treasure in heaven.** Thus freed, he could **come, follow** Jesus.

One can almost see the angels, invisibly present and striving for the salvation of all (Luke 15:10), holding their breath as they awaited the man's response. Certainly the apostles themselves looked intently and hopefully at him who could be their newest fellow-disciple. As the man continued kneeling before Christ (v. 17), it was as if a choice between two worlds opened before him. He could choose poverty and the adventure of following this wonder-working Teacher, or he could choose a life of wealth and ease, continue to wrestle with the emptiness that haunted his hours, and try to push the Teacher's words away from him. He had come to Jesus as if to his last hope. Now he was aghast at what he heard and the choice he was given.

In the end, the struggle to free himself from his wealth was too great, and he chose the bondage of riches over the joy of Christ. **His face darkened** when he heard this **word**. (The word translated *darkened* is the Gr. *stugnazo*; it is the word used to describe the threatening appearance of the sky before a storm in Matt. 16:3, and the appalled faces of those distressed over destruction in Ezek. 27:35 LXX.) His face fell, and he slowly got up from his knees. It seems that without another word, **he went away**, grieved and **sorrowful**. He was not able to obey the counsel he was so eager to receive, **for he was one who had many properties**. He walked away from the Lord, and left in the dust the Kingdom of God he was offered there. We can imagine the Lord's eyes following him as he departed, sorrowful Himself that he had turned away from eternal joy.

ॐ ॐ ॐ ॐ ॐ

23 And having looked around, Jesus says to His disciples, "How difficult it will be for those who have properties to enter into the Kingdom of God!"

24 And the disciples were astonished at His words. But Jesus answers again and says to them, "Children, how difficult it is to enter into the Kingdom of God!

25 "It is easier for a camel to go through the eye of a needle than for a rich *man* to enter into the Kingdom of God."

26 And they were even more thunderstruck and

said to Him, "And who is able to be saved?"

27 Looking at them, Jesus says, "With men *it is* impossible, but not with God, for all things are possible with God."

28 Peter began to say to Him, "Behold, we have left everything and followed You."

29 Jesus said, "Amen I say to you, there is no one who has left house or brothers or sisters or mother or father or children or fields, for My sake and for the Gospel's sake,

30 "but that he shall receive a hundredfold as much now in this time, houses and brothers and sisters and mothers and children and fields, with persecutions, and in the age to come, eternal life.

31 "But many who are first will be last, and *the* last, first."

As the Lord **looked around** at the rich man and his companions departing, He lamented **to His disciples**, teaching them the lesson that was to be learned from the rich man's failure: **how difficult it will be for those who have properties** and riches to finally **enter into the Kingdom of God**. For to become Jesus' disciple and have the assurance of final life in that Kingdom, one must deny oneself and renounce the hope of popularity and comfort (8:34), embracing instead the persecutions that were sure to come if one followed Jesus. This was exceptionally difficult for those who had wealth, and who thus had become used to the ease, pleasure, and popularity wealth alone could bring. The suffering poor had little to lose, but the rich had much!

The disciples, however, **were astonished at His words**. Contemporary thought regarded wealth as a sign of God's blessing. If even the rich had such difficulty entering the Kingdom, what hope was there for the rest, who (they assumed) had less of the divine favor! Christ did not relent when He saw the disciples confounded at this saying. He did not qualify His words, nor soften them, nor seek to console His disciples in any way, as if wealth were *not* spiritually dangerous to the human soul. Rather, He intensified His words, repeating them in an even more generalized and universal way. He addressed them affectionately as His **children** (Gr. *tekna*) and then drove the saying into their hearts a second time, saying, **"How difficult it is to enter into the Kingdom of God!"** That is, this life is full of the temptations of wealth and privilege, which tie the heart to the things of earth and dull the natural appetite for God. To finally have true life, one must shake oneself free of the bondage to possessions that characterizes this age. This is a great and difficult task, and one that is impossible for the unaided will. Indeed, **it is easier for a camel to go through the eye of a needle than for a rich *man* to enter into the Kingdom of God.** That is, it is, humanly speaking, impossible! Such is the vulnerability of the human heart to the temptations to wealth.

The disciples were **even more thunderstruck** when Jesus refused to modify or soften His words. They blurted out, **"And who is able to be saved"** if this is so? If the rich, who they assumed were rich only by the favor of God, have no hope, what about the rest of humanity? Jesus **looked at them** (Gr. *emblepo*), gazing at them as He had gazed at the rich young man (v. 21), measuring the despair in their hearts. He did have a word of assurance for them after all. **With men,** this feat of renunciation and trust in God is **impossible.** All by themselves, men such as the rich young ruler cannot be expected to shake themselves free from temptation and go through the needle's eye. But this is **not** impossible **with God.** With His help and Spirit, even this is possible. He is capable of drawing even such men to Himself, for **all things are possible with God.** (The history of monasticism would later prove the truth of this also. For many rich men were to find the power to renounce their wealth in order to follow God. The desert would later be full of many such camels who had gone through the needle's eye.)

Peter, speaking for the rest, was anxious to hear a word of reassurance. Like the rest, he was shaken by His Lord's words of verses 24–25. The rich man had not been willing to leave everything—but the disciples had! With the plaintiveness of a nervous child, he observed, "**Behold, we have left everything and followed You.**" Jesus was not slow to respond with the desired reassurance. "**Amen I say to you,**" He answered, prefacing His promise with His customary oath, "**there is no one who has left house or brothers or sisters or mother or father or children or fields, for My sake and for the Gospel's sake, but that he shall receive a hundredfold as much now in this time.**" That is, for absolutely everything a man renounces for the sake of Jesus and His message (Jesus repeats the list again to emphasize that no sacrifice would be overlooked), he will be abundantly compensated. More than that, not only will he be compensated in this age, but **in the age to come**, he will have **eternal life.**

There are, of course, other things to consider. In this age, not only will a man be fully compensated for his sacrifices, but he will receive **persecutions** as well. One must not assume that one renounces a life of worldly ease merely to have it soon restored again! The renunciation of worldly blessings will be fully rewarded, and the Christian will know a life full of blessing indeed. But these blessings are part of a life lived apart from the applause of this age. The apostles were the richest of all men, knowing the blessing of God, but by human standards they were still the dregs of all things (1 Cor. 4:13).

Also, one's status in this age does not necessarily carry over into the age to come. The Kingdom overthrows all the standards of this world, and those important here, for all their renunciation, are not necessarily important there. **Many** who are **first** and important in this age **will be last** in the age to come, **and *the* last** and least in this age may be **first** then. That is how unimportant wealth and position are! Let the apostles be cheerful in their renunciation!

§V.8   Third Passion Prediction—
James and John rebuked for seeking to be first

༺ ༺ ༺ ༺ ༺

32 And they were on the road, going up to Jerusalem, and Jesus was going before them; and

> they were astonished, and those following were afraid. And He took the Twelve again and began to tell them the things about to happen to Him,
>
> 33 saying, "Behold, we are going up to Jerusalem, and the Son of Man will be delivered *up* to the chief-priests and the scribes, and they will condemn Him to death and deliver Him *up* to the Gentiles.
>
> 34 "And they will mock Him and spit on Him, and scourge Him, and kill *Him*, and after three days He will rise."

St. Mark next narrates the third prediction of the Passion. It occurred in response to the fearful apprehension of the apostolic band as they approached **Jerusalem**. Jerusalem, as we learn from John's Gospel, had been the scene of several attempts on Jesus' life (see John 11:8), and they were appalled and **afraid** as they saw Christ **going before them**, striding boldly ahead to what seemed certain death.

Once again, Christ did not attempt to deny their fears, only to assure them that it was somehow in the divine plan. He gives them the most detailed prediction of future events yet, adding the details that He would be delivered from **the chief-priests and the scribes** over **to the Gentiles**, who would **mock Him and spit on Him, and scourge Him**. In all three predictions of the Passion, He mentions His Resurrection (8:31; 9:31; 10:34), but it is doubtful if this was much consolation to the trembling disciples. They still had too much trouble trying to understand how the Messiah could possibly be crucified, and sought to make sense of it by allegorizing the whole thing. What they *did* understand was that Jerusalem was dangerous, and that they would prefer to remain in the safety of Galilee!

ॐ ॐ ॐ ॐ ॐ

> 35 And James and John, the two sons of Zebedee, come up to Him, saying to Him, "Teacher,

we want You to do for us whatever we request of You."

36 And He said to them, "What do you want Me to do for you?"

37 And they said to Him, "Give to us that we may sit in Your glory, one on Your right and one on the left."

38 But Jesus said to them, "You do not know what you request. Are you able to drink the cup which I *Myself* drink, or to be baptized with the baptism with which I *Myself* am baptized?"

39 And they said to Him, "We are able." And Jesus said to them, "The cup that I *Myself* drink you will drink, and with the baptism with which I *Myself* am baptized you will be baptized.

40 "But to sit on My right or on the left, this is not Mine to give, but *it is* for those for whom it has been prepared."

As in the other accounts of the Passion predictions, this prediction also is followed by a lapse on the part of the apostles. This time it is **James and John** who display their ignorance of the ways of the Kingdom. Thinking (as did the other apostles) that the coming Kingdom meant only glory for them, they tried a secret ploy to cut their leader Peter out of the running for first place. It was perhaps during a moment of rest along the roadside that they made their move. In a more or less private moment, they **come up to Him** (the present indicative is used again, to highlight the drama of their request) and ask for a special (as yet unspecified!) favor. (A comparison with Matt. 20:20 reveals that they got their mother to do the talking, perhaps thinking the request would seem less self-serving if she presented it.) In the style of ancient oriental politics, He is asked for a special boon on the basis of friendship. Rather than acquiesce (does He suspect something is up, knowing them as He does?), He first asks, **"What do you want Me to do for you?"** Then comes the requested favor: assign the two best positions in the **glory** of His new Kingdom to the brothers, so that they **sit one on** the **right** of Him **and one on the left.** Peter, who before had been the first, was to be relegated to at least third place down, subordinate to the **sons of Zebedee.**

In another example of His infinite patience with human sin and stupidity, the Lord does not rebuke them for this. Instead, He simply replies that they **do not know** what they are asking for. That is, they do not realize that such positions of glory in the Kingdom are based on suffering and lowly service. He asks them a question in return: are they **able to drink the cup** which He Himself is to drink (the pronoun is emphatic in the Greek), **or to be baptized with the baptism** with which He is to be baptized? They seem to desire glory in His coming Kingdom. That is good—but are they prepared to pay the price? His own experience in establishing that Kingdom (that of drinking the cup of wrath and being drowned in suffering) will show that glory can only come as the reward for lowliness. Are they able to bear this?

They quickly answer, **"We are able."** Perhaps they did not know what they were agreeing to. Nonetheless, the Lord took them at their word, and James and John were indeed to suffer for Him. Their reply, though for the moment springing from ignorance of what lay ahead, was even so an expression of their determination to do whatever it took to follow Him. The Lord honored that determination and promised them its reward, saying, **"The cup that I *Myself* drink you will drink, and with the baptism with which I *Myself* am baptized you will be baptized."** That is, this part of your request for glory is granted. However, the main part of their request He could not grant. For they did not simply want glory in His Kingdom, they wanted *more glory than the others*. Their request was motivated partly by a noble desire to share His glory, and partly by an ignoble one to beat out the other disciples using political means. The ignoble part of their request is instantly refused, with the explanation that what they were asking for was anyway not His to give. Rather, the Father would decide such things, assigning the seats of glory as *He* willed. They were not "up for grabs" to whoever would put himself forward.

ॐ ॐ ॐ ॐ ॐ

41 And having heard this, the ten began to be indignant at James and John.

42 And calling them to *Himself*, Jesus says to them, "You know that those who are supposed to rule over the Gentiles lord it over them; and their great ones exercise *tyrannous* authority over them.

43 "But it is not thus among you, but whoever wishes to become great among you will be your servant;

44 "and whoever wishes to be first among you will be slave of all.

45 "For even the Son of Man did not come to be served, but to serve, and to give His life *as* a ransom for many."

Though the interview was meant to be private, word of it inevitably got out. When the other **ten** apostles **heard** what had happened, **they began to be indignant at James and John.** It was not, of course, that they understood that glory in the Kingdom is given as the reward of humility. Rather, it was simply that they were each coveting the best position for themselves, and resented such a sneaky ploy to snatch it away from them. Though they themselves made no such requests, it was apparent that they were in the grip of the same ignorance as James and John, thinking only of glory and privilege.

So it was that the Lord had to correct such notions, which still lay in their ambitious hearts. Taking time from their journey, and **calling them to *Himself*** for a time of teaching, He strives to show them the priority of humility. In doing this, He appeals to a reality which they all **know**—and detest. They all have had experience of **those who are supposed to rule over the Gentiles**, men such as the Emperor Tiberius and his local officials. They were **supposed to rule**, but this rule was nothing more than self-serving tyranny and oppression, not true ruling at all. The **great ones** of the Gentile world loved to **lord it over** their subjects and **exercise *tyrannous* authority** over them. How often had the disciples (with all the Jews) complained about such use of authority! Yet they are acting the same way as these hated Gentiles, for they are only concerned about their own personal self-aggrandizement.

It is to be **not thus among** them in the coming Kingdom. They are to be different from these worldly Gentiles, who consider that authority is only used for self-serving. Rather, the one who **wishes to become great** among them must prove himself the **servant** (Gr. *diakonos*), and the one who wants **first** place in the Kingdom will find it only given as the reward for being the **slave of all** (Gr. *doulos*). The Lord Himself will lead the way and demonstrate by example. Even though He is **the Son of Man** and Messiah, He still came **not to be served, but to serve** (Gr. *diakoneo*), as if He were but a servant. In this service, He will hold nothing back, but will in humility **give His** very **life** *as* **a ransom for many**. If the Master is to find glory only through lowliness and servanthood, how much more His disciples?

(We note in passing how Christ designates His death as a **ransom** for the **many** millions of the world. We have here an echo of Isaiah 53:11, which speaks of the Suffering Servant as "justifying the many" and "bearing their iniquities." Christ's death was not to be simply an execution or a martyrdom. It was to be a Sacrifice, which would take away the sins of the world. Those who wear the sign of the cross around their necks and rejoice that they are part of those ransomed many are called here to remember the humility that saved them, and imitate it in their daily lives.)

§V.9   Healing of Blind Bartimaeus

ॐ ॐ ॐ ॐ ॐ

46 And they come to Jericho. And as He was going out from Jericho with His disciples and a considerable crowd, a blind beggar Bartimaeus, the son of Timaeus, was sitting beside the way.

47 And having heard that it was Jesus the

> Nazarene, he began to cry out and say, "Jesus, Son of David, have mercy on me!"
>
> 48 And many rebuked him, that he should be silent, but he cried out all the more, "Son of David, have mercy on me!"
>
> 49 And Jesus stood *still* and said, "Call him." And they call the blind man, saying to him, "Have courage, arise! He is calling you."
>
> 50 And casting-aside his garment, he jumped up and came to Jesus.
>
> 51 And answering him, Jesus said, "What do you want Me to do for you?" And the blind man said to Him, "Rabboni, that I may see again!"
>
> 52 And Jesus said to him, "Go your way, your faith has saved you." And immediately he saw again, and followed Him on the way.

As the culmination of the Lord's journey to Jerusalem, St. Mark narrates the healing of a beggar's blindness. This is of more than historical interest. It is meant to show how those who have sight and who are saved **follow** Jesus. It is only the blind—like the Pharisees—who reject Him. Even a blind man can see that He is the messianic **Son of David**.

There is some question as to the precise location of the miracle. Matthew as well as Mark locate it at the place where Jesus *left* Jericho on the way to Jerusalem (see Matt. 20:29), whereas Luke locates it at the place where Jesus *entered* Jericho (Luke 18:35). Moreover, there are other difficulties attending the narrative as well. Mark and Luke mention only the one beggar, whereas Matthew mentions a second one (Matt. 20:30).

I would offer the following possible reconstruction of the healing. As Jesus enters Jericho, He is hailed by the notable local beggar, Bartimaeus. At that time, the beggar remains lost in the crowd, as Christ goes in to be the overnight guest of Zacchaeus (Luke 19:1f). The next morning, Bartimaeus, having learned of Christ's whereabouts, repositions himself outside the house of Zacchaeus, joined by another beggar. As Christ leaves Zacchaeus's home and the city of Jericho, He again encounters the beggars, who again cry out to Him as the Son of David, and He grants them healing. All three evangelists telescope the events, omitting as irrelevant to their purposes Bartimaeus's overnight wait and repositioning, and focusing on the healing itself. Luke chooses to regard Christ's visit to Zacchaeus as the climax of His journey to Jerusalem, and so begins the narration of the beggar's healing with Christ's *entry* into Jericho. Matthew and Mark do not tell the Zacchaeus story at all, regarding the healing of the beggars as the climax, and so narrate it as happening when Christ *left* the city.

If this reconstruction of the events is correct, then Christ indeed met Bartimaeus face to face **as He was going out from Jericho**, accompanied as usual by **His disciples and a considerable crowd**. The crowd is mentioned at the outset, to show how the **blind beggar Bartimaeus** could be lost in it and almost miss meeting Christ. That the beggar is named is unusual in the Gospels, for no other sufferers are mentioned by name. It is probable that **Bartimaeus** continued to be known in the Church as one of her oldest members. (For the non-Aramaic readers, the name is immediately translated as meaning **son of Timaeus**.)

In any case, the blind beggar was **sitting beside the way**, begging from the crowd of passersby on the way to Jerusalem. When he **heard** that the famous **Jesus the Nazarene** was near in the passing crowd, **he began to cry out and say, "Jesus, Son of David, have mercy on me!"** Like other people, he suspected Jesus might indeed be the designated Messiah (see John 7:31), and it was to better get His attention in the midst of the crowd that he hailed Him as the messianic **Son of David**.

Such relentless and continued crying out was an irritant to the crowd. Perhaps some thought it shocking that he should openly and repeatedly shout out a messianic designation that others only dared to consider privately. Certainly such a clear confession was unusual in a Jewish crowd, and perhaps that was why he used it as a way of drawing attention to himself. The crowd, hardened to the sight of blind beggars, **rebuked him, that he should be silent**. He knew, however, that with every step Jesus took away from him down the road, his only hope of healing was fading away, and **he cried out all the more**, shouting for all he was worth.

On hearing him, **Jesus stood *still*** and said, **"Call him."** When this was reported back to the seated beggar, he **cast-aside his garment** and **jumped up and came to Jesus.** This detail of throwing off his cloak in his haste is important. As a blind man, he would need to be careful not to lose his possessions, for he would never be able to find them again. But since Jesus was calling him, he did not care, for he fully expected to be able to see and find his cloak again. His outer cloak didn't matter; what mattered was that Jesus was calling him!

Christ was interested in relating to the man as a man, and not simply as a "case" or a cure which must be given before continuing on His way. Bartimaeus was not an interruption; he was a person. Therefore, Jesus did not presume, but allowed the man to state his request, even though it must have been obvious what he wanted. The Lord asked him, **"What do you want Me to do for you?"** and received the instant and breathless answer, **"That I may see again!"** Bartimaeus addressed Jesus as **Rabboni**, a strengthened form of the respectful title Rabbi.

The Lord's response is immediate. **"Go your way,"** He tells him. **"Your faith has saved you."** As soon as the Lord uttered these simple words, the blind man **saw again**, and **followed** Jesus **on the way** into Jerusalem. The words **he followed Him** denote primarily only that Bartimaeus joined the happy crowd following Jesus into the city. Given that Bartimaeus was evidently known in the later Church, it seems that we are to read into this "following" a note of discipleship as well. St. Mark means the reader to see how those who are the saved are the followers of Jesus. It is they who have been enlightened to see Him as the true Messiah and Son of David.

Notes for Section V:

_____

_____

_____

Notes for Section V:

_____

_____

_____

_____

_____

_____

_____

_____

_____

_____

_____

_____

_____

_____

_____

_____

_____

_____

_____

_____

_____

_____

_____

_____

_____

_____

_____

_____

_____

_____

_____

_____

_____

_____

_____

_____

๛ VI ๛

MINISTRY IN JERUSALEM
(11:1—13:37)

§VI.1 The Triumphal Entry

๛ ๛ ๛ ๛ ๛

11 1 And as they draw near to Jerusalem, to Bethphage and Bethany near the Mountain of Olives, He sends two of His disciples,

2 and says to them, "Go into the village opposite you, and immediately as you enter it, you will find a colt tied, on which not one man has yet sat; loose it and bring it.

3 "And if anyone says to you, 'Why are you doing this?' say, 'The Lord has need of it'; and immediately he sends it here again."

4 And they went away and found a colt tied at a door out on the street, and they loose it.

5 And some of those standing there said to them, "What are you doing, loosing the colt?"

6 And they spoke to them just as Jesus had said, and they let them *take it*.

7 And they bring the colt to Jesus and cast their garments on it; and He sat on it.

At long last the Lord entered Jerusalem in triumph. His entry, however, was carefully preplanned to be a proclamation of His identity as Messiah, as well as an indication of what kind of Messiah He was to be.

He entered the Holy City from the north, probably staying the night before in nearby Bethany. We learn from John 12:1–8 that He had spent that evening there at a banquet served by Martha and her family, in thanksgiving for His raising of her brother Lazarus from the dead. It was at this supper that their sister Mary anointed Him, in an impulsive and emotional act of devotion. (This anointing will be reported later in Mark 14:3–9, where it forms the contrasting counterpoint to Judas' act of betrayal.) It was in part due to the excitement provoked by this public and dramatic act of resurrection (narrated in John 11) that all the city of Jerusalem was stirred to a frenzy of messianic enthusiasm as they welcomed Him.

The day after this supper, therefore, they **draw near to Jerusalem** (the historic present is used throughout this account). From Bethany He **sends two of His disciples** to the suburb of Jerusalem, to **Bethphage**, which was actually reckoned as being within the city limits of Jerusalem. He has prearranged the use of a special animal for His entry into the city, and **says** to the two disciples, "**Go into the village** [of Bethphage] **opposite you, and immediately as you enter it, you will find a colt tied, on which not one man has yet sat; loose it and bring it.**" This animal was chosen to demonstrate Jesus' identity as Messiah because it had never been used before (see Num. 19:2, which stipulates that a heifer used for sacred service must be one on which a yoke has never been placed). By coming into Jerusalem on such an animal, Jesus was making a silent but public proclamation that He was Messiah and was coming to establish God's Kingdom.

Jerusalem was still, nonetheless, a dangerous place for him, since His enemies were everywhere. He therefore had arranged for this demonstration secretly beforehand. The animal had been left **tied at a door out on the street**, in plain open view for the disciples as they entered. They would need to use the password, however, before taking it, since the disciples did not know the owners by sight. If challenged "**Why are you doing this?**" they were to respond by saying, "**The Lord has need of it.**" The saying was intentionally ambiguous. The words "the Lord" could refer to the owner, giving the impression to listening bystanders that the owner of the donkey was simply claiming his own animal. Or the words "the Lord" could refer to Jesus. Hostile listeners could overhear the exchange and be none the wiser that Jesus of Nazareth was near and was coming. (We note that similar precautions for secrecy are taken in the choice of a place to celebrate the Passover meal, 14:13f.) Mark narrates the sequence of events in such detail to show how dangerous Jerusalem was at this time. At length, the disciples returned with the animal (along with its mother; see Matt. 21:2). They **bring the colt to Jesus** (again the historic present is used), **and cast their garments on it.** He then **sat on it** and began His royal entry into the Holy City.

৵ ৵ ৵ ৵ ৵

8   And many spread their garments on the way, and others, leafy branches cut from the fields.
9   And those who went before, and those who followed, cried out, "Hosanna! Blessed is He who comes in *the* Name of *the* Lord!
10 "Blessed is the coming Kingdom of our father David! Hosanna in the highest!"
11 And He entered into Jerusalem, into the Temple; and having looked around everywhere, the hour now being late, He went out to Bethany with the Twelve.

As He rode humbly into the city, accompanied by His disciples and a crowd from Bethany, **many** from Jerusalem saw His approach on the donkey, and immediately grasped its significance. They were expecting and hoping that He was come to the Passover (see John 11:56), and when they saw Him riding in royal pomp, they knew that He was coming to usher in the Kingdom. They therefore went out to meet Him and escort Him into the city in triumph. They **spread their garments on the way,** laying them on the road before His path to form a kind of carpet for Him. **Others** (perhaps those not wearing an outer cloak) cut **leafy branches** for the purpose **from the fields** nearby. The crowd swelled to a great and jubilant number, as they exulted in what they felt certain was the **coming Kingdom** of their **father David**. On all sides, both **those who went before** Him and **those who followed** after openly hailed Jesus at last as their Messiah. They **cried out, "Hosanna! Blessed is He who comes in *the* Name of *the* Lord! Hosanna in the highest!"** (The term **Hosanna**, a Hebrew word originally meaning "save us"—see its use in Ps. 118:25—was by that time used simply as an acclamation, like our "Hurray!") Though they still had a political and military understanding of the Kingdom, they were correct in hailing Jesus as Messiah.

So it was that Christ **entered into Jerusalem** and continued His path until He had come to the House of His own Father. There He dismounted and entered **into the Temple** as well. He **looked around everywhere** there, not like a tourist, or pilgrim, or worshiper, but like the Lord coming suddenly to His own place, and inspecting it as its Lord to see if it was all in order (see Mal. 3:1). When **the hour** grew **late** and evening came, **He went out to Bethany with the Twelve**, a mere mile or so distant, to spend the night in safety (probably at the home of Lazarus, Martha, and Mary).

ৠ ৠ ৠ ৠ ৠ

12 And the next day, when they had gone out from Bethany, He was hungry.

13 And seeing from a distance a fig tree in leaf, He went *to see* whether He would find anything on it; and having come to it, He found nothing but leaves, for it was not the *appointed* time for figs.

14 And He answered and said to it, "May no one any longer eat fruit from you forever!" And His disciples heard.

15 And they come into Jerusalem. And having entered into the Temple, He began to cast out those buying and those selling in the Temple, and overturned the tables of the

moneychangers and the seats of those selling the doves,

16 and He would not let anyone carry vessels through the Temple.

17 And He taught and said to them, "Is it not written, 'My House will be called a House of prayer *for* all the nations'? But you *yourselves* have made it a thieves' cave."

18 And the chief-priests and the scribes heard, and sought how to destroy Him; for they were afraid of Him, for all the crowd was thunderstruck at His teaching.

19 And whenever it became late, they would go out of the city.

On His way **from Bethany** to Jerusalem **the next day**, He saw **from a distance a fig tree in leaf**. Because **He was hungry**, He approached it *to see* **whether He would find anything on it** to eat. Its leaves drew attention to it, as if advertising its presence. When He had **come to it**, however, **He found nothing but leaves, for it was not the *appointed* time for figs**. The figs ripened in mid-August to October. At this time of the spring, there would be no figs at all. The tree's spectacular show of leaves served only to hide its fruitlessness beneath.

As the Lord looked at it, He saw not only a fig tree, but the People of Israel and their Temple. Like the fig tree, the outward pomp and glory of the Temple that He had seen the other day seemed to draw attention to itself, promising and advertising to the world how pious the Jews were. But just as the leaves of the fig tree hid its fruitlessness, so the outward glory of the Temple hid the spiritual fruitlessness of the People of Israel. Outwardly, all was splendid. Did not the prophets themselves promise that "Israel would blossom and fill the world with fruit" (Is. 27:6)? But inwardly, there was no fruitfulness at all, but only hypocrisy and rebellion. The Temple was to be abandoned by God and left to be cursed.

And so the Lord, like the prophets of old, enacted a parable, and cursed the fig tree. Jeremiah had undertaken symbolic actions in order to teach the people (Jer. 13:1f), as had Ezekiel (Ezek. 4:9f). Here Jesus also symbolically curses the fruitlessness and hypocrisy of the Temple and the city, saying, **"May no one any longer eat fruit from you forever!"** The **disciples heard** this curse, and doubtless wondered at His seemingly irrational action. Enlightenment and lessons would follow later.

At length **they come into Jerusalem** itself. St. Mark paints the following scenes of zeal with vivid colors, preparing for them by using the historic present. Christ, finding the Temple a place not of spiritual faithfulness and fruitfulness but of worldliness and greed, **began to cast out those buying and those selling**.

The problem, of course, was not the idea of sacred commerce itself. The many kinds of coinage in circulation throughout the world necessitated the use of moneychangers and their tables, as only the coinage of the Temple was allowed. Also, people would come from afar and buy their sacrifices (such as the doves, the cheapest of offerings) on site, so as to ensure that the animals were properly unblemished and fit for sacrifice (see Deut. 14:24–26). There were markets on the Mount of Olives nearby for that very purpose. The problem with these tables and markets was that they were located within the Temple itself, in the Court of the Gentiles. (This was a fairly recent development, having been established there as recently as about AD 30.) The Gentiles were not permitted to enter the inner courts of the Temple. It was punishable by death for them to enter into the Court of the Women or the Court of the Israelites beyond that. The only place that these Gentiles had to pray in, as they came from **all the nations** of the world, was the outer Court of the Gentiles, and it was just here that these markets had been lately set up. The Gentiles were therefore hindered in their communion with the God of Israel, and unable to pray in peace because of the commotion and noise that inevitably accompanied any Eastern bazaar.

Jesus was indignant on behalf of His Father's House. He **overturned the tables of the moneychangers and the seats of those selling the doves** and drove all of those engaged in the sacrilegious business out of the Temple. His only concern was to restore the proper sanctity of the place. Those who tried to **carry vessels through the Temple**, using it as a shortcut, were refused access.

As He sat in the Temple and **taught** them there, He reminded them of the sanctity of God's House. Had it not been written in Isaiah 56:7, "**My House will be called a House of prayer *for* all the nations**"? God's will, revealed by the prophets, was for all the nations of the world to come and find Him in His House, to see His glory and come to worship Him. The Temple was to have been a standing universal witness to the God of Israel, who called all the world to Himself. But what had it become? It was no witness to the Gentiles at all, and the very place set aside for them had been co-opted for base commerce. They themselves (the pronoun is emphatic in the Greek) had transformed the holy House into a **thieves' cave**, a place where the unrighteous huddled and hid in safety, avoiding detection and righteous punishment for their deeds, even as the prophets had said (see Jer. 7:11). The **chief-priests and the scribes heard** Him give this public teaching in the courts and colonnades (see John 10:23). They were the ones ultimately responsible for the markets which He had so peremptorily ejected. This act was a defiant challenge to their authority, and they burned with impotent anger, which they dared not yet express. They could only meet secretly and seek **how to destroy Him**.

ॐ ॐ ॐ ॐ ॐ

20 And passing by early, they saw the fig tree withered from *the* roots.

21 And remembering, Peter says to Him, "Rabbi, behold, the fig tree which You cursed has withered."

22 And Jesus answers, saying to them, "Believe in God.

23 "Amen I say to you, whoever says to this mountain, 'Be taken up and cast into the sea,' and does not doubt in his heart, but believes that what he says is occurring, it will be *thus* for him.

> 24 "Therefore I say to you, all things for which you pray and request, believe that you have received, and it will be *thus* for you.
>
> 25 "And whenever you stand praying, forgive, if you have anything against anyone, that your Father also who is in the heavens may forgive you your offenses."
>
> (*Verse 26 is omitted, since it is not original to Mark, but seems to have been added in conformity with Matthew 6:15.)

The next day, as Jesus and His disciples were again **passing by early** in the morning and going from their place in Bethany back to the Temple, **they saw the fig tree** that Jesus had cursed just the other day, **withered from *the* roots** up, so that it was completely dead. **Remembering** what Jesus had said, **Peter says to Him** (the historic present is used in this exchange), **"Rabbi, behold, the fig tree which You cursed has withered."** That is, Peter was mentioning such a thing as if it were a marvel, something to be forever beyond them.

The Lord is calling them to do His own works (see John 14:12), and the sonship and closeness to God which He has, He will share with them (insofar as mere human beings can share the gift offered by the uncreated Word), if they will only **believe in God**. They may think that they could never do such wonders, but they will do even greater wonders than these.

He therefore encourages them to trust that God will work in their midst, prefacing His promise with the solemn oath, **"Amen I say to you."** Not only He, but **whoever believes** will be able to do wonders. Indeed, such a one could **say to this mountain** beside them (the Mount of Olives), **"Be taken up and cast into the sea"** (the Dead Sea, nearby and visible to them from where they stood). God's power in His Church will not be limited by anything but their doubt. If the man speaking such a word does **not doubt in His heart** but **believes that what he says is occurring** as he speaks, **it will be *thus* for him** and what he says will happen. Whatever they would **pray and request**, they must **believe** that they had **received** it, and it would be given.

This assumes, of course, that they are pure of heart. **Whenever** they **stand praying** (for standing was the universal posture for prayer), they must **forgive** all offenses, if they have **anything against anyone**. It does not matter whether the grudge one holds is justified or not. All must be forgiven—otherwise, they will not be forgiven themselves, nor granted their requests. As they stand on earth, they must be humble and tender of heart, for only thus will their **Father who is in the heavens** above **forgive** them and accept their prayers.

§VI.2 The Pharisees Challenge Jesus' Authority

ॐ ॐ ॐ ॐ ॐ

27 And they come again into Jerusalem. And as He was walking in the Temple, the chief-priests and scribes and elders come to Him,

28 and said to Him, "By what authority are You doing these things, or who gave You this authority to do these things?"

29 And Jesus said to them, "I will ask you one word, and you answer Me, and I will tell you by what authority I do these things.

30 "The baptism of John—was it from heaven, or from men? Answer Me."

31 And they questioned among themselves, saying, "If we say, 'From heaven,' He will say, 'Then why did you not believe in him?'

32 "But shall we say, 'From men'?"—they feared the crowd, for all had *it that* John was indeed a prophet.

33 And answering Jesus, they say, "We do not know." And Jesus says to them, "Neither will I *Myself* tell you by what authority I do these things."

When they **come again into Jerusalem** after stopping for a moment beside the fig tree (we note the historic present used to narrate the conflict), His adversaries were waiting for Him. **As He was walking in the Temple** (probably in the colonnade, on the way to give His daily teaching to the people), **the chief-priests and scribes and elders come to Him, and said to Him, "By what authority are You doing these things, or who gave You this authority to do these things?"** They had been caught off guard by His boldness the previous day, but now were ready with their counter-challenge. It was they, they felt, who had been charged by God to keep order in His House. Who did He think He was to challenge and override this authority? If He were to declare that He had an authority from God superior to theirs, they doubtless would have further demanded that He prove it, possibly by asking for a sign (see 8:11). If He refused to perform such a sign (and they felt certain He would refuse), He would seem to forfeit the right to override their authority and take over the Temple.

Jesus was not caught off-guard. Before He answered their question, they must first answer one of His. That seemed only fair! He would ask them only **one word**. If they proved themselves wise and worthy by answering it, He would acquiesce in their demand and answer their question in return.

His question was a simple one: **"The baptism of John—was it from heaven, or from men?"** He demanded that they **answer** Him immediately, and they had no choice but to go into a huddle then and there and produce a response.

This was a problem for them, for they cared for the glory of men (see John 5:44)—and for their own safety! As they **questioned** and debated **among themselves**, they considered the two possible responses. If they said that John's baptism and authority were **from heaven**, then Jesus would reply, **"Then why did you not believe in him?"** and they would be confounded. But they could, they felt, hardly tell the truth! They could not say that they actually rejected John as a false prophet and thought that his authority was simply **from men**. If they did that, they **feared** that the crowd would tear them to pieces, **for all had** *it that* **John was indeed a prophet.** They broke from their huddle and reported their findings to Jesus: "**We do not know.**" In other words, "No comment!"

In saying this, they proved themselves unworthy of receiving a straight answer, and the Lord would throw no pearls before them (see Matt. 7:6). If they could not recognize the authority of John, they certainly could not recognize the authority of Jesus, and there was nothing further to be said to them. One can almost see Jesus smiling as they gave their feeble reply. He could only reply in return, "**Neither will I** *Myself* **tell you by what authority I do these things.**" His foes had come forward in bold confidence to challenge and oust Him, and had been utterly confounded. Laughter and derision from the crowd would have attended their humiliating retreat.

ॐ ॐ ॐ ॐ ॐ

12 1 And He began to speak to them in parables: "A man planted a vineyard and put a hedge around *it*, and dug a vat, and built a tower, and rented it out to farmers and left home.

2 "And he sent a slave to the farmers at the *appointed* time, that he might receive from the farmers *some* of the fruit of the vineyard.

3 "And they took him and beat *him* and sent *him* away empty.

4 "And again he sent to them another slave, and that one they *wounded* in the head and dishonored.

5 "And he sent another, and that one they killed, and *so with* many others, beating some and killing others.

6 "He still had one, a beloved son; he sent him last to them, saying, 'They will respect my son.'

7 "But those farmers said to themselves, 'This is the heir; come, let us kill him, and the inheritance will be ours!'

8 "And they took him and killed him and cast him out of the vineyard.

9 "What will the lord of the vineyard do? He will come and destroy the farmers and will give the vineyard to others.

10 "Have you not read this Scripture: 'The stone which the builders rejected, this has become the head of the corner;

11 "'This occurred from the Lord, and it is marvelous in our eyes'?"

12 And they sought to seize Him; and *yet* they feared the crowd, for they knew that He told the parable against them. And they left Him, and went away.

After this, Jesus **began to speak to them in parables**—perhaps as soon as He reached His destination in the Temple after being stopped by the Temple authorities on His way there (as narrated in the previous verses). Fresh from this challenge to His authority, He told a parable about how those who rejected Him would come under judgment from God.

The parable begins in a familiar way, evoking a similar parable of judgment from Isaiah 5:1–7. It posits a scene that was common in Palestine, that of an absentee landlord who rented out his lands to tenant farmers. The preparation of the land—planting a vineyard and putting a hedge around it, and digging a vat, and building a tower—is rehearsed in detail, not simply to evoke the comparison with Isaiah 5, but also to show that the owner of the vineyard has a moral right to some of the fruit he collects as the rent. He has done all this work and put his money into the land, and he has a right to collect a benefit from it. It is his land. After he **rented it out to farmers and left home** to sojourn elsewhere, he fully expected to receive his due.

So it was that **he sent a slave to the farmers at the *appointed* time** of harvest **that he might receive from the farmers *some* of the fruit of the vineyard**. To his shock, they defied his authority. More than that, **they took** the slave he had sent **and beat** *him* **and sent** *him* **away empty**. The lord of the vineyard, however, did not instantly retaliate against such an outrage. Rather, with exceptional patience, **again he sent to them another slave**. This one fared the same as the first, proving that the owner's policy of patience was ill-conceived, for **that one they** *wounded* **in the head and dishonored** with insults and defiance. Astonishingly, the owner **sent another**—and **that one they killed!** The lord of the vineyard, however, continued with unheard-of patience, sending **many others**, even though some of these they beat and others they killed.

The hearers of the parable by now must have thought this all sounded too familiar for comfort. It sounded far too reminiscent of God's response to the People of Israel as described in their Law (see Neh. 9:26; Jer. 7:25, 26), when He sent prophet after prophet to them in days of old, only to have them rejected and killed. It was apparent that the lord of the vineyard was an image of God, and the defiant farmers, an image of the rebellious in Israel.

Then the parable took a new turn: the owner **still had one** left to send, **a beloved son**. Thinking that his son would command more respect than slaves, **he sent him last** of all **to them**, thinking that surely **they will respect my son**.

It was not to be. The rebels were implacable in their defiance of the owner's love and patience. Instead of respecting the son, as might have been expected, in their insane rage they saw only a further opportunity for their selfishness. **"This is the heir!"** they crowed. If they killed him, the land would be left legally ownerless on the death of the father, and then **the inheritance** would be theirs. So it was that **they took him and killed him and cast him out of the vineyard**, heaping the final indignity on the son by leaving his corpse unburied.

The parable held its listeners spellbound—both the Lord's supporters who came to hear His teaching and His foes, who listened in horror. The Lord asked a final rhetorical question: **"What will the lord of the vineyard do?"** What could one expect as the inevitable response to such a culminating atrocity? We learn from Matthew's version of the parable that some in His audience, carried away by indignation, shouted out the obvious answer (Matt. 21:41)—that **he will come and destroy the farmers and will give the vineyard to others.** Christ's foes were aghast, for by this time they had no doubt that He had cast them in the part of the rebels, who were to be judged and dispossessed by God. They reacted, probably in a sputter of incoherent protest (see Luke 20:16). But the Lord was insistent: it had to be, for it was prophesied in the Scriptures. Had they **not read** it themselves, many times? " **'The stone which the builders rejected, this has become the head of the corner; this occurred from the Lord, and it is marvelous in our eyes'?"** (Ps. 118:22). That is, David himself had prophesied that his messianic descendant would be rejected, even though He had been chosen by God. Christ's foes thought it impossible that one whom they rejected could turn out to be the true Messiah. Jesus demonstrates from the Scriptures that this was exactly what was prophesied.

It was no wonder, therefore, that **they sought to seize** and have Him arrested. This was impossible, however, as long as He was in public. **They feared the crowd** and knew that they would never allow Him to be taken. Even though **they knew that He told the parable against them**, they had no choice but to slink away.

ॐ ॐ ॐ ॐ ॐ

13 And they send some of the Pharisees and Herodians to Him, that they might catch Him in a word.

14 And they come and say to Him, "Teacher, we know that You are truthful, and it is not a concern to you about anyone, for You do not look at men's faces, but teach the way of God in truth. Is it permitted to pay a poll-tax to Caesar, or not?

15 "Shall we give, or shall we not give?" But He, knowing their hypocrisy, said to them, "Why do you test Me? Bring Me a denarius that I may look *at it.*"

> 16 And they brought *it*. And He says to them, "Whose image and inscription *is* this?" And they said to Him, "Caesar's."
> 17 And Jesus said to them, "Render to Caesar the things that are Caesar's—and to God the things that are God's." And they marveled greatly at Him.

The next time (possibly later that same day?), a delegation of His foes again approached Him. This delegation was a combination of **some of the Pharisees and Herodians**, who had long since formed an alliance against Jesus (3:6). The Temple authorities **send** these to Him, **that they might catch Him in a word**. That is, they tried to get Him to say something that they could use against Him legally. (Once again the historic present is used, to allow us to stand with the crowd and hear the whole exchange.)

They decided they would focus on the issue of Roman taxation. The Romans collected tribute tax from every Israelite, as they did from all the people they conquered. The tax was thus a sign of Rome's sovereignty over Israel and of Israel's lowly state as an occupied territory. It was bitterly resented by every patriotic Jew as a tyrannous imposition by a foreign power. The Zealots, a Jewish group dedicated to the violent overthrow of Roman authority, categorically refused to pay the tax, since it was an acknowledgment of Caesar's authority over them. To pay the poll-tax, they felt, was to insult God; it was an act of spiritual betrayal, for God was to be Israel's only King. To the Zealots, those who paid the tax to Rome were refusing to give God His due. The Romans, for their part, considered such refusal to pay the tax a form of treason, and they were prepared to punish to the limit any man who seemed to be stirring up the populace to such revolt.

The Lord's foes remembered their first encounter with Him (11:27f), and how Jesus had refused to answer their question. They made sure that He would have no choice but to answer this one, and began with flattery designed to press Him into replying. **"Teacher,"** they began, with feigned deferential respect, **"we know that You are** truthful, and it is not a concern to you about anyone, for You do not look at men's faces, but teach the way of God in truth." That is, He was not one to defer to anyone in authority when it came to teaching God's will, nor to water down the truth for the sake of partiality before the powerful. He was one who always answered forthrightly! By prefacing their question with such flattery, they made it impossible for Him to refuse to answer as He had before, lest it seem as if He was indeed pandering to the powerful and showing partiality.

Having laid the groundwork, they sprang the trap. Was it **permitted** by God **to pay a poll-tax to Caesar, or not?** To make the trap doubly secure and impale Him on the horns of their dilemma, they asked a second time, a straight yes-or-no question: **Shall we give, or shall we not give** to Caesar?

It was a clever trap. If He answered, "We must give to Caesar," then He would lose popularity with the people, for all hated the tax. Moreover, they would compare Him unfavorably to John, who had been prepared to give his life in standing up to the secular authorities for the sake of truth. And if He answered, "We must not give to Caesar," then they had Him in their clutches, for this was a seditious utterance and one which could serve as a serious accusation before the Romans.

The Lord was untroubled. **Knowing their hypocrisy** and that they were not really asking because they wanted to be taught **the way of God in truth**, He asked them **why** they persisted in **testing** Him with such useless verbal games. We can almost hear Him sighing as He says, **"Bring Me a denarius that I may look** *at it.*" They found someone in the crowd who had the coin with which the poll-tax was to be paid, and they handed it to Him. Did He study the coin for a moment with mock seriousness before holding it up for them to scrutinize? But hold it up He did, and asked them a question, the answer to which everyone in the crowd already knew: **"Whose image and inscription** *is* **this?"** They had no choice but to state the obvious: **"Caesar's."** The Lord handed their coin back to them, with instructions to pass it along as tax to Caesar. **"Render to Caesar the things that are Caesar's."** The coin had both his face and his name on it—it obviously belonged to him! If it was his, then give it to him! Pay the tax. But take care to give him no more than his humble due. They must equally render **to God the things that are God's.** The Zealots had said that one must not give what belongs to God to Caesar instead. In this they were correct. Caesar could have his money—since it was his in the first place! But only God could have the ultimate loyalty of the human heart. The Romans might tax the People of God, but they could not usurp the place of their true and heavenly King. Israel's ultimate allegiance belonged only to Him.

It was a staggering answer, cutting to the core of a multitude of complex spiritual and political issues in a mere ten words (as counted in the Greek). All His hearers, including His foes, **marveled greatly** at such penetrating wisdom.

ॐ ॐ ॐ ॐ ॐ

18 And Sadducees come to Him (who say *there is not* to be a resurrection), and asked Him, saying,

19 "Teacher, Moses wrote to us that if one's brother dies, and leaves behind a wife, and does not leave a child, his brother should take the wife and raise up seed to his brother.

20 "There were seven brothers, and the first took a wife, and died, and did not leave a seed.

21 "And the second one took her, and died, not having left behind a seed; and the third likewise,

22 "and the seven did not leave a seed. Last of all the woman died also.

23 "In the resurrection, when they rise again, of which one will she be wife? For the seven had her *as* wife."

24 Jesus said to them, "Is it not for this that you are deceived, not having known the Scriptures, nor the power of God?

> 25 "For when they rise from the dead, they neither marry nor are given in marriage, but are like angels in the heavens.
> 26 "But concerning the dead that they are raised, have you not read in the Book of Moses, in *the passage* about the bush, how God spoke to him, saying, 'I am *the* God of Abraham, and *the* God of Isaac, and *the* God of Jacob'?
> 27 "He is not *the* God of the dead, but of the living; you are much deceived."

The next challenge came from the **Sadducees**. These were a sect consisting of the high-priestly family and other leading aristocratic families of Jerusalem. They were known to be in disagreement with the Pharisees, in that they say *there is* **not to be a resurrection** of the dead. The Sadducees believed that the dead no longer existed, and could not be united with their bodies and raised up. They also did not acknowledge the present supernatural ministries of angels (see Acts 23:8). Further, they only acknowledged the original five Books of Moses as true Scripture, rejecting everything that came after as merely human invention. Some of these rationalists came to challenge the Lord. As one who taught the existence of angels and spirits and who proclaimed a future resurrection and judgment, He would have aroused their disdain too.

They approached Him with feigned deference, calling Him **Teacher**, supposedly to receive a rabbinical ruling on a point of Law. They proposed a scenario, based on the part in the Law of **Moses** which said that **if one's brother dies, and leaves behind a wife, and does not leave a child, his brother should take the wife and raise up seed to his brother**. This was the so-called "levirate law," which was motivated by a desire to have a man's ancestral inheritance stay within his family (Deut. 25:5f). The children of the union would be legally the children of the dead man, and would inherit his property and so preserve the name of the family within Israel.

Given this law, they present the following situation: **There were seven brothers, and the first took a wife, and died, and did not leave** a seed (that is, a descendant). **And the second one took her, and died, not having left behind a seed; and the third likewise, and the seven did not leave a seed. Last of all the woman died also.** That is, it was proposed that all seven men married the same woman, one after the other, in a series of vain attempts to implement the law of levirate marriage. It was apparent by now that this was not a real situation requiring a rabbinical ruling. Rather, it was based more on literary precedents (such as the story in Tobit 3:8 of seven husbands having the same wife, as they died one after another). Then came their actual question: **"In the resurrection, when they rise again, of which one will she be wife? For the seven had her *as* wife."**

It was not a silly question, nor one aimed simply at "stumping" Jesus so that He could not answer. On the contrary, it was an attempt to show the incompatibility of a belief in the final resurrection with the world presupposed by the Law of Moses. For (they argued) if one tried to combine that Mosaic worldview with a belief in the resurrection of the dead, then such insoluble and absurd situations arose. One simply could not sensibly apply the Mosaic Law to situations envisaged by the world of the resurrection. Therefore, since the Law was divine and universal in application, *that world of the resurrection did not exist.* The Sadducees were attempting to show that the world presupposed by the Law was a naturalistic one, not the supernaturalistic one proclaimed by those who believed in the future resurrection.

The Lord quickly cut through their arrogance. For Jesus, the Sadducees were not simply wrong; they were **deceived** and in grave spiritual peril. And **this** was the reason why they were mired in deception: they did **not know the Scriptures, nor the power of God.** That is, they had rejected large parts of **the Scriptures** by accepting as Scripture only the five Books of Moses, and so had rejected the revelation of God Himself. How could they possibly know the truth, when they rejected the truth that God had spoken? Also, they were ignorant of the true **power of God.** Their God was too small; they thought it impossible that He could raise from the dust men who had been long dead and restore them to vitality again. In their rationalism they had dishonored God, by thinking such feats of power were beyond Him.

Then, having diagnosed their illness so that they might repent, He answered their question. His answer was brief, for their question was not a real question, but simply an attempt to show the absurdity of the idea of resurrection. Replying to their stated query, He said, **"When they rise from the dead, they neither marry nor are given in marriage, but are like angels in the heavens."** That is, the social institutions of our age—marrying and being given in marriage, birth and childrearing, sowing and harvesting, governing and making war—all these realities were for this age only. In the age to come, they are to pass away and give place to the Presence of God, which will transcend all such earthly pastimes. As the **angels in the heavens** do not engage in such mundane activities, but spend their time in ceaseless contemplation and adoration, so will it be with those who **rise from the dead.** Questions of who will have her as wife will then be meaningless. In that age, the time for taking a wife and raising children will be past.

The Lord had yet more for the Sadducees, in His desire to help them see the truth. He wanted them to know the truth **concerning the dead** and know **that they are raised**. He could not appeal to such passages as Daniel 12, however (which spoke clearly of the resurrection), for they did not accept that such passages were really Scripture. Only the five Books of Moses were Scripture in their eyes.

In His condescension, the Lord reaches down to help them in their infirmity. He could have simply insisted that they renounce their limited view of Scripture. Instead, He proves His point about the resurrection from the Mosaic Law itself, which they accepted. He quotes from *the passage* **about the bush** in Exodus 3. There **God spoke** to Moses and said, **"I am *the* God of Abraham, and *the* God of Isaac, and *the* God of Jacob"** (Ex. 3:6). This must mean that the dead do *not* perish, as the Sadducees imagined. For to be someone's God means to be their protector. And God declares that He is still the protector of Abraham, Isaac, and Jacob. To be a protector of the dead is a contradiction in terms. He is not *the* **God of the dead**, uselessly watching over those now beyond His care. Rather,

He is the God **of the living**, protecting and caring for them. If this is so, then Abraham, Isaac, and Jacob must still be alive before God—able to be raised up and waiting for this glorious provision from their Protector. The Sadducees were therefore **much deceived** in rejecting the future resurrection, for even their own Mosaic Law taught it.

ॐ ॐ ॐ ॐ ॐ

28 And one of the scribes came to *them* and heard them debating, and seeing that He had answered them well, asked Him, "Which is *the* first commandment of all?"

29 Jesus answered, "*The* first is, 'Hear, O Israel! *The* Lord our God is one Lord,

30 "'and you shall love *the* Lord your God with all your heart, and with all your soul, and with all your mind, and with all your strength.'

31 "*The* second *is* this, 'You shall love your neighbor as yourself.' There is not another commandment greater than these."

32 And the scribe said to Him, "Well *said*, Teacher! You have truly said that *He* is one, and there is not another except Him,

33 "and to love Him with all the heart and with all the insight and with all the strength and to love one's neighbor as oneself is more than all the burnt-offerings and sacrifices."

34 And when Jesus saw that he had answered intelligently, He said to him, "You are not far from the Kingdom of God." And after that, no one dared to ask Him *questions*.

After this exchange, **one of the scribes came** to where they were **debating**, and saw that Jesus had **answered** the Sadducees **well**. That is, He had completely vanquished that sect which the Pharisees also considered their ideological foes. Though a **scribe**, he was true of heart, and had not lost sight of what God really wanted in the midst of the multitude of legal distinctions and scribal debates. Jesus seemed to him to have real wisdom. Could He measure up, however, to the wisdom that *he*, the scribe, had found? He came to Jesus, not so much to be instructed, as to see how Jesus measured up (see Matt. 22:3–35).

His question presupposed that some commandments were more important than others. There were traditionally 613 commandments in the Law, with some being "weightier" than others. What did Jesus regard as the weightiest, *the* **first commandment of all?** Jesus had a reputation among the Pharisees as a lawbreaker, one who disregarded God's Law (see 2:24; 7:5). What would He say when asked about the Law?

Perhaps the scribe expected Him to say something about how the Law could be disregarded (which could be used against Him). If so, he would have been surprised, for Jesus took His stand in the heart of the Law, uttering the *Shema*, the standard proclamation of loyalty to God from Deuteronomy 6:4–5, which pious Jews recited every day. Jesus said that the first and weightiest commandment was love for God as the sole focus of Israel's existence: **Hear, O Israel!** *The* **Lord our God is one Lord, and you shall love** *the* **Lord your God with all your heart, and with all your soul, and with all your mind, and with all your strength.** Without being asked, Jesus also added what was *the* **second** commandment—that is, the corollary which followed inevitably from the first: **You shall love your neighbor as yourself** (a citation from Lev. 19:18). No other commandment in the entire Law could be **greater than these.** That is, all the others existed only as expressions of these two basic principles. Any scribal interpretation which did not further them was invalid (see 7:9–13).

The scribe was no narrow-minded partisan. Though not coming as a humble seeker, he still knew truth when he heard it, and he applauded the Lord's answer. **"Well** *said,* **Teacher!"** he responded. **"You have truly said that** *He* **is one, and there is not another except Him, and to love Him with all the heart and with all the insight** and with all the strength and to love one's neighbor as oneself is more than all the burnt-offerings and sacrifices." The scribe recognized that love for God was the only goal of the Law, and that the mindless offering of sacrifices in a mercenary attempt to buy His favor was useless. God wanted relationship with His people, and ritual separated from that relationship had no value.

This was an insight and a stance rare in Pharisaism, which legalistically tended to lose sight of the goal of the Law and confuse the means with the end. When Jesus **saw that he had answered intelligently**, He wanted to confirm the scribe in his insight and to encourage him to follow it to its final and logical conclusion, which was discipleship to Him. He therefore told him that he was **not far from the Kingdom of God**. If the scribe would continue in this trajectory, he would find himself one of Jesus' disciples.

ॐ ॐ ॐ ॐ ॐ

35 And Jesus answering said, as He taught in the Temple, "How do the scribes say that the Christ is *the* son of David?

36 "David himself said in the Holy Spirit, 'The Lord said to my Lord, "Sit on My right until I put Your enemies under Your feet." '

37 "David himself calls Him 'Lord', and how is He *his* son?" And the large crowd heard him gladly.

After He had dealt with all the challenges and silenced all His foes, it seems that there was a silence. The string of questions and series of opposing delegations ceased, and "after that, no one dared to ask Him *questions*" (v. 34). The Lord then **answered** this silence and continued to teach with a challenge and question of His own: "**How do the scribes say that the Christ is *the* son of David?**"

The significance of the question is not readily apparent today, but it was the burning question of the day as Jesus sat and **taught** in the Temple. It had to do with the nature of Messiahship. When the common man referred to the Messiah as *the* son of David, he meant that Messiah was to be a military hero as David had been—a "chip off the old block." He expected the Messiah to appear in glory, raise an army, and liberate Israel from the Romans. The Kingdom of David that followed (see 11:10) was to be a political one, and Israel's glory an earthly one.

This was all wrong. If they believed this, they would never recognize Jesus as the Messiah, for He repeatedly insisted that His Kingdom was *not* of this world (John 18:36), and its glory was heavenly. The Messiah was not to be a military figure like David, but a transcendent one.

This was apparent, Jesus said, from the words of David himself. In his own Psalm 110, uttered as a prophet in the Holy Spirit, David wrote, "The Lord said to my Lord, 'Sit on My right until I put Your enemies under Your feet'" (Ps. 110:1). The first Lord David referred to was God; the second Lord whom God addressed was the Messiah. So much was uncontroversial, for Jesus' hearers all considered this psalm to be a description of the Messiah who would sit at God's right hand. What Jesus points out is that David himself refers to the Messiah as his own Lord. David evidently then acknowledged the Messiah as superior to himself and as utterly transcendent. How could Messiah be said to be David's son, his derivative and inferior? The *title* son of David for Messiah was not the problem (Bartimaeus used it and was not rebuked, 10:47); the *politicized understanding* of Messiah was the problem. Jesus was teaching the people that in their understanding of Messiah, they must see Him not as a military revolutionary like David, but as a heavenly Lord.

ॐ   ॐ   ॐ   ॐ   ॐ

38 And in His teaching He said, "Watch out for the scribes, the ones wanting to walk *about* in robes and *who want* greetings in the market-places,

39 "and first-seats in the synagogues, and first-places at suppers,
40 "the ones eating up widows' houses and for pretense praying long. These will receive more judgment."

St. Mark then relates other things that the Lord taught during that week. In particular, He warned the people to **watch out for the scribes** of the Pharisees and avoid their hypocritical ways. Jesus focused on their pride as dangerous to any real spirituality. They **wanted to walk *about* in robes.** These were not liturgical vestments (only the priests would wear them); they were the clothes one would normally wear for outdoor daily living. But they were of a better quality than most. The scribes made a point of wearing long flowing white robes (white clothes were a mark of distinction) in order to better call attention to their high social position. They also wanted to receive respectful **greetings** as they passed through **the market-places**, delighting as people stood up and bowed as they passed by, addressing them as "Rabbi," "my Master," "my Father" (see Matt. 23:7–10). They coveted the **first-seats in the synagogue,** up at the front, facing the people, where all could see them and admire their preeminence. They took the **first-places at suppers** as their right (for one's place at the table nearest the host was determined by one's social standing). They insisted on these external marks of honor because they felt that their scribal knowledge made them better than everyone else. Their pride in position was evident in all they did, and it was this pride that was rebuked, not the mere fact of wearing robes, or being greeted, or sitting in places of honor.

They were, however, *not* better than everyone else. Rather, their outward show masked an inner greed and rapacity (see Matt. 23:25–28). They were always **eating up widows' houses.** That is, they would live with pious widows and sponge off them, using up all their resources until there was nothing left. They would **for pretense** and mere outer show **pray long** in public, extending their prayers to let everyone listening know how holy they were. All they did was directed at feeding their own passions, not at truly pleasing God.

When the time came for God's sentence to be handed down on the Last Day, they would **receive more judgment** and condemnation for it all. Let not the people imitate these scribes, however much they proclaimed themselves as examples of piety!

ॐ ॐ ॐ ॐ ॐ

41 And He sat down opposite the treasury, and observed how the crowd were casting copper-*coins* into the treasury, and many rich *people* were casting *in* many *coins.*

42 And one poor widow came and cast in two leptas (which is a quadrans).

43 And calling His disciples to *Him,* He said to them, "Amen I say to you, this poor widow cast in more than all the ones casting into the treasury;

44 "for they all cast in from their abundance, but she, out of her lack, cast in as much as she had, all her living."

As a true example of piety, St. Mark narrates the actions of a **poor widow** whom the Lord observed in the Temple treasury. In the outer Court of the Women (so named because it was accessible to all Jews, including the women), there were thirteen trumpet-shaped receptacles placed against the wall, into which people could deposit their gifts. Jesus **sat down opposite** some of these and **observed how the crowd were casting copper-*coins*** into them. There were **many rich *people*** there who came and **cast *in* many *coins.***

The Lord noticed **one poor widow** who came to one of the offering receptacles and **cast in two leptas.** A *lepta* was the smallest coin then used; its value was 1/128 of a denarius. Since a denarius was a day's pay for a laborer, two leptas were a small offering indeed, amounting to 1/64 of a day's wage. (St. Mark translates the amount for the benefit of his Roman readers, who would not know what a *lepta* was. He says the two *leptas* amounted to a Roman **quadrans**.)

Many may have been tempted to think her offering insignificant. The Lord, however, saw its true worth, and commended it to His disciples as an example for their own piety. **"Amen I say to you,"** He assured them, **"this poor widow cast in more than all"** the others. That is, God esteemed her gift as larger than even the impressive sums put in by the wealthy, and would reward her accordingly. The rich **cast in** to the treasury **from their abundance**, and they could easily afford it. **She, out of her lack** and poverty (most widows in those days were poor), **cast in as much as she had**, all that she had to live on. Note: She had *two* leptas, and could have kept one back. But she did not; she put in both, **all her living**. It was this total self-giving that was the *true* sign of piety, not the proud flashiness of the scribes. Let the Lord's disciples imitate this poor woman—and receive her reward!

§VI.3 The Olivet Discourse

ॐ ॐ ॐ ॐ ॐ

13 1 And as He came out of the Temple, one of His disciples says to Him, "Teacher, behold—what stones and what buildings!"

2 And Jesus said to him, "Do you see these great buildings? There will by no means be left *one* stone on *another* stone which will not be torn down."

3 And as He sat on the Mountain of Olives opposite the Temple, Peter and James and John and Andrew asked Him privately,

4 "Tell us, when will these things be, and what *will be* the sign when all these things are about to be consummated?"

Immediately after the challenges in the Temple, Christ and His disciples **came out of the Temple** to rest in the comparative privacy of the Mount of Olives (or Olivet). As they were leaving the area, one of them **says to Him** (the historic present is used), **"Teacher, behold—what stones and what buildings!"** The Temple site was indeed one of the wonders of the ancient world. The Temple itself was made of huge white stones, each about 25 cubits long, 8 cubits high, and 12 cubits wide, and ornate with gold. When the sun struck it, it shone with brilliance, "the perfection of beauty" (Ps. 50:2). Like all who saw it, they were awestruck at its splendor. The Lord, however, was not so impressed by the Temple, for He saw the proud defiance that lurked beneath the outward glory. He had spent the last hours meeting proud challenges to His authority—challenges and pride that would soon result in His death. And He knew that God would punish such rebellion by destroying the Temple—as indeed it was destroyed by the Romans in AD 70. He responded to their enthusiasm by saying, **"Do you see these great buildings? There will by no means be left *one* stone on *another* stone which will not be torn down."** The glory of the Temple resulted in pride and self-sufficiency growing in the hearts of the worshipers, and God would overthrow the Temple along with their pride.

The disciples were stunned by this reply. They were perhaps silent as they left the city by the north gate and then went eastward across the Kidron Valley. As they **sat** on the western slope of **the Mountain of Olives opposite the Temple**, they had a full panoramic view of the whole Temple mount. It seemed incredible that all that glittering façade could one day cease to be. Surely the Temple would last until the end of the world, and Jesus was speaking of its destruction as part of that final conflagration. **Peter, James, John, and Andrew**, the first ones called by the Lord and a kind of inner circle, **asked Him privately** for further clarification. In particular they wanted to know, **when will these things be?** He must have been speaking of His Coming and final glorification. **"What *will* be the sign,"** they asked, **"when all these things are about to be consummated?"** They wanted to know what the sign was that would signal the imminent End, that they might have time to prepare themselves for it.

ॐ ॐ ॐ ॐ ॐ

5 And Jesus began to say to them, "Watch out that no one deceives you.

6 "Many will come in My Name, saying, 'I am *He!*' and will deceive many.

7 "And when you hear of wars and reports of wars, do not be disturbed. It is necessary *that they* happen, but *it is* not yet the end.

8 "For nation will be raised against nation, and kingdom against kingdom; there will be earthquakes in *various* places; there will be famines. These things *are the* beginning of birthpangs.

In His response, Christ is concerned both to answer their question about the destruction of the Temple (for that was what they meant by "these things," v. 4) and to warn them about the end. His reply consists largely of telling them to **watch out** that they are not misled (Gr. *blepo*), and He tells them this four times (vv. 5, 9, 23, 33).

His reply needed to be long, for the disciples had confused two things that were actually separate. As pious Jews, they had assumed that the destruction of the Temple would herald the imminent end of the age. In point of fact, the Temple would be destroyed within one generation, in AD 70, whereas the end of the age would be at least two millennia distant. Christ undertook to teach them about both the destruction of the Temple and the end of the age.

He begins, therefore, by warning them to **watch out that no one deceives** them. Much uproar will soon begin—**many will come** in His **Name** (that is, claiming to be Messiah), saying **I am *He*** who will deliver Jerusalem, and they **will deceive many**. Many Jews will believe their messianic claims, and will fight for the city, thinking their new Messiah can deliver them. The Lord's disciples will **hear of wars and reports of wars**, so that all worldly stability will seem to be coming down around their ears. Surely that will mean that the end is at hand! But they are **not** to **be disturbed** by such events, nor shaken into thinking that the end is imminent. It is **necessary** that such things **happen**, for they have been decreed by God. Nonetheless, it will **not yet** be the time for **the end**. Such false Christs and wars do *not* herald the consummation, and are *not* signs of the End. **Nation will be raised against nation** (we note the passive voice used, indicating that these events come from the hand of God) and even **kingdom against kingdom**. More than this, even the earth itself will lose its stability, as there will be **earthquakes** (and not just in one place, but many, **in *various* places**), and **there will be famines** too. These also are not signs of the end. On the contrary, they are but the **beginning of birthpangs**. In the apocalyptic vocabulary of that day, people spoke of "the birthpangs of the Messiah"—that is, the increasing and painful catastrophes that would characterize the end of the age, leading up to the coming and reign of the Messiah. Jesus says that these disasters are *not* those birthpangs, but only the **beginning** of them. Birthpangs begin slowly and are spaced far apart. When they begin, birth is not imminent. The pangs have to grow in severity and frequency before birth is at hand. In the same way, He says, these disasters will have to grow much worse before the end is in sight.

ॐ ॐ ॐ ॐ ॐ

9   "But watch out for yourselves! For they will deliver you *up* to councils and you will be beaten in synagogues and you will stand before governors and kings for My sake as a witness to them.

10   "And it is necessary that the Gospel first be heralded to all the nations.

11   "And when they lead you *away*, delivering you *up*, do not be concerned beforehand about what you are to speak, but speak whatever is given you in that hour, for it is not you *yourselves* who speak, but the Holy Spirit.

12 "And brother will deliver *up* brother to death, and a father *his* child, and children will rise up against parents and put them to death.

13 "And you will *surely* be hated by all because of My Name, but the one who perseveres to *the* end, this one will be saved.

But they must **watch out** for themselves, for they will soon have more pressing problems. Persecution against them is soon to begin. Their Jewish foes will **deliver** them up **to councils** and they will be **beaten in synagogues**. The word translated here *councils* is the Greek word *sunedria*. Every local Jewish community had its own council or *sanhedrin*. (The nation had its own Great Sanhedrin—which would soon come together to condemn Jesus, see 14:55.) These local councils were responsible for regulating and punishing the conduct of Jews in the community. The Lord's followers will be arraigned before these courts and tried for heresy, found guilty, and then **beaten in** the **synagogues**, given the customary thirty-nine lashes with a plaited leather strap (see 2 Cor. 11:24).

Moreover, they will even be tried beyond the local Jewish courts; they will **stand before governors** and even **kings** for the sake of Jesus and **as a witness** to Him. For the Gospel is not just destined for Israel. It is **necessary that the Gospel first be heralded to all the nations**. They must be prepared to witness to their faith and suffer on the *world* stage, not just at home among fellow Jews.

For they will indeed be **delivered** *up* to suffering. (The word *delivered up*—Gr. *paradidomi*—is used three times in the next few verses.) When they are **led** *away* under arrest, however, and **delivered** *up* to prison, they are **not** to **be concerned beforehand** or worried **about what** they are **to speak** at their defense. In giving their testimony, they need not rely on worldly rhetoric or try to hire a good lawyer. They are called to be prophets, and as such need only **speak whatever is given** them by the prophetic Spirit **in that hour**. Their heavenly Father will not abandon them, but will give them irrefutable wisdom (see Luke 21:15). At their trials, it will not be they alone who speak, **but the Holy Spirit** within them.

They should not think, however, that such spiritual assistance means that they will be acquitted, or that they can avoid suffering. On the contrary, **brother** would **deliver** *up* **brother to death, and a father** *his* **child, and children will rise up against parents and put them to death**. It will be a time of unparalleled betrayal and suffering, and they will learn that the Gospel will divide even the previously indivisible unity of families (see Matt. 10:35–38). Faith in Jesus as Messiah will cause them to be disowned even by family members, who will side with those persecuting them. In fact, they will *surely* **be hated** (the Greek is emphatic: *esesthe misoumenoi*, "exist as hated") **by all** because they are loyal to Him and bear His **Name**. The world will contain no safe corners. All people everywhere will hate and persecute them, simply because they are His followers. One must expect this and **persevere to** *the* **end** of the age, enduring whatever suffering will come. For **this one**—the one who perseveres and does not apostatize—and this one alone, will finally **be saved**. If they would enter into life at the Last Day, they must cling to their faith now and not deny their Lord when the persecution begins.

ॐ ॐ ॐ ॐ ॐ

14 "But when you see the abomination of the desolation standing where it ought not to be (let the reader understand), then let those in Judea flee to the mountains.

15 "And let the one on the housetop not go down, nor enter in to take anything from his house;

16 "and let the one in the field not turn back to the things behind to take his garment.

17 "But woe to the ones having *children* in *the* womb and the ones nursing *babies* in those days!

18 "But pray that it may not occur in winter.

19 "For those days will be a tribulation such as has not occurred from *the* beginning of creation which God created until now, and by no means will *ever* occur *again*.

---

20 "And unless *the* Lord had shortened the days, no flesh would have been saved, but because of the chosen whom He chose, He shortened the days.

21 "And then if anyone says to you, 'Behold, here *is* the Christ!' or 'Behold, there!' do not believe in *him*;

22 "for false-christs and false-prophets will be raised up and will give signs and wonders so as to *completely* deceive, if possible, the chosen.

23 "But you *yourselves* watch out! Behold, I have foretold you everything.

After warning them not to be misled into thinking that the upheaval of their day means that the End is at hand, He turns to their original question: the sign preceding the destruction of Jerusalem. They had asked, "What *will be* the sign when all these things [i.e. the destruction of Jerusalem and—as they thought—the end of the age] are about to be consummated?" (v. 4). The Lord therefore tells them what "the sign" (Gr. *semeion*) is that Jerusalem is about to be destroyed. They will know its destruction is at hand when they **see the abomination of the desolation standing where it ought not to be.**

What was this sign? The parallels in the other two synoptic Gospels of Matthew and Luke can help us. In Matthew 24:15, Jesus is reported as saying the sign is "the abomination of desolation standing in the holy place." In Luke 21:20, this Jewish expression is paraphrased for a Gentile audience as meaning "Jerusalem surrounded by armies." That is, the "holy place" where the foreign armies **ought not to be,** because of the sacrilegious **abomination** of their idolatrous military banners, was the sacred area around Jerusalem itself. When the disciples saw them with their banners standing encamped within the city limits (such as at Bethphage), then they should recognize that the **desolation** of the city was at hand (see Luke 21:20). That would be the sign that God had abandoned Jerusalem to her sins, and that divine judgment was soon to fall. All those in the surrounding area of **Judea** should **flee to the mountains** nearby, and seek safety there until it was all over.

(St. Mark adds a parenthesis, suitably cryptic, so that only his Christian audience in Rome would comprehend it. He adds the phrase, **let the reader understand.** That is, Mark adds his own editorial comment, even as he did in a parenthesis in 7:19, and says here that those who read the Book of Daniel, which refers to "the abomination of desolation" in 9:27, 11:31, and 12:11, should **understand** how this disaster will fulfill all the ancient prophecies about God's judgment on Israel. St. Mark adds this in such a cryptic way because he does not want to write openly that the Roman armies are the prophesied abomination. Such openness would have been considered treasonous in that day, and Mark takes care to cloak his meaning from all but Christian eyes, even as Paul did when he referred to the Roman power in 2 Thess. 2:5–7 as that which will be "taken out of the way.")

The Lord therefore tells His disciples to flee the city when they see this sign, and not to return. They must utterly separate themselves from the world they knew, and not let worldliness tie them down, nor delay their departure (see the use of flight in Luke 17:31 as an image of spiritual detachment). They must hasten to get away, and not postpone their departure, waiting until they wound up their business affairs. Such delay would prove fatal, as days stretched to weeks and weeks stretched to months and years. They must have an inner detachment which allowed **the one on the housetop not** to **go down** to **enter in** to his home **to take anything from his house.** Let him flee instantly, abandoning everything to save his life! And **the one** working **in the field**—when he saw the sign, let him **not turn back to the things** left **behind** (such as the **garment** he took off to work in the heat). Let him too flee from where he was, giving up all his possessions if he would save his life. This was a parabolic utterance, of course. When the sign came, the disciples had a matter of weeks and months to flee. But the Lord tells this parable of instant and panicked flight to impress on them the dangers of staying behind for the sake of gain.

For when the disaster came, it would be unparalleled. **Woe to the** ones having *children* in *the* womb and the ones nursing *babies* in those days, for these would thus be encumbered in their flight and unable to get away quickly enough. Similarly, the disciples should then **pray that** the disaster **may not occur in winter**, for then the rivers would be swollen and flight would also be difficult.

For those days will be a tribulation such as has not occurred from *the* **beginning of creation which God created until now, and by no means will** *ever* **occur** *again.* The disaster will be so great that **unless** *the* **Lord had shortened the days, no flesh would have been saved.** As that great **tribulation** and affliction went out, it would destroy all **flesh,** every human being, in Jerusalem. But because of **the chosen** ones, the Christians who prayed for mercy on Jerusalem, God would **shorten the days,** so that some inhabitants of the city would be spared.

The temptation for everyone living during that dreadful time was to believe that God would intervene and save Zion. Had He not promised to do so, and was not the Christ to be a military and political revolutionary who would overthrow all their Gentile foes? In the days preceding the final disaster of AD 70, in fact many would come and claim to be the promised messianic deliverer. Jesus therefore warned His disciples not to believe any who would claim they would lead Jerusalem to victory. **If anyone** were to say to them, "**Behold, here** *is* **the Christ!** Follow that man and he will save us!" or "**Behold, there!** There he is! Join his army and we will be rescued!" the disciples were **not** to **believe in** *him,* nor believe that he could rescue Zion. Such imposters would surely come. **False-christs and false-prophets** would **be raised up,** and would even **give signs and wonders so as to** *completely* **deceive, if possible** even them, **the chosen.** They must **watch out** and be forewarned. For Jesus had **foretold everything.**

It all happened exactly as the Lord said. In the days leading up to AD 70, there were indeed wars and earthquakes and famines. Jewish nationalism became more violently intense and more apocalyptic. Jesus' followers were indeed tried and flogged in the synagogues and put to death, and even brought before Gentile rulers (the experience of St. Paul is the most shining example). And in

October of 66, the Roman armies under Cestius Gallus marched against Jerusalem and surrounded her. The Christians of Jerusalem remembered the Lord's words and fled to the mountain city of Pella. In 70, the Roman armies returned under Titus and laid siege to the Holy City again. Jerusalem put up a valiant struggle, even though suffering starvation which reduced the inhabitants to cannibalism. At last the city fell, and the Temple was burned to the ground, with not one stone left on another. A few from the city survived, spared by the prayers of the Christians. These were led captive into all nations, and Jerusalem continued to be trampled underfoot and fought over. This was no temporary setback (as some Jewish holdouts thought, fighting in AD 130). It was to last until the end of the age, until the time of Gentile domination of the world would cease (Luke 21:24). (The story of Jerusalem's fall and the Christians' escape is narrated by Eusebius in his *History of the Church*, 5.5–8.)

༄ ༄ ༄ ༄ ༄

24 "But in those days, after that tribulation, the sun will be darkened, and the moon will not give its radiance,

25 "and the stars will be falling from heaven, and the powers, in the heavens, will be shaken.

26 "And then they will see the Son of Man coming in clouds with much power and glory.

27 "And then He will send the angels and will gather together His chosen from the four winds, from the end of earth to the end of heaven.

28 "Now from the fig tree learn the parable: when its branch has already become tender and puts forth the leaves, you know the summer draws near.

29 "Thus, you *yourselves* also, when you see the things occurring, know that it is near, at *the* doors.

Finally, the Lord teaches them about His Coming and the end. The disciples thought it would come soon, and that the wars in their day were signs of it. But it will come much later—only **after that tribulation**, and after **those days** of this age, with the long humiliation of Jerusalem. When it is at hand, **the sun will be darkened, and the moon will not give its radiance, and the stars will be falling from heaven, and the powers, in the heavens, will be shaken**. The false-Christs may show signs and wonders to try to prove their false claims to be Messiah (v. 22), but here are the real and irrefutable signs! Let the false-Christs reproduce these! When the true Christ at last appears, all the order in the cosmos will be overthrown, as His Coming will shatter the foundations of this age and replace them with those of the age to come.

In using such language, Jesus is speaking with the classic imagery of the prophets (see Is. 13:10; Ezek. 32:7; Joel 2:10). This does not mean, however, that He is simply using metaphors. St. Luke, who paraphrases the Jewish phraseology of the accounts found in St. Matthew and St. Mark to make them clearer to a Gentile audience, still reports Jesus as predicting "signs in the sun and moon and stars" as "the powers of the heavens" are "shaken" (Luke 21:25, 26). It is apparent, then, that prior to the Second Coming, the heavens above will abound with disturbing phenomena.

It is **then** and only then that **they will see the Son of Man coming in clouds with much power and glory**. *How* all the earth will see the Son of Man coming in heavenly glory is not explained, nor can it be. The Second Coming is, by definition, the event by which this age, which we can see and imagine, becomes the age to come, which we cannot imagine. St. Peter would later write that on that day "the heavens will pass away with a roar and the elements will be destroyed with intense heat," giving way to "a new heavens and a new earth in which righteousness dwells" (2 Pet. 3:10, 13). When all reality as we know it is dissolved and transformed into the more enduring realities filled with the Presence of God, we will know the answer to such questions. The Lord does not speak of His final Coming to tantalize our curiosity, like one showing the preview scenes of a movie. Rather, He speaks to assure His disciples that He will indeed return and that there is no danger of them missing it.

At that time, like God gathering the exiles home (see Deut. 30:4; Is. 43:6; Zech. 2:6), so Jesus will **gather together His chosen from the four winds**, wherever they may be scattered and sojourning in all the earth. None will be lost, none overlooked. Though they be buried at **the end** and farthest limit **of earth** and even **to the end of heaven** (that is, far beyond the horizon), still He will find them and gather them safely into His Kingdom. They may rest assured and confident in His care—**He will send** His invincible messengers **the angels** to escort them safely home.

To encourage His disciples not to "faint with fear and the expectation of the things coming on the world" (Luke 21:26), He concludes His teaching on His Second Coming with a **parable**. They must **learn** from the **fig tree**: unlike most other trees in Palestine, which blossomed in the spring, the fig tree blossomed later, in the summer. All people knew that **when its branch** had **become tender and put forth the leaves**, the **summer** was drawing near and was just around the corner. Men know how to read the nearness of summer. In the same way, the disciples themselves (the Greek pronoun is emphatic) must learn how to read the nearness of the Kingdom. When they **see** those fearful things **occurring** (described in vv. 24, 25), they will also **know that** the Kingdom of God is **near**—even at **the** very **doors**, about to enter this age (see Luke 21:31). The shaking of the powers of heaven should not be a cause for cowering, but for straightening up in joyful anticipation. What is coming is not more disaster, but their redemption (Luke 21:28). The change in the fig tree meant good news of summer, and these changes in the world will mean the good news of the coming Kingdom.

ॐ ॐ ॐ ॐ ॐ

30 "Amen I say to you, this generation will by no means pass away until all these things occur.
31 "The heaven and the earth will pass away, but My words will not pass away.

The Lord then concludes His entire discourse with an assurance of the certainty of His predictions. **This generation**, He promises— the one then living and resisting His word (see 8:38; Matt. 23:36)— would **by no means pass away until all these things** would **occur**. That is, the entire sequence of events He had described, beginning from verse 5, would begin to occur before all of that current generation had died. (Not, of course, that the Second Coming would occur, but that His words would begin to find their fulfillment.) When Daniel received his revelation, he was told to "conceal these words and seal up the book until the end of time," for their fulfillment was not due for a long time after (Dan. 12:4). The Lord here makes it clear that it is otherwise with this revelation—the time for fulfillment was immediate.

And so it was. The Lord uttered these words on Mount Olivet about AD 30, and within one generation, Jerusalem lay in ruins. His words therefore were living and powerful, the very words which brought the world into being (Gen. 1:3f). As such, they would outlive the world. **The heaven and the earth** would one day **pass away**, but Christ's eternal and divine **words** would **not pass away**. The disciples might be sure, therefore, that His predictions would be speedily fulfilled.

(We may note in passing the implied claim to divinity that Christ was hereby making. Only God could speak such eternal words [see Is. 40:8]. In the mouth of any created being, such a claim to speak words more eternal than the cosmos would be blasphemous. Christ makes such a claim because He is not a merely created being, but the everlasting God, eternally one with the Father.)

ॐ ॐ ॐ ॐ ॐ

32 "But concerning that day or hour no one knows, neither the angels in heaven, nor the Son, but the Father.

33 "Watch out, keep awake, for you do not know when the *appointed* time is.

34 "*It is* like a man who left home, leaving his

> house and giving his slaves the authority, each
> one his work, who also commanded the door-
> keeper to keep alert.
>
> 35 "Therefore, keep alert, for you do not know
> when the lord of the house is coming, whether
> in the evening, at midnight, at cockcrow, or
> early,
>
> 36 "lest he come suddenly and find you sleeping.
> 37 "And what I say to you, I say to all: Keep alert!"

Christ adds a final warning. The disciples must not conclude from His words about Jerusalem being destroyed within one generation that they may also predict the time when the Kingdom will come. They very much wanted to know this, so that they might plan their lives. There is something buried deep in the human heart, some fatal desire, which wants to settle down in this age, which resists spiritual detachment from possessions, which feels uncomfortable with the thought of finding security in God alone. If we could only know when the Kingdom would come, we could get on with our worldly lives and make the necessary repentance later on! But the Lord warns that this is impossible.

There is no man wise enough to be able to read all the contours of history and discern the hand of God in it all and accurately calculate the Day. **Concerning that** final **day or hour, no one knows.** No one on earth has what it takes to unravel the fathomless purposes of God. Indeed, not even **the angels in heaven** have such wisdom, for all their high and transcendent vision of God and their knowledge of heavenly mysteries. **Nor,** Jesus says, does **the Son** Himself. That is, **the Father** has hidden the secret in the abyss of His own counsels, and not even Jesus Himself, in His self-emptied incarnate state, has access to it. The disciples then may be sure that no other man living may be wise enough to predict it! They must therefore **watch out,** being careful to **keep awake** and be vigilant, for they **do not know when** the *appointed* time of that Coming will be.

A Christological note may be added here. Though Jesus says

that He did not then have access to the Father's secret in the state of His earthly existence, one should not conclude that He is essentially inferior to the Father, or that He is not truly one with Him (see John 10:30). Indeed, the Lord earlier affirmed that the Son has full knowledge of the Father (Matt. 11:27). In His essential union with the Father, it would seem that He does indeed have inner and heavenly access to all that the Father knows. It was during His earthly existence, when He emptied Himself by uniting human nature to Himself and shared our human condition, that He shared all of our experiences. Thus He hungered and thirsted, and marveled at unbelief, and asked who touched Him in a crowd (5:30; 6:6; John 4:7). It was in this state also that He walked in humility with us, having laid aside and veiled His glory. This verse is not meant to explain the limitations of Jesus' subjective knowledge; it is meant to teach us that vigilance, and not calculation of the times, is what is required of us.

In order to help them understand this need for constant vigilance, He tells a parable about **a man who left home, leaving his house and giving his slaves** their **authority** and assigned **work**, and then **commanded the doorkeeper to keep alert**. The disciples knew what the duty of the slaves was. They were not to slack off the moment their lord was gone, and return to their tasks just before he returned. They were expected to work diligently all the time he was away. And, since they could not possibly know when their master was returning, whether it was to be **in the evening, at midnight, at cockcrow** at dawn, or **early** the next morning, they must **keep alert** all the time, lest he return **suddenly** and without warning and find them **sleeping**.

The word translated here in verse 33 as *keep awake* is the Greek *agrupneo*, cognate with the word for sleepless vigil and watching, *agrupnia*, translated "sleepless nights" in 2 Corinthians 11:27. The Lord is therefore telling His disciples to maintain a constant inner vigilance. Like one who refuses to nod off to sleep on his assigned watch, so Christ's disciple must not let the spirit of the age lull him into spiritual slumber. He must remain spiritually awake and attuned to the things of God. If he takes the Lord's earthly absence as an excuse to live in disregard of His commandments, His Coming will find him unprepared (Luke 21:34–36). Christ ends His discourse with this sober word of warning. He is not speaking just to the four disciples who asked Him these questions (v. 3), He is speaking **to all** who would heed Him throughout the present age. Unlike the destruction of Jerusalem, His Coming would be without warning. They therefore must live in a constant state of preparedness for it. Christ's last word to us is, **Keep alert!**

Notes for Section VI:

_____

_____

_____

_____

_____

_____

_____

_____

_____

_____

_____

_____

_____

_____

_____

_____

_____

_____

_____

_____

_____

_____

_____

_____

_____

ॐ VII ॐ

THE PASSION
(14:1—15:47)

§VII.1 Judas's Plan to Betray Jesus and the Anointing at Bethany

---

14 ॐ ॐ ॐ ॐ ॐ

1 Now the Passover and the Unleavened *Bread* was two days away; and the chief-priests and the scribes were seeking how to seize Him by guile, and kill Him,

2 for they were saying, "Not in the festal *crowd*, lest there be an uproar of the people."

Having sketched the story of Jesus' ministry, St. Mark moves to his climax, telling the story of His arrest, Crucifixion, and Resurrection. This begins with the defection of Judas Iscariot. Judas had for a long time been growing apart from Jesus and had alienation growing like a cancer in his heart (see John 6:70; 12:6). His growing disaffection with his Master would boil over into a determination to betray Christ during His final week.

To show how Judas's betrayal worked in the overall plan of Jesus' foes, St. Mark first explains how when **the Passover** (Gr. *Pascha*) and the feast of **the Unleavened *Bread* was two days away** (that is, on Tuesday of that final week), **the chief-priests and the scribes were seeking how to seize** Jesus **by guile**. That is, Christ's foes in the Temple were determined to have Him arrested, but wanted to do it secretly. He was still popular with the crowd, and if they sent officers to arrest Him as He was teaching in the midst of the Temple, there would be **an uproar** and a riot and the officers would be torn to pieces by **the festal** *crowd* (i.e. those who assembled in Jerusalem for the Passover feast). Jerusalem's population swelled from 50,000 to about 250,000 at Passover time, and many of these were Galileans. Christ's foes therefore were trying to find a way to get Him alone. Judas's willingness to betray Jesus therefore fit right in with their objectives.

ॐ ॐ ॐ ॐ ॐ

3 And while He was in Bethany in the house of Simon the leper, and reclining, a woman came, having an alabaster *flask* of costly perfume of pistic nard; she broke the alabaster *flask* and poured *it* over His head.

4 But some indignantly *said* to themselves, "Why has this loss of perfume occurred?

5 "For this perfume might have been sold for more than three hundred denarii and given to the poor." And they scolded her.

6 But Jesus said, "Leave her; why do you cause her toil? She has worked a good work for Me.

7 "For you always have the poor with you, and whenever you want, you can do good to them; but Me you do not always have.

8 "She has done what she could; she has taken My body beforehand to anoint *it* for the burial.

9 "And amen I say to you, wherever the Gospel is heralded throughout all the world, what this *woman* has done will also be spoken for a memorial of her."

10 And Judas Iscariot, who was one of the Twelve, went away to the chief-priests, that he might deliver Him *up* to them.

11 And they rejoiced when they heard, and promised to give him silver. And he sought how to deliver Him *up* at an opportune *time*.

Having shown how Jesus' foes were seeking a way to find Jesus alone, St. Mark then "flashes back" to a time before His Triumphal Entry into Jerusalem, to narrate the event that pushed Judas over the edge. It occurred before He had even entered Jerusalem, when **He was in Bethany in the house of Simon the leper** (i.e. Simon who had *formerly* been a leper; it is inconceivable that one would host a gathering still being a leper). That is, it occurred six days before the Passover, when He was at a party held in His honor by Lazarus, Martha, and Mary (John 12:1–8). (Perhaps it was held **in the house of Simon the leper** because their friend Simon had a house big enough to accommodate the large crowd invited, and the home of Lazarus and his sisters was too small.) It was during this feast, as Jesus was **reclining** at table during the meal, that **a woman came** to Him.

We know from the account in John 12:3 that this woman was Mary, the sister of Lazarus. This is important, for it makes her actions more understandable. Mary was desolated by the untimely death of her brother (John 11:32, 33), and overwhelmed with gratitude at his restoration and resurrection. It was customary for a host to provide some oil for anointing the heads of his guests. Simon had doubtless done this, but it would seem that Mary intended to make her own offering of anointing oil in token of her immense gratitude. She had a special perfume for the purpose, one probably preserved down the generations as a family heirloom. It was kept in **an alabaster *flask***, as precious perfumes often were. These flasks would preserve the perfume, but the long neck of the flask would have to be **broken** to pour out the contents. It could not be stoppered after that; its contents had to be used all at one time. The perfume was **costly** indeed, being **pistic nard** (Gr. *nardou pistikes*— a transliteration of the Aramaic), the aromatic oil made from the pistachio nut.

As in all such anointings, Mary **poured *it* over His head**. Then, suddenly overwhelmed with love and thankfulness (and having to use the rest of the flask), she poured the rest on His feet, removed her veil, and wiped His feet with her hair (see John 12:3). The unveiling of her hair in public was a shocking display, and one which would cause much murmuring all around. (Mary, it seems, was used to shocking people; see Luke 10:39f.)

For Judas, whose heart was rapidly growing colder toward his Lord, this was all he could stand. All thought it a tremendous waste, and Judas gave voice to their concerns (John 12:4, 5). The perfume that Mary used up in one extravagant and impulsive act (just like a woman, they thought!) **might have been sold for more than three hundred denarii**—almost a year's wages—**and given to the poor**. Jesus had a great and abiding concern for the poor, and they felt sure this was His attitude too. Thus **they scolded her** over **this loss of perfume**. Stupid woman! Now the perfume was gone for good!

Jesus, however, did *not* have this attitude, and He instantly sprang to her defense. **Leave her** alone, He commanded them, silencing their superficial and self-righteous scolding. **Why do you cause her toil** and trouble? For she had done nothing wrong, nothing worthy of censure. Rather, she had **worked a good work for Me**. The word translated here *worked* is the Greek *ergazomai*, meaning not just "to do," but "to accomplish." It is the word used in Romans 2:10 to describe the accomplishing of good works leading to eternal life. Christ says here that Mary had accomplished a true *mitzvah*, a good deed worthy of the divine reward. Were they so concerned with the poor? Then let them know that they **always have the poor** with them, and **whenever** they want, they can **do good to them** and give alms.

It was otherwise with Jesus. Him they would **not always have**. Mary had **done what she could** to help Him, she had **taken His body beforehand to anoint** *it* **for the burial**. The anointing of a dead body in preparation for burial was known as a good work—how could anyone blame her for this? Who would deny the dead their customary anointing? This was a true and worthy act she was doing for Him. Indeed, He says, prefacing the promise with His usual oath, **amen I say to you, wherever the Gospel is heralded throughout all the world**, her act of devotion **will also be spoken** along with that message **for a memorial of her**.

It was an astounding response. A **memorial** (Gr. *mnemosunon*) was something done or offered as a memorial before God, so that He would remember the person thus commended and reward him or her. (The word is used in Lev. 2:2 LXX for a memorial sacrifice, and the phrase here used, Gr. *eis mnemosunon*, is also used in Acts 10:4 to describe how Cornelius' prayers and alms ascended as a memorial before God.) What Jesus meant was that Mary's act of devotion would function as her memorial before God on the Last Day. Every time the Gospel was preached, this act would be rehearsed along with it, so that the Gospel preachers would continually offer this memorial on her behalf. Far from being a waste worthy of censure, her outpouring of love was worthy of eternal reward, and would be memorialized, not just in Palestine, but the world over.

The disciples were doubtless amazed at Jesus' fervency in her defense. Judas was more than amazed. For him this was the last straw: to be publicly rebuked in favor of a woman. After they had left the party, he nurtured the resentment within. When he had opportunity to see **the chief-priests** (probably during the Wednesday of that final week), he secretly **went away** to them **that he might deliver Him up** to them. This was the break they had been hoping for, and **they rejoiced when they heard** his offer. To show their gratitude for his help, they **promised to give him silver**, and he, for his part, **sought how to deliver Him up at an opportune** *time*. St. Mark discloses the final component of the bargain to show how tawdry and reprehensible it all was. Judas, when all was said and done, was not acting out of loyalty to any great principle, but was moved by envy and greed, like the lowest of traitors.

It must be stressed that the disciples, hearing the words of Christ to Mary about her **taking** His **body beforehand to anoint** *it* **for the burial**, must have been perplexed. His death and burial, they assumed, would not be for some years yet, for He was only thirty-three. What could *this* parable mean? By this word, however, Christ gives them a veiled reference to the imminence of His death. Mary's act of devotion had a significance that none could see. Now was the time for such extravagant acts of love. The time was fast approaching when there would be no more such opportunities.

§VII.2 The Last Supper

ॐ ॐ ॐ ॐ ॐ

12 And on the first day of Unleavened *Bread*, when the Passover was being sacrificed, His disciples say to Him, "Where do You want us to go and prepare that You may eat the Passover?"

13 And He sends two of His disciples, and says to them, "Go into the city, and a man will meet you bearing a jar of water; follow him;

14 "and wherever he enters, say to the house-master, 'The Teacher says, "Where is my lodging-room where I may eat the Passover with My disciples?"'

15 "And he *himself* will show you a large upper-room spread, ready; and prepare for us there."

16 And the disciples went out and came into the city, and found it just as He had told them, and they prepared the Passover.

Having narrated Judas's secret meeting with the chief-priests in the middle of that final week, St. Mark then tells of the events immediately following that meeting. On **the first day** of the Paschal feast **of Unleavened** *Bread*, the Thursday of that week, **when the Passover** lambs were **being sacrificed**, Jesus gave instructions to His disciples to arrange for their Passover meal. It was required that the Passover be eaten within Jerusalem. This presented a problem, for the city was swarming with Jesus' foes, so that each evening He left the city for the safety of Bethany (11:11, 19). He was safe while in the public eye in the Temple, but eating in private would give His foes an opportunity to arrest Him. If He were to remain safe, the place of His meal must be kept secret.

So it was that He had prearranged for the meal's preparation. A brave resident of Jerusalem offered secret hospitality to the outlawed Galilean (perhaps the husband of Mary, the mother of young John

Mark, the writer of this Gospel; that was a house in the city which the disciples would later use, see Acts 12:12). As the disciples waited and watched, they would see **a man bearing a jar of water**. This would be the prearranged signal, and the man would lead them to the proper house. (This action was unusual enough to be a signal, since men did not normally carry water jars; that was women's work.) The disciples were to **follow** that man, enter the house after him, and **say to the house-master, "The Teacher says, 'Where is my lodging-room where I may eat the Passover with My disciples?'"** That was to be the password which would identify the disciples to the householder, since they were not known to him by sight (see 11:3), and the owner of the rooms would take them upstairs to **a large upper-room** which he had **spread** with rugs for reclining, **ready** for the Passover meal. They were to take the Passover lamb there to be eaten after it had been sacrificed in the Temple. The disciples obeyed and followed these secret plans. After obtaining their lamb in the Temple and having it sacrificed in the usual way, they took the lamb to the room to roast it and thus **prepare** for the sacred Paschal meal.

ॐ ॐ ॐ ॐ ॐ

17 And when it was evening, He comes with the Twelve.

18 And as they were reclining and eating, Jesus said, "Amen I say to you, one of you will deliver Me up—one eating with Me."

19 And they began to be sorrowful and to say to Him, one by one, "Not me, surely?"

20 And He said to them, "*It is* one of the Twelve, one dipping with Me into the dish.

21 "For the Son of Man goes just as it is written about Him; but woe to that man through whom the Son of Man is delivered *up*! *It would have been* good for him if that man had not been born."

On Thursday, **when it was evening** and time for the annual Paschal meal, **He comes with the Twelve** to the prearranged room in Jerusalem (the historic present is again used).

The Passover meal followed a prescribed ritual. Like all feasts, by this time in Israel's history it was eaten **reclining** on couches, after the Roman manner. A number of couches would be arranged around a low table. The participants in the feast would come clothed in their best festive garments and take their places, in order of importance and precedence, around the host, who reclined at the end of the table. They would all face toward the table and lean on their left arms, eating with their right.

The meal would begin with the host or head of the family chanting a blessing over the first cup of wine (the "cup of *Kiddush*," or sanctification), giving thanks to God both for the wine and for the feastday, and beginning with the words, "Blessed are You, O Lord our God, King of the universe, who created the fruit of the vine." Each then drank the first cup of wine that lay before him. A basin of water was then brought in and all would rise from the table to wash their hands. Then the table of food was brought in, the meal consisting of the Passover itself (i.e. the lamb that had been offered in the Temple), unleavened bread, bitter herbs, greens, and a dish of stewed fruit. The host dipped some of the bitter herbs in the fruit and handed them to each, as a kind of appetizer. A second cup of wine (the "cup of *Haggadah*" or storytelling) was filled and blessed with a chanted prayer.

The Passover story from Exodus was then recounted. This story concluded with singing a hymn—the first part of the so-called Great Hallel or Great Praise, consisting of Psalms 113 and 114. The second cup was then drunk.

The head of the family would then take the unleavened bread, chant a blessing or thanksgiving over it (such as the standard "Blessed are You, O Lord our God, King of the universe, who brings forth bread from the earth"), break the bread, and distribute it, usually in silence. Then the bitter herbs were eaten, the host dipping them into the stewed fruit dish.

The meal then began, as everyone ate the Passover and enjoyed a night of fellowship, rejoicing in the freedom God had given them. Talk would be prolonged, though not past midnight. The meal would end with the blessing of a third cup of wine (the "cup of blessing"). The entire evening closed with the drinking of the fourth and final cup (the "cup of *Hallel*" or praise), over which was sung the second half of the Hallel, Psalms 115—118.

It was **as they were reclining and eating** the preliminary course (the bitter herbs and stewed fruit) that Jesus began to be troubled. He was embracing them and folding them to His heart, having longed to share one last meal with them (see Luke 22:15), yet one of them was resisting that love. Jesus solemnly affirmed (with His **Amen I say to you**) that **one of** them would **deliver** Him **up—one eating with** Him. Even in that atmosphere of cozy secrecy and supposed safety, a traitor lurked among them. The disciples were devastated at such news and **began to be sorrowful** themselves, feeling sick inside. Such was their trust in His word that, even though it seemed impossible to each of them (or all but one) that they could do this thing, they nonetheless believed Him, trusting His words over their own self-confidence. With faltering voices, they each said **one by one, "Not me, surely?"** (The personal pronoun is emphatic in the Greek.) The Lord would openly affirm only that it was indeed **one of the Twelve**, His supposedly trustworthy inner circle of confidants (see 4:11); the traitor was one of those who were even now sharing table fellowship and **dipping** with Him **into the dish** of stewed fruit which they all were sharing. (In John's Gospel we learn how Jesus revealed to John the identity of the traitor by whispering that it was the next person to whom He would give the sop of bitter herbs; John 13:23–26.) This betrayal was in God's plan, for **the Son of Man** was to go **just as it** was **written about Him** in the prophetic Scriptures. This betrayal could not sidetrack or derail His work. Nonetheless, it was a terrible thing, and **woe to that man through whom** He was **delivered** *up*! Such would be his fate on the Last Day that *it would have been* good *for him* if he **had not been born**. The disciples doubtless trembled at such a judgment hanging over them. Judas, however, hardened his heart, determined not to let fear deflect him from his task of betrayal. When Christ gave him the sop, he received it and went out (John 13:26–30). He left the light-filled room to embrace the darkness.

ৡ৵ ৡ৵ ৡ৵ ৡ৵ ৡ৵

22 And as they were eating, having taken Bread, *and* having blessed, He broke *it*, and gave to them, and said, "Take, this is My Body."

23 And having taken a Cup, *and* having given thanks, He gave *it* to them and all drank from it.

24 And He said to them, "This is My Blood of the covenant, which is poured out for many.

25 "Amen I say to you, I will no longer by any means drink of the fruit of the vine until that day when I drink it new in the Kingdom of God."

26 And having *sung a* hymn, they went out into the Mountain of Olives.

So it was, after the defection of the traitor, that Jesus was alone with His loyal disciples for the institution of the Mystical Supper. St. Mark omits all the details of the Passover meal itself, and focuses only on the two details that were unique to that meal. Thus he leaves out how the second cup of wine was filled and the Passover *haggadah* recounted. He omits how they sang the first part of the Great Hallel, Psalms 113 and 114, and then drank the second cup together, rejoicing in how God had led them out of Egypt.

After the appetizers and the Passover liturgy came the meal itself. Like all meals, it began with the breaking of bread. **Having taken** the **Bread**, Jesus **blessed** God and chanted the customary blessing, "Blessed are You, O Lord our God, King of the universe, who brings forth bread from the earth," and **broke** the bread. He then **gave** the Bread to them, saying the cryptic and bone-chilling words, **"Take** and eat; **this is My Body."** The words were bewildering. They were no part of the normal distribution of bread. What could He mean? The apostles ate the bread with heavy hearts, perhaps remembering His previous words about eating His Flesh (John 6:51; 53–58).

The meal continued as usual, everyone eating the Paschal lamb and the other food. Then, at the end of the meal, came the blessing and drinking of the third cup, the so-called "cup of blessing" (see 1 Cor. 10:16). **Having taken** His **Cup**, and **having given thanks** by reciting the usual blessing, **He gave** *it* **to them and** they **all drank from it**. This was somewhat unusual, for it was normal for each one present to drink from his own cup. And as they passed from person to person the Lord's own Cup, He again uttered the chilling words, **"This is My Blood of the covenant, which is poured out for many."** Once again, the apostles did not know what to make of this. The Lord told them that this was all to be for His remembrance, His memorial before God (see Luke 22:19; 1 Cor. 11:24, 25). Tonight's meal was a preparation for what they would do ever after, so that God would remember His sacrificial death and make its power present among them. By eating the Bread and drinking the Cup, they would eat His Body and drink His Blood, and live forever (see John 6:58). This meal, shared forever among them as the unique sign of their fellowship and mutual belonging, would manifest His sacrifice in their midst, proclaiming that death forever, until He would come again (1 Cor. 11:26).

The Paschal meal was almost over. It ended with a final cup of wine, the "cup of *Hallel*" or praise, so called because they sang the rest of the Hallel, Psalms 115—118, over it and drank it afterwards. This was the joyful cup of praise, of high exaltation and rejoicing for all God had done. It was this cup that Jesus said He would forgo. With His solemn **Amen I say to you**, He affirmed that He would not join them in drinking this festive cup. He had another cup to drink, the cup of sorrow and suffering (see 14:36), and already its grim contents were weighing on His heart. Not for Him the wine of this age which makes glad the heart of man (Ps. 104:15)! He would **no longer by any means drink** of that **fruit of the vine** and know joy **until that day when** He would **drink it new in the Kingdom of God**. The time for joy, for Him, was over. Now was the time for suffering and death. Soon He would be safe in God's

Kingdom, and *then* He would feast and rejoice. By forgoing the final cup with them, the Lord steeled Himself for the final mile of His grim journey. Over the filled wine cups, they all *sang a* **hymn,** the final Psalms 115—118 of the Paschal liturgy, and then **went out into the Mountain of Olives**—a fifteen-minute walk from their upper-room in Jerusalem.

§VII.3 Gethsemane and Jesus' Arrest

ॐ ॐ ॐ ॐ ॐ

27 And Jesus says to them, "You will all stumble, for it is written, 'I will strike the Shepherd and the sheep will be scattered out.'

28 "But after I have been raised, I will go before you into Galilee."

29 But Peter said to Him, "Even if all stumble— yet I *myself will* not!"

30 And Jesus says to him, "Amen I say to you, that today, this night, before a rooster sounds two *times*, you *yourself* will *completely* deny Me three *times*."

31 But he said emphatically, "If it is necessary for me to die with You, I will by no means *completely* deny You!" And they all said the same.

St. Mark now relates how Jesus tried to prepare His disciples for the coming catastrophe. (It would seem from John 13:36–38 that this exchange took place during the Paschal meal. Mark includes it here to show more clearly how Christ's Word was fulfilled, and how the coming events did not take Him by surprise. Their desertion was exactly what He predicted and expected.)

You will all stumble and fall away from faith, He told them. Unlikely as it seemed to them, it was inevitable, for it was **written** in Scripture. Though the prophecy of Scripture (in Zech. 13:7) of course in no sense *caused* their lapse, it did *accurately* predict it:

God would allow men to **strike the Shepherd**, and that one stroke would **scatter out** all **the sheep** He was guarding too. As sheep were dispersed abroad when their shepherd was not there to gather and protect them, so too the disciples would scatter and flee away when the blow fell on Christ. But that would not be the end. He predicted their lapse and scattering only in order to instruct them to regather again **after** He had **been raised**. When it was all over, they must go back into the safety of **Galilee**, where He would meet them again.

Peter, with his customary impetuosity (see 8:32), immediately contradicted Him. He felt that He loved Christ more than the others did (see John 21:15) and would remain steadfast even if they did not. **Even if all** the others would **stumble** and desert Him, **yet** he himself would **not**! (The pronoun is emphatic in the Greek.)

With sadness, Christ strove to deflate Peter's pride. **Amen I say to you**, He assured him, **today**, even **this** very **night**, Peter would prove himself more faithless than all the others. **Before a rooster** would **sound two** *times*, Peter himself would sound off and *completely* **deny** Him **three** *times*! He would crow out his denial sooner and more spectacularly than the roosters crowing out the morning hour. (The verb is an intensive one; not *arneomai*, "deny," but *aparneomai*, "completely deny.") The roosters began their crowing in Palestine about one or two A.M. Jesus is saying that Peter's denial is just around the corner. Peter is aghast at such a word. As if to overcome Christ's word, he pledges his loyalty all the more **emphatically**, and says that even **if it** were **necessary** for him **to die** with Jesus, he would **by no means** *completely* **deny** Him as He said. The other apostles, not to be outdone by Peter, **all said the same**, pledging their loyalty to the death. Having narrated this exchange, St. Mark is ready to show the results of such overconfidence, and he goes on to narrate Christ's arrest.

༄ ༄ ༄ ༄ ༄

32 **And they come to a place named Gethsemane; and He says to His disciples, "Sit here until I pray."**

33 And He takes along with Him Peter and James and John, and began to be startled and upset.

34 And He says to them, "My soul is very sorrowful, *even* to death; remain here and keep alert."

35 And He went *before* them a little and fell on the ground and prayed that if it were possible, the hour might pass from Him.

36 And He said, "Abba! Father! All things are possible to You; remove this cup from Me; yet not what I *Myself* will but what You *Yourself* will."

They arrived finally at their destination—a garden olive orchard (probably enclosed by a hedge or low wall), named **Gethsemane** (or "oil press"). The long shadows of the coming Cross begin to fall over His heart as He starts His descent into death. The subjective inner experience of the Son of God as He wrestled with death and finally vanquished it will remain forever beyond the veil and hidden from us mere children of men. We are permitted only to observe from the outside His tremendous struggle and to tremble as we try to imagine what He faced when He embraced and took away the sin of the world. It is enough to observe that He needed to fortify Himself with prayer as He braced Himself for the final battle.

So it was that **He says to His disciples, "Sit here until I pray."** (The historic present is used throughout this account, to allow us to take our silent places with the disciples in the Garden and see the Master from afar.) He seeks solitude for a time of prayer, and yet knows that soon Judas will come with others to arrest Him. In order to have this time of solitude, **He takes along with Him Peter and James and John** in order to post them as a kind of guard. They were to **remain** where they were and **keep alert**, watching for any disturbances, that He might not have His prayer interrupted by the coming intruders.

This time of prayer was necessary for Him. What caused Him grief was not the thought of enduring physical pain, but the unfathomable desolation of darkness that would descend on Him as He bore the sin of the world and suffered abandonment by the Father (see 15:34). As He steadfastly entered those shadows, He **began to be startled and upset** and **says to them, "My soul is very sorrowful,** *even* **to death."** They were therefore to watch for approaching intruders, and so give Him space to pray.

The words translated *startled and upset* may be examined somewhat. The word translated *startled* (Gr. *ekthambeo*) is used in 9:15 to denote the amazement of the crowd when startled by Jesus' sudden appearance, and in 16:5 to describe the amazement of the myrrhbearers when startled by the angel at the Tomb. Its use here shows how Christ was suddenly shaken by the approaching crisis and visibly agitated. The word translated *upset* (Gr. *ademoneo*) is used in Philippians 2:26 to describe the distress of Epaphroditus as he yearned for those back at home. Its use here shows how keenly the Lord felt the isolation brought on Him as He entered the darkness of the way to Calvary. By these words, St. Mark reveals the immensity of the burden that Christ was to bear in the coming hours. Indeed, that descending weight of the world nearly crushed Him, so that His **soul** was **very sorrowful,** *even* **to death.**

While the inner circle of the disciples stood guard, **He went** *before* **them a little and fell on the ground and prayed.** The normal posture for prayer was standing—to pray on the knees or in a prostrate position indicated overwhelming emotion in prayer. (It would seem that Christ first prayed on His knees—see Luke 22:41—and then, as He prayed even more intensely, fell on His face—Matt. 26:39.) The gist of His prayer (doubtless heard by Peter, James, and John before they dozed off) was that **if it were possible,** and according to God's will, **the hour** of betrayal and suffering **might pass from Him.** With tearful fervency (see Heb. 5:7), He cried out to His **Abba** or **Father. All things** were **possible** to Him! Perhaps He could fulfill His plan for the salvation of the world without His Son having to be betrayed into the hands of sinners. Let Him therefore **remove this cup** of suffering from Him, and save the world some other way. **Yet not what** He Himself might **will** (the pronoun is emphatic), **but what** God Himself would **will.** That is, even in this agony of spirit, Christ still aligned His human will with the divine will of the Father, choosing whatever the Father would decide. In that dreadful hour, as throughout His life, Jesus always unfailingly chose what God wanted, whatever the personal cost. Here was the courage that overcame the world, and here was the example to guide His Church in the days to come. When horror gripped His heart so tightly as to make sweat flow like blood (see Luke 22:44), Jesus did not falter, but walked relentlessly into the will of God. By so doing, He blazed a path for all the martyrs, and showed them the way home.

ॐ ॐ ॐ ॐ ॐ

37 And He comes and finds them sleeping, and says to Peter, "Simon, are you asleep? Were you not strong *enough* to keep alert *for* one hour?

38 "Keep alert and pray, that you may not enter into testing; the spirit indeed *is* ready, but the flesh *is* weak."

39 And again He went away and prayed, saying the same word.

40 And again He came and found them sleeping, for their eyes were burdened down; and they did not know what to answer Him.

41 And He comes the third time and says to them, "Are you still sleeping and taking your rest? It is settled; the hour has come; behold, the Son of Man is being delivered *up* into the hands of sinners.

42 "Arise, let us go; behold, the one who delivers Me *up* has drawn near!"

After a time of prayer, **He comes** to those He left to guard His solitude **and finds them sleeping**. (This was not surprising, given the stress they had been under the past week, and the emotional high of their supper with Him.) We may imagine Him shaking them gently awake, as He **says to Peter** (as to the spokesman for them all), **"Simon, are you asleep? Were you not strong *enough*** to keep alert *for* one hour? Keep alert and pray, that you may not enter into testing."

It is noteworthy that, in the midst of His own mortal agony, the Lord still had thought for the welfare of His own. He urged them to pray, not for Him, but for themselves, that they might have the strength to face the coming trial and not utterly and permanently fall away from Him. This was indeed a possibility, for Satan was at work to test them through the coming trial, that they might be rejected as chaff is sifted out from the wheat (see Luke 22:31). The coming hours would tell the tale. They must therefore **keep alert and pray** now, that they might **not enter into testing**.

The word translated here *testing* is the Greek *peirasmos*, sometimes rendered "temptation." Christ does not mean that the disciples should pray that they might be spared the psychological experience of temptation, and remain untouched by any difficulty. Rather, He means that they should pray to avoid Satan's fiery onslaught, that they might not be overwhelmed by the suffering brought on by the enemy, but instead emerge with their faith intact. This **testing**, this time of trial and temptation to apostasy, was the special work of the devil; it was from this hour that Christ had always taught His disciples to pray that God would rescue them (Matt. 6:13, "lead us not into *peirasmos*"). As the hour of His arrest and death drew near, He was concerned lest this suffering cause them finally to lose their faith in Him. Certainly their **spirit** and inner motivation to be faithful was **ready** and willing to cling to Him, but their **flesh** was **weak**, being full of fear. They must therefore **keep alert** and stay awake, **and pray** for the strength to emerge faithful at the end.

After this, **again He went away and prayed** to His Father, **saying the same word** and request as before, asking that the cup might pass from Him.

And again He came to them, still concerned for their spiritual safety and survival. Again, however, He **found them sleeping, for their eyes were burdened down** with exhaustion. They were chagrined that they had again disappointed the Master they loved, **and they did not know what to answer Him**. What could they say?

Their faithlessness and disobedience left them speechless and without excuse.

This retreat for private prayer and return to the disciples happens for **the third time** (foreshadowing Peter's threefold denial, vv. 66–72). St. Mark narrates it in the historic present (saying that Jesus **comes** and **says**) so that we may stand beside the disciples and experience with them their final fall and the arrest of their Master. Jesus, in His compassion for them in their weakness, does not rebuke or scold them for their continued failures. He simply asks them, "**Are you still sleeping and taking your rest?**" Were they still taking thought only for their own comfort? It was **settled**: He had asked the Father for **the hour** to pass from Him (v. 35), and the Father had decided otherwise. The word translated *settled* is the Greek *apexei*; it is used in Philippians 4:18 as a commercial word, meaning "to receive an account in full; to deem it settled." Here it is used to mean that the issue for which Jesus prayed was **settled, the hour** had **come** on Him and not passed from Him—they could **behold** and see it for themselves—**the Son of Man** was even then **being delivered *up* into the hands of sinners** and Gentiles! The disciples must now **arise** from where they were lying and **go** with Jesus to meet them; **the one** who was **delivering Him *up*** and betraying Him **had drawn near.**

ॐ ॐ ॐ ॐ ॐ

43 And immediately while He *Himself* was speaking, Judas, one of the Twelve, arrives, and with him a crowd with swords and wooden *clubs*, from the chief-priests and the scribes and the elders.

44 Now he who was delivering Him up had given them a signal, saying, "Whomever I will kiss, He Himself is *the one*; seize Him, and lead Him away securely."

45 And after coming, he immediately came up to Him, saying, "Rabbi!" and *fervently* kissed Him.

46 And they laid hands on Him, and seized Him.
47 But a certain one of the bystanders drew his sword, and hit the slave of the high priest and took off his ear.
48 And Jesus answered and said to them, "Have you come out as against a thief, with swords and wooden *clubs*, to take Me?
49 "Every day I was with you in the Temple teaching, and you did not seize Me; but *it is* that the Scriptures might be fulfilled."
50 And everyone left Him and fled.
51 And a certain young man was following along with Him, having put on a linen *cloth* over his nakedness; and they seize him.
52 But he left behind the linen *cloth* and fled naked.

As if to prove the truth of His words and His divine foreknowledge, **immediately while He *Himself* was speaking, Judas**, formerly His confidant and **one of the Twelve, arrives.** (We note the historic present.) Though Judas left alone, he did not return alone, but **with him**, at a distance off and shrouded in the darkness of the Garden, was **a crowd**, consisting both of Temple guards and Roman soldiers. (The presence of soldiers from a Roman cohort as part of the crowd is specifically mentioned in John 18:3.) The Jewish Temple guards probably (and the Roman soldiers certainly) had **swords**; others in the crowd had **wooden *clubs*.** All came **from the chief-priests and the scribes and the elders** to arrest Jesus and take Him back to stand trial before them, at the Jewish Sanhedrin or High Court.

Why did they come with weapons? Certainly they were taking no chances. They wanted to arrest Jesus when He could be found alone, far from the protecting crowd, and this was their only chance. They were determined that He should not escape, and perhaps expected that His disciples might attempt an armed defense, enabling Him to slip away under cover of night. Certainly He had slipped away from such trouble before (see Luke 4:30; John 8:59; 10:39), and they feared it might be easier for Him to do so again at night. The weapons would assure them that the disciples could not mount an effective armed defense.

But was that all? Perhaps not. Jesus was commonly held to be a prophet, and all the Jews remembered how disastrous it could be to try to arrest a prophet against his will. A similar band of soldiers had tried to arrest Elijah and been struck down by God (2 Kings 1:9, 10). Jesus certainly had some kind of power at His disposal (see John 12:9–11). Perhaps the weapons were not carried as a practical insurance only, but also were expressive of an unnamed fear that gripped them as they went to arrest such a mysteriously powerful figure.

The crowd, with their torches and weapons, held back, hiding in the shadows. Judas (not called here by his name, but referred to simply as **he who was delivering Him up**, his treason having supplanted his personhood) had **given them a signal**, and they watched him by the flickering light of their torches. He had told them that **whomever** he would **kiss** in respectful greeting, that very one (the Greek pronoun is emphatic) was the one they wanted; they must **seize Him, and lead Him away securely**, taking care He did not escape.

The traitor was taking no chances. He was not content to simply point at Jesus and run, for in the dim light a mistake was possible, and they could arrest the wrong person. Arresting all twelve of them was problematic, even for such an armed crowd, and they wanted to concentrate their efforts on Jesus alone. Judas was to single out Jesus in the darkness by kissing Him and Him alone.

He faithfully fulfilled his faithless work. **After coming** back to his former comrades, **he immediately came up** to Jesus and gave Him the respectful greeting of **Rabbi**, as if he were His humble disciple. In greeting, he *fervently* kissed Him.

The word translated *fervently kissed* is the Greek *kataphileo*; it is a different and more intensive word than *phileo*, which is translated *kiss* in verse 44. By using this more intensive verb, St. Mark stresses the hypocrisy of the act. Judas gave Christ no perfunctory kiss of greeting, but kissed Him with great ardor (the verb is used of the father's kiss welcoming his beloved son in Luke 15:20). Judas behaved as if he were Christ's devoted servant, all the while basely betraying Him to His murderers. The crowd waiting and watching lost no time when they saw this. As soon as Jesus was singled out, **they laid hands on Him, and seized Him.**

The disciples, though previously sleepy, were not slow to respond. They had said that they would die defending Him (v. 31) and were determined to prove themselves true to their word. Two of them had swords (Luke 22:38), one of whom was Peter (John 18:10). He **drew** it and **hit the slave of the high priest and took off his ear.** Mark, writing the Gospel in Rome, thinks it best even at that time, years later, not to mention who it was who made the attack. He conceals Peter's name and simply identifies the attacker as **a certain one of the bystanders.** (No doubt Peter meant to take off his *head*, not just his *ear*! But after all, he was a fisherman, not a soldier!)

Though the disciples were determined to resist, their Lord was not. He **answered** the arresting crowd by saying to them, **"Have you come out as against a thief, with swords and wooden *clubs*, to take Me? Every day I was with you in the Temple teaching, and you did not seize Me."** That is, if He were truly a criminal and needed to be forcibly restrained with such weapons, why did they not arrest Him sooner, while He openly taught in the Temple? The Temple crowds would not object to a criminal being arrested. The fact that they were arresting Him secretly and far from the crowds proved that He was in fact no criminal, and that their arrest was wrong. This was allowed by God, however, not because Jesus was an evildoer, but **that the Scriptures might be fulfilled.** The Scriptures prophesied that Messiah must be numbered with the transgressors and die (e.g. Is. 53:12), and so it must be. Because of this, the arrest was successfully made. **Everyone left Him**, even those who had pledged their lives in His defense, **and fled.**

St. Mark then narrates the story of **a certain young man** who was then **following along with** Jesus, **having put on a linen *cloth* over his nakedness.** Most people wore wool for their outer garment; the use of linen indicated a greater wealth. Also, the fact that the young man had nothing on beneath the cloth indicated that he had dressed hurriedly to follow Jesus and His disciples as they left their upper room to go pray in the Garden of Gethsemane, probably tagging along secretly and uninvited. In the ensuing melee, **they seize him** (the historic present indicates the vividness of the memory). He squirms away from their grasp and **left behind the linen *cloth* and fled naked**. The panic of his escape (seen in his determination to escape, even if he had to go naked) reflects the panic of *all* the disciples. They had promised to guard and defend Him. But when the moment for action came, after a brief and ineffective lashing out, they all abandoned Him to flee for their own lives.

(We may ask in passing, who was that nameless **young man**? The most probable answer, and the one long favored by the Fathers, is that it was St. Mark himself, as a young boy of perhaps fourteen years. He may well have listened outside the door of his parents' upper room while Jesus and His apostles used it for their Passover supper, and dressed hastily to follow them when he heard them leaving later that night. Like many young boys, he was keen to share an adventure—but found this adventure more than he had bargained for!)

§VI.4 Jesus' Trial

ॐ ॐ ॐ ॐ ॐ

53 And they led Jesus away to the chief-priest; and all the chief-priests and the elders and the scribes come together.

54 And Peter had followed Him from a distance, until *he was* inside the courtyard of the chief-priest; and he was sitting together with the attendants and warming himself near the light.

55 Now the chief-priests and the whole Council sought a witness against Jesus to put Him to death; and they did not find *one*.

56 For many bore false-witness against Him, and the witnesses were not identical.

57 And some stood up and bore false-witness against Him, saying,

58 "We *ourselves* heard Him say, 'I *Myself* will tear down this sanctuary made-with-hands, and in three days I will build another one made-without-hands.'"

59 And not even thus was their witness identical.

60 And the chief-priest stood up in *the* midst and asked Jesus, saying, "Do You make no answer *to* what these *men* witness against You?"

61 But He was silent, and did not answer anything. Again the chief-priest asked Him, and says to Him, "Are You *Yourself* the Christ, the Son of the Blessed *One*?"

62 And Jesus said, "I *Myself* am; and you will see the Son of Man sitting on *the* right of the Power and coming with the clouds of heaven."

63 And the chief-priest tore his shirt, and says, "What further need do we have of witnesses?

64 "You heard the blasphemy; how does it appear to you?" And they all condemned Him to be liable to death.

65 And some began to spit at Him, and to cover around His face and to buffet Him, and to say to Him, "Prophesy!" And the attendants received Him with slaps.

66 And, Peter being below in the courtyard, one of the servant-girls of the chief-priest comes,

67 and seeing Peter warming himself, she looked at him, and says, "You *yourself* also were with Jesus the Nazarene!"

68 But he denied, saying, "I neither know nor understand what you *yourself* say." And he went outside into the forecourt.

> 69 And the servant-girl saw him, and began again to say to the bystanders, "This one is one of them!"
>
> 70 But again he denied. And after a little, the bystanders again said to Peter, "Truly you are, for you also are a Galilean."
>
> 71 But he began to curse and swear, "I do not know this man of whom you speak!"
>
> 72 And immediately a rooster sounded a second *time*. And Peter remembered the word Jesus spoke to him, "Before a rooster sounds two *times*, you will *completely* deny Me three *times*." And he threw *himself* down and wept.

St. Mark summarizes the events connected with Christ's trial, which took up the entire night. Although night trials of capital offenses were, strictly speaking, illegal, the great Council (or Sanhedrin) no doubt felt that they had no choice. As a volatile and occupied territory, Israel did not have the right to exercise the death penalty. That legal privilege was jealously guarded by the Romans; they alone had the right to execute criminals. If Jesus were to be condemned to death, He must be found guilty by a *Roman* court—that is, by the governor, Pontius Pilate. Also, He must be found guilty and condemned quickly, before the populace had time to be mobilized by His disciples in His defense. That meant that He must be brought to Pilate for trial as soon as day broke and the courts were open. And *that* meant that He must be found guilty by a Jewish court *before* daybreak. Thus, even though night trials were contrary to their legal custom, He must be tried at night anyway.

Assuming that He was arrested after eleven P.M., it would have been almost midnight when He was brought to trial before the supreme court or Sanhedrin. After a quick appearance before the former high priest Annas (the real power behind the high-priestly throne, and the father-in-law of Caiaphas, the present high priest; see John 18:13, 19–24), He was led bound to His actual trial. The location is a matter of some dispute, but it appears that it took place at the palatial residence of Caiaphas, which would explain why a servant-girl was the doorkeeper (see John 18:17). If the Council met in the Temple courts, one would have expected a male Levite as doorkeeper.

They then **led Jesus away** to His trial, where **all the chief-priests** (the Temple executive officers), **the elders** (the heads of the influential families of Jerusalem), and **the scribes** (the experts in Jewish law, mostly drawn from the Pharisees) awaited. There were officially seventy members of the Council. It is not necessary to insist that all the members were called there for the trial (those who had expressed sympathy with Jesus' mission were perhaps not summoned), only that the Council met in formal plenary session.

True to his word, **Peter had followed** the band arresting Jesus **from a distance**. After his initial panic and flight, Peter seems to have recovered himself. With his friend John, he followed his Master as closely as he dared, keeping back enough to avoid arrest himself. It would seem that he stayed at a distance not simply out of cowardice and fear of arrest, but also because he felt he must stay free if he was to be of any help to his Lord.

He trailed His Master **until** *he was* **inside the courtyard of the chief-priest** Caiaphas. It would seem that there was a forecourt and then an inner court, kept by a door (see John 18:15, 16). Jesus was brought through these to a room overlooking the courtyard below (Mark 14:66). Peter would not have been allowed into the inner rooms, but came as close as he could in the inner court, waiting for the outcome as he fought a sick sense of dread and helplessness.

It was by now perhaps one A.M. and the night air was cold. To stay warm, **he was sitting together with the attendants** and servants of Caiaphas, **warming himself near the light** of a charcoal fire which had been kindled in the courtyard. (As well as seeking warmth, Peter perhaps felt he would be safer from detection if he blended with the crowd. If he stayed apart from them, he would be the more obvious.)

It was this **light** that proved his undoing. As he hunched over the fire, the light revealed his features, and he was quickly identified by the crowd that surrounded him. (Peter's denials occurred at the same time as Christ's trial, and in order to convey these as contemporaneous events, St. Mark mentions Peter's presence both before narrating Jesus' trial and after it; vv. 54, 66–72.) It was **one of the servant-girls** of the household who first sounded the alarm. (Mark means us not to miss the irony: Peter vowed he would remain true whatever the odds, yet is cowed by a mere servant-girl.) She **looked at him**, staring closely (Gr. *emblepo*) to be sure that she had the right man. Then she blurted out accusingly, "**You *yourself* also were with Jesus the Nazarene!**" (The pronoun is emphatic in the Greek.) That is, this man was one of them—he should be arrested too! Peter was horrified at being identified, and felt he must at all costs avoid arrest if there was to be any hope of saving the Master. So he emphatically and formally **denied** the charge, saying, "**I neither know nor understand what you *yourself* say.**" The girl was dangerous for him to be around, and he prudently moved away, going **outside into the forecourt.**

There was, however, to be no safety for Peter that night. The **servant-girl** (with one of her fellow servants; see Matt. 27:71) pursued him, insisting **again** and saying **to the bystanders, "This one is one of them!"** Once **again he denied** knowing the Lord or being His disciple. His passionate denial seemed to have silenced the accusations. The minutes ticked by. **After a little** (that is, after about an hour—see Luke 22:59—at perhaps between two and three o'clock in the morning), the accusations began again. He had tried to say as little as possible and so melt into the crowd, but his passionate denials had made his voice heard, and with his voice, his accent, for Peter spoke with the accent peculiar to all Galileans. This accent was recognized by one of the crowd (by one of the slaves of the high priest, a relative of the one whose ear Peter had cut off in the Garden several hours earlier; see John 18:26), and this one piped up, "**Truly you are** [one of them], **for you also are a Galilean**" like Jesus. Everyone knew that most of His supporters came from Galilee!

Peter was desperate to maintain his freedom, and the passionate, impulsive nature that had led him into trouble before (see 8:32, 33) asserted itself now. He **began to curse and swear**—that is, to invoke a series of oaths and curses on himself to the effect that he did **not even know this man of whom** they were speaking. Note that Peter avoids using the name Jesus in his answer, as if He were so much a stranger to him that he scarcely knew His Name. May God do so to him and more also if he had even met the Man!

No sooner had he said these words than **immediately a rooster sounded a second** *time*. Peter remembered the words of the Lord, spoken a few short hours before, that **before a rooster sounded two** *times* he would *completely* **deny** Him **three** *times*. Horrified remorse overwhelmed him, as he suddenly realized the significance of what he had just done. He had thought he had been maintaining his freedom in order to serve the Lord. In fact he had been deny-ing Him, as foretold. Rushing out and collapsing in grief, **he threw** *himself* **down and wept.**

Meanwhile (St. Mark narrates Peter's denial in flashback), the Lord's trial was going on upstairs. As Peter was denying Christ below, Israel was judicially disowning Him above. It was a long, drawn-out affair, as they all **sought a witness against Jesus to put Him to death.** That is, they brought many witnesses before them (dragging them from their homes in the middle of the night), hoping to substanti-ate a charge that could be considered worthy of death under Jewish Law. If they were to justify His condemnation before the people the next day, this was absolutely necessary. Witness followed witness, as each one repeated what he had heard Him say, but **they did not find** *one* who had anything they could use against Jesus. These were not impartial witnesses, but rather hand-picked men who bore false-witness against Him, repeating with malevolent intent what they thought they had heard Him say.

St. Mark gives one example of their false-witness. **Some** of them **stood up** in the court and affirmed, **We** *ourselves* (the pronoun is emphatic) **heard Him say, "I** *Myself* **will tear down this sanctu-ary made-with-hands, and in three days I will build another one made-without-hands."** The reported words are interesting, and refer to an utterance Jesus made in the Temple some years earlier, near the beginning of His ministry (see John 2:19). It had electrified and scandalized them at the time, and they repeated it again now. To desecrate or attempt the destruction of a sacred edifice such as the Temple was indeed a capital offense. But to substantiate such a charge, detailed corroboration that He had said such a thing was necessary, and differences even in trivial details could render such evidence inadmissible (see Susanna 52). Such was the case now, and the **witness** offered was **not identical**.

The night wore on, and the Council was no closer to finding a capital offense that they could make stick than they had been when they began hours earlier. If Jesus remained silent and did not Himself provide some evidence they could use, they ran the risk of letting this unique opportunity of condemning Him slip away. Finally, in desperation, **the chief-priest stood up in** *the* **midst**, determined to break the deadlock and get something that could be used against Jesus. That piece of evidence, it was now clear, could only come from Jesus Himself, and he must get Him to speak. Caiaphas therefore **asked Jesus** if He had anything to say in His own defense, or would make any **answer** *to* **what** His accuser **witnessed against** Him. Again Jesus **was silent.** The opportunity was slipping away. Soon it would be daybreak and time for the scheduled meeting with Pilate. Jesus must be found guilty before then.

At last, Caiaphas turned on Christ with vehement passion, placing Him on oath by adjuring Him by the living God (see Matt. 26:63) to declare whether or not He Himself (the pronoun is emphatic) was **the Christ, the Son of the Blessed** *One*. Many had been saying this secretly and claiming this for Him (see John 7:31)—what did *He* say? Was it true, or not?

The One who was the Truth could only tell the truth, for silence here would be taken for denial. "**I** *Myself* **am**," He affirmed (the pronoun again is emphatic in the Greek, *ego eimi*). He was indeed the promised Messiah. More than this, this claim would be vindicated by God Himself, for they would **see** Him **sitting on** *the* **right of the Power**, of God Himself (Ps. 110:1), and **coming with the clouds of heaven** (Dan. 7:13). By quoting these Scriptures as referring to Himself, Jesus was claiming in the strongest way possible that He was the true Messiah. His claim was no mere self-promotion. The all-powerful God Himself would vindicate His claim and bring Him to His Throne, placing Him on His right hand as Lord of all.

The high-priest at last had his desired piece of evidence. With mock horror at the supposed blasphemy, **the chief-priest tore his shirt**. To rend one's robe was the classic response to hearing about a catastrophe (see 2 Kings 18:37), and Jesus' words, Caiaphas asserted, were a catastrophic blasphemy. What could be more impious than for a mere man, a sinner, to impersonate the glorious Messiah? (For to falsely claim to be the Messiah when one was not was sacrilegious.) And the Pharisees took it as self-evident that He was not the Messiah, for He did not, as they thought, keep the Law (see John 9:24). Here He was, a lawbreaker, claiming to be God's Anointed Savior! What could be more blasphemous?

The trial was over. **What further need** was there to call more **witnesses**? They themselves all **heard the blasphemy** for themselves. He instantly called for a verdict, saying, **"How does it appear to you?"** The Council, stacked and biased from the start, delivered the verdict they had come to give: **they all condemned Him to be liable to death**. This was the signal for the arresting officers to vent their hatred for the prisoner, now that He was "safely" condemned. **Some** of them **began to spit at Him** in contempt, as they **cover around His face** with a blindfold and invite Him to **prophesy** and reveal who was His attacker. The Messiah was supposed to be able to know such things without seeing them: if He was indeed the Messiah, let Him do His stuff! The **attendants** and officers **received Him with slaps**. He who timelessly received the adoration of the seraphim and cherubim now was struck on the cheek by the hands that He Himself had formed (see Antiphon 10 for Holy Friday Matins). Christ's final humiliation had begun.

🦋 🦋 🦋 🦋 🦋

15 1 And early the chief-priests with the elders and scribes and the whole Council immediately held a consultation, and having bound Jesus, they led Him away, and delivered *Him* up to Pilate.

2 And Pilate asked Him, "Are You *Yourself* the

King of the Jews?" And answering, He says to him, "*As* you *yourself* say."

3　And the chief-priests accused Him of much.

4　And Pilate again asked Him, saying, "Do You not answer anything? Behold how many things they accuse You of!"

5　But Jesus no longer answered anything, so that Pilate marveled.

6　Now at the feast he used to release to them one prisoner whom they asked for.

7　Now there was one called Barabbas who had been bound with the rioters who had in the riot done murder.

8　And the crowd went up and began asking *him* to do as he had done for them.

9　And Pilate answered them, saying, "Do you want me to release to you the King of the Jews?"

10　For he knew that the chief-priests had delivered *Him* up because of envy.

11　But the chief-priests stirred up the crowd *to ask him* to release Barabbas to them instead.

12　Pilate again answered them and said, "Then what shall I do with Him whom you call the King of the Jews?"

13　And again they cried out, "Crucify Him!"

14　But Pilate said to them, "Why, what wickedness has He done?" But they cried out all the more, "Crucify Him!"

15　And intending to satisfy the crowd, Pilate released Barabbas to them, and after having Jesus scourged, he delivered *Him* up to be crucified.

Next comes the official trial before Pilate. It was **early** in the morning, in the predawn hour, that **the whole Council** held a hasty **consultation**. That is, they took a final decision as to what formal charges they were to bring to the Roman governor. Impersonating the Messiah might have been a sin in Jewish eyes, but the Romans cared little for such Jewish delusions. If the Romans were to find Him guilty, He must be charged with something that was a capital offense under Roman law. Accordingly (and ironically), they would charge Him with being a political Messiah and with inciting armed rebellion against Rome (the very thing Jesus had been careful to avoid). This was indeed a capital crime in the eyes of Rome. With this plan in mind, **having bound Jesus, they led Him away, and delivered** *Him* **up to Pilate**, once it was daybreak and Pilate was available to receive legal charges.

Once the trial before Pilate began, the charge was simple: that of sedition. **Pilate asked Him** if He were guilty of this charge, of being the Messiah: "**Are You** *Yourself* [the Greek is emphatic] **the King of the Jews?**" There is a note of incredulity in the emphatic **You**, as if Pilate can scarcely credit such a charge. Is *this one* the dreaded rebel? One styling himself the King of the Jews could be expected to look more formidable and commanding, yet this one standing before him looked harmless enough! Jesus answered the charge affirmatively, saying, "*As* you *yourself* say." (His response—literally, "You say so," or "the words are yours," which looks somewhat ambiguous in English—conveys no such ambiguity in its original cultural setting. It was the usual respectful way of answering a question affirmatively.)

The **chief-priests** and delegation from the Sanhedrin launched into an extended accusation, and **accused Him of much**, saying that He claimed to be the rightful King of Israel, rather than Caesar, and that He told the people they should not pay the poll-tax to Rome (Luke 23:2). These were serious matters indeed. When Pilate at length allowed Jesus to answer the charges and speak in His own defense, the Lord **no longer answered anything**, refusing to address the charges at all. **Pilate marveled** at such serenity in the face of passionate hatred.

Pilate was a shrewd governor, of many years' experience. He could tell by looking at Jesus that He was no military threat to Rome, and **he knew** too that **the chief-priests had delivered** *Him* **up because of envy**. Moreover, his wife had sent him a message, warning him to stay clear of the whole controversy, citing a dream she had had the night before (Matt. 27:19). Pilate was a cynical and worldly man, but he was a Roman after all, and had a Roman's sense of justice. He therefore began to do all he could to find Jesus not guilty and to acquit Him of any capital offense.

At length Pilate came out to address the whole assembled **crowd** which had gone up to Jerusalem for the festal week. It was the custom that Rome would grant a pardon and **release to them one prisoner whom they asked for** to honor the Jews' feastday, as a gesture of goodwill (and as an investment in pacific relations with the local populace), and they insisted that Pilate do so now. Pilate strove with the crowd to **release** to them **the King of the Jews**.

Pilate had, however, underestimated the Council's determination to have Jesus destroyed. When Pilate asked the assembling crowd whom he should release, they all shouted back that he should release **Barabbas**, having been **stirred up** to the purpose by **the chief-priests**. When asked whether he should not rather **release to** them Jesus, the popular so-called **King of the Jews**, who was so manifestly harmless and innocent, they cried out in reply that He should be crucified. All the four Gospels record Pilate's awareness of this as a miscarriage of Roman justice and his reluctance to acquiesce. Instead of simply granting the crowd's wish immediately, he attempted to reason with the mob, asking, **"Why, what wickedness has He done?"** But all attempts to secure His release inflamed the mob even more, to the extent that a riot was in danger of breaking out unless he granted their request (Matt. 27:24).

We may pause to examine this determined preference for Barabbas. It was produced by the agitation of the chief-priests, but their incitement must have found a responsive chord in the hearts of the crowd. Barabbas was a well-known figure, one **who had been bound** and arrested by the Romans along with some **rioters** and who had **done murder** in the riot. It would appear that Barabbas was a Zealot, or at least one of Zealot sympathies, and that the riot in question was an anti-Roman demonstration. He appeared before the crowd therefore as a patriot, and as one in whom their messianic and revolutionary aspirations would find an effective welcome. Jesus, on the other hand, by allowing Himself to be arrested and mocked by the Romans, had proved Himself in the people's eyes to be a false-Messiah, a fraud, a pretender. All their fervent hopes in Him had been disappointed, and the crowd felt that He had deluded them into thinking He was the promised Messiah, when He was now manifestly nothing of the kind. No wonder their enthusiasm turned so quickly to rage.

Pilate, for his part, had no intention of risking a riot in Jerusalem when the city was overflowing with Passover pilgrims, and was quite prepared to sacrifice principle to expediency. With a minimum of words, St. Mark relates that, **after having Jesus scourged, he delivered *Him* up to be crucified**. The Lord's repeated predictions of His Passion were being fulfilled.

ॐ ॐ ॐ ॐ ॐ

16 And the soldiers led Him away into the court-yard (that is, the Praetorium), and they call together the whole cohort.

17 And they clothe Him *in* purple, and put around Him a woven crown of thorns,

18 and began to greet Him, "Hail, King of the Jews!"

19 And they struck Him *on* the head with a reed, and spat on Him and bent the knee, worshipping *before* Him.

20 And after they had mocked Him, they stripped Him *of* the purple and clothed Him in His own garments. And they lead Him out to crucify Him.

St. Mark now focuses on a part of that scourging (which occurred, so John 19:1–4 informs us, as part of Pilate's extended wrangling with the crowd prior to his final condemnation of Jesus). In order to humiliate Jesus (and, as Pilate hoped, excite sympathy from the multitude; John 19:4, 5), he allowed the soldiers freedom to indulge in some crude and brutal anti-Semitic horseplay.

First of all, Jesus is scourged in **the courtyard**, before representatives of **the whole cohort** or detachment of soldiers who accompanied Pilate to Jerusalem for the Passover. This scourging was in itself a fearful punishment, and one that Rome did not allow her citizens to undergo. The one to be scourged was first bound to a post, with his back exposed. He was then lashed repeatedly with an instrument called a *flagellum*, which was a number of leather thongs plaited with pieces of bone or metal. The effect was to lay the whole back open to the bone, and it was not uncommon for men to die while being scourged.

After this scourging, the soldiers began to mock the Jews in the person of Jesus. They had nothing but contempt for the popular Jewish messianic and revolutionary aspirations, and delighted to heap abuse on these aspirations by mocking the would-be Messiah. After Jesus had been scourged, as He stood in their midst bleeding and reeling, some of them enacted a grotesque dramatic skit. Was Jesus the King of the Jews? Then a King must look the part! He needed the imperial purple and a proper crown! This was hastily provided, as some **clothe** Him in **purple** (the historic present is used), throwing a scarlet cloak around His shoulders (the term "purple" was a loose one, denoting colors from rose to true purple) —possibly the short military cloak worn by soldiers. A crown was provided too, as one of them constructs a **woven crown** out of the **thorn** bushes growing nearby and presses it on His scalp. For a scepter, they gave Him a **reed** found nearby as well. Then they seated Him on a chair and came up, in a hideous pantomime, to offer the King their allegiance. They came up to **greet Him** in acclamation. As they would greet their own king by saying, "Hail, Caesar!" so they greeted Him by saying, **"Hail, King of the Jews!"** Then, instead of giving Him the customary kiss of allegiance, they took the reedy scepter from His hand and **struck Him *on* the head** with it, and **spat on Him**. They then **bent the knee** and knelt in mock humility, **worshipping *before* Him** and bowing down in allegiance, as they would do to a true king.

At length it was all over. After Jesus had been finally condemned, they stripped Him *of* the purple and clothed Him in His own garments. Laboriously, Jesus picked up the crossbeam to which He would soon be nailed, bearing it across His shoulders, and began to walk to the hill outside the city gates. St. Mark uses the historic present, saying, **they lead Him out to crucify Him**. Through this use of the historic present, we are allowed to accompany Him on His way. One can almost hear the jeers of the crowd and the shouts of the soldiers, and smell the blood from the lacerated wounds. The final hours were at hand.

§VI.5 The Crucifixion

༃ ༃ ༃ ༃ ༃

21 And they conscript a passerby, a certain Simon of Cyrene, coming from the countryside (the father of Alexander and Rufus), that he might take up His Cross.

22 And they bring Him to the place "Golgotha," which is interpreted, "Place of a Skull."

23 And they gave Him wine *mixed with* myrrh; but He did not take it.

24 And they crucify Him, and divide up His garments, casting lots for them, *to see* who should take what.

25 Now it was the third hour and they crucified Him.

26 And the inscription of the charge *against* Him was inscribed, "The King of the Jews."

27 And they crucify two thieves with Him, one on His right and one on His left.*

29 And the ones going by slandered Him, wagging their heads and saying, "Ha! You who

(*Verse 28, which refers to the scripture of Is. 53:9 being fulfilled, is not original to Mark's Gospel, and is not in most manuscripts.)

> would tear down the Sanctuary and rebuild *it*
> in three days,
>
> 30 "save Yourself, and come down from the
> Cross!"
>
> 31 Likewise, the chief-priests also mocked to one
> another, with the scribes, saying, "He saved
> others; Himself He is not able to save!
>
> 32 "Let the Christ, the King of Israel, now come
> down from the Cross, that we may see and
> believe!" And the ones crucified with Him
> reproached Him.

St. Mark now reaches the climax of his story—the death of the Messiah. For him, the entire ministry of Jesus has been leading up to this moment, when He would give His life as a ransom for many (10:45). (Indeed, the Gospel of Mark has been called "a Passion story with an extended introduction.")

After Jesus' final judicial condemnation by Pilate, He was led by Roman soldiers out from the Praetorium where He was being held to a place where executions customarily took place—the so-called **Place of a Skull**, or, in Aramaic, **Golgotha**, a bare hillock just outside the city walls. Its name, Skull Hill, was perhaps suggested by its rounded bare height (resembling the top of a skull) as much as by the grisly executions which were held there.

The Lord was greatly weakened by the scourging He had received, and fell in exhaustion as He attempted to lumber toward His final destination with the crossbeam tied across His shoulders. So it was that **they conscript a passerby, a certain Simon of Cyrene** to carry His Cross for Him (the historic present is used throughout the description of the Crucifixion). This Simon was evidently a Jew from the Diaspora, now coming into Jerusalem, perhaps for the Passover sacrifices during the Week of Unleavened Bread. Roman soldiers had the right to conscript the locals to carry goods to a distance of one mile (see Matt. 5:41), and they made use of this in conscripting Simon **that he might take up** Jesus' **Cross**. This Simon had sons, **Alexander and Rufus**, who (with him?) became disciples of Jesus;

one of them was perhaps resident in the Roman church. Certainly it is interesting that St. Paul would later write to the Romans, sending greetings to "Rufus" (Rom. 16:13).

At length, **they bring Him to the place "Golgotha,"** along with the two thieves crucified with Him. (Presumably Simon dropped his burden there and departed. Or did he stay and observe the final hours of the controversial celebrity whose cross he was forced to carry?) Once there, the pious Jewish women of Jerusalem **gave Him wine** *mixed with* **myrrh**. It was their charitable custom to offer this narcotic drink to their countrymen about to be crucified, in order to dull the pain. The Lord, however, though offered the cup, **did not take it**. The Father had willed that He drink another chalice, the cup of suffering (14:36), and He was determined to drain it to the dregs. He would not turn from any of the suffering which the Father had decreed for the salvation of the world.

There **they crucify Him**. St. Mark does not dwell on the sufferings involved in this most brutal of executions. Its horrors were known and notorious throughout the world. Josephus, a Jewish historian and contemporary of St. Paul, described it as "the most wretched of all ways of dying" (*Wars*, 7,5,4). It was exquisitely calculated to stretch out mortal agony to the maximum, and those tied to crosses sometimes took days to die of exhaustion.

When Jesus reached the site, He was nailed to the crossbeam carried by Simon, a nail piercing each hand (Gr. *cheir*, what we would call a forearm). The crossbeam would then be hoisted up and secured to the vertical post planted in the earth, and the feet would be nailed, often with one nail piercing the two feet overlapped. The one executed would sit against a small seat which carried much of his weight, though he would slump forward and would have to press up with the feet to draw each breath. If the legs were broken, therefore, the one crucified would be unable to push up and draw a breath, and would die by asphyxiation. The height of the cross need not be very tall, and often the one crucified was suspended just barely above the earth. In cases where the Romans particularly wanted to make an example of the criminal, the cross was made higher. Jesus' Cross was such a high one, since one standing nearby could only reach His lips by placing a sponge on the end of a reed and reaching up with it (v. 36). The Lord was also crucified on a "†"-shaped cross, as the board listing the charge against Him was hung above His head (Matt. 27:37).

The detachment of soldiers guarding Him settled down to wait until He and those crucified with Him were dead. To pass the time, they decided they would **divide up His garments** among them. These would have included His inner and outer garments, His belt, sandals, and headcovering. Some were valued more than others, and so they **cast lots for them,** *to see* **who should take what.** This soldier's game would have passed some of the time, which hung heavy on their hands. They had seen many die like this; for them it was just another job. In including this detail here, St. Mark shows how complete was Christ's humiliation and despoliation: He was deprived of *everything*—even the clothes on His back.

There were many passing by, since it was the Week of Unleavened Bread. At **the third hour** (i.e. nine A.M.) many would have come to the Temple to be in Jerusalem and would be there to see the extraordinary execution of the controversial Nazarene. By saying **they crucified Him** after the third hour had come (probably nothing more precise than midmorning is meant here), St. Mark means to show that Christ died in the most public way and time possible, in full view of the city. And He died publicly *as the Messiah*—for **the inscription of the charge** *against* **Him was inscribed, "The King of the Jews."** The charge for which the criminal was condemned was displayed to make an example of him, so that no one else would dare to imitate the crime. It was written on a board whitened with chalk and hung on the cross or around his neck. In saying that Jesus was "the King of the Jews," the Romans doubtless meant simply that He was dying as a revolutionary and traitor against Caesar. For the Christians, however, it had a deeper significance, and revealed a truth not intended by the Romans who wrote it. Jesus was indeed the King of the Jews, the Messiah, and as the Messiah He was suffering, offering a ransom for the world.

Jesus' humiliation was augmented by the company of those with Him, for He was crucified along with **two thieves,** possibly two men who had been arrested in the riot along with Barabbas. Jesus was classed along with such criminals, being positioned in the middle of them, so that the thieves were executed **one on His right and one on His left.**

Once He was crucified, His foes considered their victory to be complete. They had been trying for years to destroy Him (see 3:6) and were now triumphant. They could not resist crowing and taunting Him in His hour of defeat. He had claimed to be God's Messiah! He had claimed to be even holier than the holy **Sanctuary** of the Temple, and to be able to **tear** it **down** and **rebuild** *it* **in three days!** His execution was the final and undeniable refutation (they thought) of such blasphemous claims, and He had at last been proven a deluded blasphemer, for God would never allow His Messiah to be so treated. They **slandered Him**, heaping insults on Him, **wagging their heads** in contemptuous agitation. **Ha!** they called out. If He still thought He was the Messiah, let Him **save** Himself, and **come down from the Cross!** That would be a miracle worthy of the Messiah! **He saved others**, healing them with His pretended wonders, worked by the devil's power (see 3:22)—but **Himself** He was obviously **not able to save.** What kind of Messiah or Christ was that? **Let the Christ, the King of Israel** as He styled Himself, **now come down from the Cross**—then they would **believe.** Let Him now prove His Messiahship and act like Messiah, and they would be the first to enlist as His disciples! All were unanimous in this chorus of victorious abuse: **the ones going by** on the road, **the chief-priests**, joined by **the scribes**—even (the crowning indignity) **the ones crucified with Him.**

ॐ ॐ ॐ ॐ ॐ

33 And when the sixth hour had come, darkness occurred over the whole land until the ninth hour.

34 And at the ninth hour, Jesus shouted with a great voice, "Eloi, eloi, lama sabachthani?" which is interpreted, "My God, My God, why

have You left Me behind?"

35 And some of the ones standing by hearing it said, "Behold, He is calling Elijah."

36 And someone ran and filled a sponge with vinegar, put it on a reed, and gave a drink to Him, saying, "Leave *Him*; let us see if Elijah comes to take Him down."

The cup of suffering was not yet empty, and more yet had to be drunk. The Lord, obedient to the end, drained it to the dregs. As well as being abandoned by God's Israel, He was, in some indefinable way which human intellect cannot comprehend, abandoned by God Himself. As the outward and cosmic expression of His entering His final darkness when He bore in Himself the sins of the world, the sun was blackened from the sky. From **the sixth hour** (i.e. noon) **until the ninth hour** (i.e. three P.M.), **darkness occurred over the whole land**. This was no normal eclipse, but the poetic and fit expression of the creation's horror at seeing its Creator so outraged. Like one hiding his face from an unbearable crime, so the sun's face was hidden from mortal men.

In speaking of the alienation of Jesus from His Father, we enter on a subject the reality of which is largely hidden behind the veil. What happened in those hours when the Lamb of God bore away the sins of the world and became a curse for us (see Gal. 3:13)? Ours is not to attempt to pry into such divine enormities. Rather, we may simply tremble with fear and gratitude that the Lord has plumbed such depths for us, to which we may never have to descend.

Of the measure of those depths we may get some clue from the Lord's cry at the end. **At the ninth hour, Jesus shouted with a great voice, "Eloi, eloi, lama sabachthani?"** This was Hebrew for **"My God, My God, why have You left Me behind?"** It was also the beginning of Psalm 22, in which the righteous sufferer, by his afflictions, turned all the families of the earth to God (Ps. 22:27) and was vindicated by God. It was not, however, that Christ was quoting the Scripture. Rather, the prophetic Scripture was quoting *Him*. Christ **shouted** in dereliction and agony; He was not reciting

Bible verses. It was this abandonment which the Psalmist foretold (along with His being despised, mocked, surrounded, pierced, and despoiled of His garments; see Ps. 22:6, 7, 8, 16, 18). St. Mark wants the reader to see how Jesus' suffering fulfills the Scripture and proves Him to be the true Christ.

The ones **standing by**, however, did not understand this. Their vernacular was Aramaic, not Hebrew. Hebrew was no longer popularly understood, and when the Hebrew Scriptures were read in the synagogue, the reading had to be followed by an Aramaic translation. So it was that the bystanders did not realize that **Eloi** was **My God** in Hebrew, and thought that Jesus was calling for "Eli" or **Elijah**. This seemed to make sense to them, for there was a tradition that Elijah would come to rescue the innocent sufferer. They thought that He was **calling Elijah** to come and **take Him down**. When Jesus called for some **vinegar** (a sour wine drunk by laborers; see Ruth 2:14) to moisten His lips, so that He could speak (John 19:28–30), someone gave it to Him, saying that they should **leave *Him*** be so that they could **see if Elijah** was indeed coming **to take Him down** and save Him. He had invoked Elijah, as if He were innocent— would Elijah indeed come and prove Him so? As it was for the soldiers, it was all but a game to them. By narrating the incomprehension of the bystanders, St. Mark increases the sense of Christ's isolation.

ॐ ॐ ॐ ॐ ॐ

37 And Jesus, having released a great cry, expired.

38 And the curtain of the Sanctuary was torn in two from top to bottom.

39 And when the centurion, who stood by opposite Him, saw that He expired thus, he said, "Truly this man was *the* Son of God!"

40 Now there were also women observing from a distance, among whom *were* Mary Magdalene, and Mary the mother of James the little and Joses, and Salome,

---

> 41 who when He was in Galilee, followed Him
> and served Him, and many other *women* who
> came up with Him into Jerusalem.

Having moistened His lips, Jesus was able to **release** and utter a final **great cry**, lifting up His voice in a mighty sound of triumph. His work had been finished; darkness had been taken away from the heart of the world. He cried out, "It is completed! Father, into Your hands I commit My spirit" (Luke 23:46; John 19:30). Then, having said these words, immediately He **expired** and died. This was significant. No sooner had He given His spirit leave to depart than He died. To all others dying on crosses, death came slowly, as life gradually ebbed from their bodies. Their final audible words were curses, which came in a continuous stream until exhaustion rendered them too weak to speak further. But here was something different. This One was alive and articulate until the end, and His final words were not futile curses, but words of victory and of serene confidence in God. He committed His life to God and then immediately died, as One who had power over life and death, and whose death was somehow voluntary.

More than that, the divine response to that death was instantaneous and dramatic. **The curtain of the Sanctuary** (the large curtain separating the Sanctuary from the forecourt, visible to all in the Temple) **was torn in two from top to bottom**. This was a clearly supernatural rending. A man might somehow tear that veil (standing high above the heads of all) if he seized the bottom and ripped it up to the top. But the veil was ripped in two **from top to bottom**, and no man could be tall enough to seize it from the top. It was as if God were rending His garments, desecrating His own Temple at the catastrophe of the death of His Son. The violence in the Temple (a foreshadowing of its final destruction in AD 70), coming at the same time as Jesus' death, revealed Him as the true Messiah.

Even the pagan **centurion** who **stood by opposite Him**, and so was able to watch Him as He **expired thus** (i.e. triumphantly and voluntarily), recognized that He was Messiah. The centurion had no doubt heard of Jesus' claims to be *the* **Son of God**, and also witnessed the taunts of those who derided Him for those claims (Matt. 27:43). The Roman soldier concluded then that He **truly was what He claimed to be**, even if he did not appreciate all that was meant by this title. By narrating this confession of the pagan centurion, St. Mark means to foreshadow the conversion of all the Gentiles in the Church, and to rebuke Israel for their unbelief. If even the pagan centurion could see that Jesus **was truly *the* Son of God**, why couldn't Israel see that too?

As well as the Roman soldiers, **there were also women observing from a distance**. They had **followed Him and served Him** for a long time, journeying with Him from Galilee and accompanying Him as He entered **into Jerusalem**. St. Mark mentions them by name, as if listing official witnesses. He names them now as witnessing His death and burial (15:47), for he will bring them forward later as witnesses to His Resurrection as well (16:1f). They were well known in the Christian community: **Mary Magdalene** (i.e. from the town of Magdala in Galilee), **Mary the mother of James the little and Joses** (i.e. the mother of Jesus' kinsmen, see 6:3 and the Excursus "On the Brothers of the Lord," page 85), **and Salome** (probably the mother of the sons of Zebedee; see Matt. 27:56).

§VI.6 Jesus' Burial

ॐ ॐ ॐ ॐ ॐ

42 And evening having already come, since it was Friday, that is, the *day* before the Sabbath,

43 Joseph from Arimathea came, a prominent Councilor, who was himself anticipating the Kingdom of God, and he became daring and went in before Pilate and asked for the body of Jesus.

44 And Pilate marveled that He had already died, and calling in the centurion, he asked him if He was already dead.

> 45 And knowing *this* from the centurion, he gave
> the fallen to Joseph.
> 46 And he bought a linen *cloth*, took Him down,
> wrapped *Him* in the linen *cloth* and put Him
> in a tomb which had been hewn from *the* rock,
> and rolled a stone to the door of the tomb.
> 47 And Mary Magdalene and Mary the *mother* of
> Joses were observing where He was put.

St. Mark next carefully relates the circumstances surrounding Jesus' burial. This was not simply a matter of tying up loose ends. Rather, it was an important prelude to the Resurrection. The Church in Jerusalem was able to point to the empty tomb in confirmation of its preaching (see Acts 2:29–31), and this was only possible because it was able to say with assurance in which tomb the body of Jesus had been laid.

After the Lord's death, when **evening** had **already come** on Friday, **before the Sabbath, Joseph from Arimathea came**. Having his ancestral home in Ramathaim-Zophim, about twenty miles northwest of Jerusalem (see 1 Sam. 1:1), he is described as **a prominent Councilor**, an esteemed member of the Sanhedrin. He was an admirer of Jesus and a secret disciple (John 19:38), who, like the other disciples, was **anticipating the Kingdom of God**. He had not consented to the Sanhedrin's murderous plan (Luke 23:51) and perhaps was not even present during the session of the past night. He **became daring and went in before Pilate and asked for the body of Jesus**.

Such a course of action required daring indeed. Though the bodies of those crucified were usually granted to their families for burial if requested, it was otherwise with those who had been executed for high treason, as Christ had been. Burial in such cases involved getting special permission from the governor. Making the request and giving Jesus honorable burial would have its cost for Joseph, for by so doing he was placing himself at odds with all his colleagues on the Council and aligning himself publicly with the discredited and criminal heretic. Nonetheless, Joseph did so. (The family of Jesus, to whom such duty would normally fall, were obviously in no position to make the request: His Mother was prostrate with grief, His disciples were all in hiding, and none of them had any stature with which to approach the Roman governor.) The alternative was to leave the body to a common grave or to be eaten by wild animals. This last was particularly abhorrent to Jews, who felt that a body would defile the land if it remained unburied after sundown. So it was that during the brief space between the time Jesus died at three P.M. and sunset, Joseph took steps to secure Jesus' body.

First of all, he had to take custody of the corpse. He arranged for a hasty audience with the governor and made his daring request. Pilate had finished with the affair just a few hours before and therefore **marveled that He had already died**, for often it took several days for men to die on the cross. Summoning **the centurion** responsible, **he asked him if He was already dead.** The centurion had seen Him die with his own eyes (v. 39) and assured Pilate that He was indeed dead. Being assured of this fact, Pilate **gave the fallen to Joseph.**

The corpse was probably being guarded at the Cross by Joseph's servants. With an eye on the setting sun, Joseph (assisted by his fellow Councilor, Nicodemus; John 19:39) **took Him down** and performed the usual Jewish rites of burial, wrapping Him **in the linen** *cloth*. Haste was essential if Jesus was to be buried before the day faded. Rather than transport the corpse for burial elsewhere, Joseph **put Him** in his own **tomb** nearby, **which had been hewn from** *the* rock. The **door** or entrance to the tomb was covered by a disc-shaped **stone** which was **rolled** against it. There was no chance, therefore, of the body being moved or stolen. And since **Mary Magdalene and Mary the** *mother* **of Joses were observing** the whole scene from a distance, there was also no chance of the location being mistaken.

Notes for Section VII:

_____

_____

_____

Notes for Section VII:

❧ VIII ❧

THE RESURRECTION
(16:1–8)

161 And when the Sabbath had passed, Mary Magdalene and Mary the *mother* of James, and Salome, bought aromatic *spices* that they might come and anoint Him.

2 And very early on the first *day* of the week, they come on the tomb, the sun having risen.

3 And they were saying to themselves, "Who will roll away the stone from the door of the tomb for us?"

4 And looking up, they observe that the stone had been rolled away, for it was extremely great.

5 And entering into the tomb, they saw a young man sitting on the right, clothed in a white robe, and they were startled.

6 And he says to them, "Do not be startled; you seek Jesus the Nazarene, who was crucified. He has risen; He is not here; behold the place where they put Him.

7 "But go; tell His disciples and Peter, 'He is going before you into Galilee; there you will see Him, as He told you.'"

8 And having gone out, they fled from the tomb, for trembling and distraction had *seized* them; and they told nothing to anyone, for they were afraid.

The story of Jesus now reaches its earthly climax. Christ had been crucified on the Friday before the Sabbath, and **when the Sabbath had passed**, on Saturday evening, **Mary Magdalene and Mary the** *mother* **of James, and Salome, bought aromatic** *spices* that they might **anoint** His dead body. They did not have the spices on hand, and this would have been the first opportunity they had to buy them, since such things could not be bought on the Sabbath.

Orthodox who are trained by their liturgical tradition to think of the Myrrhbearers as a single group may lose sight of the confusion that gripped the women in those dark hours and the difficulty of concerted action. They came from dramatically different backgrounds (Mary Magdalene was once afflicted by seven demons, whereas Mary the mother of James was part of Jesus' extended family), and they almost certainly did not live together in the same house in Jerusalem. They had little to bind them together, apart from their common devotion to the Master. This devotion drove them to perform one final act together—they were determined to meet together for another time to anoint Jesus' body. After a hastily convened and hushed conversation in the gathering darkness of Friday evening, they agreed to rendezvous again at His tomb, bringing the **aromatic** *spices* they would buy at the first opportunity.

The chaos of those days must be remembered to fully appreciate the courage of these women. Jesus had perished amidst awe-inspiring phenomena: the sun was blackened from the sky for three hours, and there was an earthquake when He died (Matt. 27:45, 51). The crowd left the scene in terrified tears (Luke 23:48), and even the hardened centurion who crucified Him was sobered (Luke 23:47). The Sanhedrin had secured a seal on His tomb and a Roman guard was placed there (Matt. 27:66). His disciples were hiding behind locked doors, fearful that their arrests and executions were next (see John 20:19). It was in this atmosphere that the women decided, as all the rest fled from the site of crucifixion, that they would return. They set out from their various dwellings **very early on the first** *day* **of the week**, starting out when it was yet dark and **coming on the tomb** a bit later, **the sun having** just **risen**.

Their conversation, tensely whispered in the predawn hour as they walked the deserted city streets to the tomb, was full of apprehension. They faced a seemingly insuperable problem: **Who** would **roll away the stone from the door of the tomb** for them? This was not just a matter of the stone being **extremely great** and difficult to move. It was also a matter of the Roman guard. The stone had been sealed by imperial order, and it was a capital offense to break it and open the tomb. The guards would certainly not do so on behalf of a few Jewish women. In the absence of men, the women were risking their personal safety by approaching the Roman guards at all. How would they fulfill their goal and gain access to the dead body of Jesus?

When they came to the tomb (at different times, apparently; see John 20:1–18), those arriving had a shock. They were focused on the question of how to **roll away the stone from the door**, but when they entered the cemetery and **looked up** at the tomb, **they observe that the stone had been rolled away** (the historic present is used, allowing us to observe their shock). (We note in passing how carefully St. Mark chooses his words: he says that the stone had been rolled away, **for it was extremely great**. Not "although" it was great, but **for** it was great; Gr. *en gar megas sphodra*. That is, the angel moved the stone to allow the women to see the emptiness of the tomb, knowing they could never move it themselves.)

Naturally, they **entered into the tomb** to find the Lord's body. Suddenly an angelic vision appeared to them, as they **saw** what seemed to be **a young man sitting on the right** of where the Lord's Body had been laid, **clothed in a white robe**, shining with the brilliance of heaven. They were **startled** and prostrated themselves to the ground in fear (Luke 24:5).

The angel told them **not** to be **startled** and frightened. He knew that they were **seeking Jesus the Nazarene, who was crucified**. They were not mistaken; they had the right place. But He had **risen** and so was **not here**. They could **behold** for themselves **the place where they put Him.**

This last remark was probably in reference to the graveclothes which the Lord had folded up and left behind in the place where

He had been laid (John 20:6, 7). By seeing the graveclothes left behind (and unoccupied!), they could deduce for themselves that Christ had not been moved to another place—for who would strip a corpse of its graveclothes before moving it? Rather, He was risen indeed.

What then was left for them to do? Not to anoint Him with the spices they still carried in their trembling hands. Rather, they must **go** from there, find and **tell His disciples**—including especially **Peter**, even though he had denied Him—that **He** was **going before** them **into Galilee** as He had previously arranged (14:28). Let them all go and meet Him again there for a grand reunion with all His disciples (see Matt. 28:16; 1 Cor. 15:6).

Having received this word, they went out, and **fled from the tomb, for trembling and distraction had** *seized* **them**. The word translated here *distraction* is the Greek *ekstasis*, meaning to be beside oneself (see the English word "ecstasy"). It is the word used for St. Peter falling into a trance in Acts 10:10, and for the fearful amazement of the crowd at a miracle of healing in Luke 5:26 and Acts 3:10. Its use here indicates that the women were left stunned with amazement, unable to talk, dazed at the power of God. As they ran from the tomb, **they told nothing to anyone** all the way back to the apostles, **for they were afraid**.

On this note of fear (the Greek ends with the words *ephobounta gar*), the Gospel ends. Their fear shows that they had witnessed the mighty work of God. As Moses trembled at the burning bush (Ex. 3:6), as Isaiah shook in the Temple (Is. 6:5), so the revelation of God's power always cows the children of men. The Myrrhbearers had seen evidence of this power manifested before their eyes, and they also were cowed and trembling before it. The Lord had risen! He who walked among us as the Son of Man would walk among us no more. By His Resurrection He had been glorified and now walked in the Kingdom of God. He would meet His disciples in Galilee and prove to them that He was alive again. But now He belonged to the age to come and to the right hand of the Power on high.

ॐ ॐ ॐ ॐ ॐ

❧ EXCURSUS
ON THE LONGER ENDING OF ST. MARK'S GOSPEL

The best manuscripts witness to the fact that St. Mark ended his Gospel with 16:8. Other manuscripts, however, contain other endings.

One manuscript ends with the words of an alternate verse 9: "And they briefly reported all these instructions to Peter and those with him. And after this, Jesus Himself sent out through them, from east to west, the sacred and incorruptible heralding of eternal salvation."

Another manuscript has the so-called "Freer logion" or saying, in which Jesus upbraided His disciples for their hardness of heart, and they excused themselves, saying, "This age of lawlessness and unbelief is under Satan. Therefore reveal Your righteousness now."

Other manuscripts end with alternate verses 9 to 20, and it is this (the so-called "longer ending") that is the traditional alternate ending. This ending first records a series of Resurrection appearances of Christ to His disciples. It begins by saying that "He appeared first to Mary Magdalene, from whom He cast out seven demons," and then, "After this He appeared in another form to two of them as they walked on the way to the country." Then "afterward He appeared to the Eleven" and "reproached them for the unbelief." Then comes the famous commission, "Go into all the world and preach the Gospel to all creation. He who believes and is baptized will be saved; but he who disbelieves will be condemned." The Lord then speaks of "signs following along with" the Church, such as casting out demons, speaking in new tongues, picking up serpents, drinking deadly things without suffering harm, and laying hands on the sick for their recovery. Finally, Christ's Ascension is mentioned, when He "was taken up to heaven and sat down at the right hand of God."

What are we to make of this longer ending, the more popular alternate appendix to Mark's Gospel? There is no difficulty in considering the commission to "preach the Gospel to all creation" as authentic (the core of vv. 15–18). Individual sayings of Jesus circulated in the apostolic community (compare the saying preserved in Acts 20:35), and there seems no reason why these words could not be judged one of these authentic sayings.

The series of Resurrection appearances, however, cannot be judged to be original to Mark's Gospel. It seems, along with the brief mention of the Ascension in verse 19, to have been created by an early church writer to form the context for the otherwise disconnected sayings of Jesus.

That it was not written by St. Mark is apparent even apart from a study of manuscripts. The appearances of verses 9–14 are a summary of the Resurrection appearances as recorded in the other Gospels. Thus, the appearance to Mary Magdalene is a summary of that recorded in John 20:1–18; the appearance to the two disciples as they walked to the country is a summary of the Emmaus road appearance recorded in Luke 24:13–35; the appearance to the Eleven is a summary of that recorded in Luke 24:36–43. The writer of this collection of summaries obviously had the other Gospels before him when he wrote. He could not possibly then have been St. Mark, for there is no evidence that Mark used the other Gospels, nor that those Gospels were written before his. (Indeed, many would date St. John's Gospel in the final decades of the first century, long after St. Mark finished his work.) It seems clear, then, that a church writer, probably in the second century, constructed an ending to be appended to the authentic Markan ending in 16:8.

Once appended to 16:8, the longer ending was immensely popular, and soon became "the" traditional ending for Mark's Gospel. Why was this? Obviously, many people then (as now) felt the original ending of Mark's Gospel was too abrupt. They were used to reading about the Resurrection appearances of Christ in the other Gospels, and Mark's Gospel seemed to them unfinished without it. The question may be asked, Why did Mark not include any Resurrection appearances in his Gospel?

In the absence of a word from St. Mark himself, this question of "why" cannot receive an authoritative answer, and we are left to speculate about his motives and purposes.

We may say, however, that to assert that a Gospel *must* conclude with a Resurrection appearance is to impose our own later categories on it. Mark was not writing a complete life of Christ. It was not a part of his purpose to narrate Christ's Resurrection appearance, any more than it was his purpose to narrate His Birth. Rather, St. Mark's purpose is stated in his very first words: he wanted to tell the story of "the beginning of the Gospel of Jesus Christ" (1:1). That is, he wanted to share what Christ did on the world stage, His public ministry to Israel, which formed the "beginning" or source of the Church's preaching of the Gospel. The hidden events of His conception, birth, and childhood were not a part of this public ministry. Neither were His Resurrection appearances, which were privileged and private manifestations to His own. The Resurrection appearances belonged not to the world stage, but to the Church's hidden life of communion with Christ, and to the world to come. When Mark wrote his Gospel, there was no standard literary Gospel genre to which he thought he needed to conform. (This would come later, when the Church compared all four of the Gospels.) Mark simply wrote what was according to his purpose. He concluded his Gospel with the discovery of the empty tomb, for that was the last thing that open and public historical process could see. The Resurrection appearances that came after belonged to the realm of faith.

His Gospel story was written for the Church community, not only to edify them and preserve the words and deeds of Jesus, but also to provide a resource in their proclamation to the world. It is possible that St. Mark focuses only on those events that occurred on the world stage because it was those events that were incontrovertible due to their public nature. The world might deny the secret Resurrection appearances to the apostles, but none could deny the open fact of the empty tomb. The Church would indeed go on to proclaim the Resurrection of Christ as central to its faith. St. Mark provides the Church with a dossier of evidence to support that proclamation, recording the undeniable public ministry of the Master, when He walked among us in power as the Son of Man.

About the Author

Archpriest Lawrence Farley currently pastors St. Herman of Alaska Orthodox Church (OCA) in Langley, B.C., Canada. He received his B.A. from Trinity College, Toronto, and his M.Div. from Wycliffe College, Toronto. A former Anglican priest, he converted to Orthodoxy in 1985 and studied for two years at St. Tikhon's Orthodox Seminary in Pennsylvania. In addition to the books in the Orthodox Bible Study Companion series, he has also published *The Christian Old Testament: Looking at the Hebrew Scriptures through Christian Eyes; A Song in the Furnace: The Message of the Book of Daniel; Unquenchable Fire: The Traditional Christian Teaching about Hell; A Daily Calendar of Saints: A Synaxarion for Today's North American Church; Let Us Attend: A Journey Through the Orthodox Divine Liturgy; One Flesh: Salvation through Marriage in the Orthodox Church; The Empty Throne: Reflections on the History and Future of the Orthodox Episcopacy;* and *Following Egeria: A Visit to the Holy Land through Time and Space.*

✠ ANCIENT FAITH RADIO

Visit www.ancientfaithradio.com to listen to Fr. Lawrence Farley's regular podcast, "No Other Foundation: Reflections on Orthodox Theology and Biblical Studies."

A Complete List of the Books in the Orthodox Bible Study Companion Series

The Gospel of Matthew
Torah for the Church
• Paperback, 400 pages, ISBN 978-0-9822770-7-2

The Gospel of Mark
The Suffering Servant
• Paperback, 280 pages, ISBN 978-1-888212-54-9

The Gospel of Luke
Good News for the Poor
• Paperback, 432 pages, ISBN 978-1-936270-12-5

The Gospel of John
Beholding the Glory
• Paperback, 376 pages, ISBN 978-1-888212-55-6

The Acts of the Apostles
Spreading the Word
• Paperback, 352 pages, ISBN 978-1-936270-62-0

The Epistle to the Romans
A Gospel for All
• Paperback, 208 pages, ISBN 978-1-888212-51-8

First and Second Corinthians
Straight from the Heart
• Paperback, 319 pages, ISBN 978-1-888212-53-2

Words of Fire
The Early Epistles of St. Paul to the Thessalonians and the Galatians
• Paperback, 172 pages, ISBN 978-1-936270-02-6

The Prison Epistles
Philippians – Ephesians – Colossians – Philemon
• Paperback, 224 pages, ISBN 978-1-888212-52-5

Shepherding the Flock
The Pastoral Epistles of St. Paul the Apostle to Timothy and Titus
• Paperback, 144 pages, ISBN 978-1-888212-56-3

The Epistle to the Hebrews
High Priest in Heaven
• Paperback, 184 pages, ISBN 978-1-936270-74-3

Universal Truth
The Catholic Epistles of James, Peter, Jude, and John
• Paperback, 232 pages, ISBN 978-1-888212-60-0

The Apocalypse of St. John
A Revelation of Love and Power
• Paperback, 240 pages, ISBN 978-1-936270-40-8

Other Books by the Author

The Christian Old Testament
Looking at the Hebrew Scriptures through Christian Eyes
Many Christians see the Old Testament as "the other Testament": a source of exciting stories to tell the kids, but not very relevant to the Christian life. *The Christian Old Testament* reveals the Hebrew Scriptures as the essential context of Christianity, as well as a many-layered revelation of Christ Himself. Follow along as Fr. Lawrence Farley explores the Christian significance of every book of the Old Testament.
• Paperback, 200 pages, ISBN 978-1-936270-53-8

A Song in the Furnace
The Message of the Book of Daniel
The Book of Daniel should be read with the eyes of a child. It's a book of wonders and extremes—mad kings, baffling dreams with gifted interpreters, breathtaking deliverances, astounding prophecies—with even what may be the world's first detective stories added in for good measure. To argue over the book's historicity, as scholars have done for centuries, is to miss the point. In *A Song in the Furnace*, Fr. Lawrence Farley reveals all the wonders of this unique book to the receptive eye.
• Paperback, 248 pages, ISBN 978-1-944967-31-4

A Daily Calendar of Saints
A Synaxarion for Today's North American Church
Popular biblical commentator and church historian Fr. Lawrence Farley turns his hand to hagiography in this collection of lives of saints, one or more for each day of the calendar year. His accessible prose and contemporary approach make these ancient lives easy for modern Christians to relate to and understand.
• Paperback, 304 pages, ISBN 978-1-944967-41-3

Unquenchable Fire
The Traditional Christian Teaching about Hell
The doctrine of hell as a place of eternal punishment has never been easy for Christians to accept. The temptation to retreat from and reject the Church's traditional teaching about hell is particularly strong in our current culture, which has demonstrably lost its sense of sin. Fr. Lawrence Farley examines the Orthodox Church's teaching on this difficult subject through the lens of Scripture and patristic writings, making the case that the existence of hell does not negate that of a loving and forgiving God.
• Paperback, 240 pages, ISBN 978-1-944967-18-5

Let Us Attend
A Journey Through the Orthodox Divine Liturgy
Fr. Lawrence Farley provides a guide to understanding the Divine Liturgy, and a vibrant reminder of the centrality of the Eucharist in living the Christian life, guiding believers in a devotional and historical walk through the Orthodox Liturgy. Examining the Liturgy section by section, he provides both historical explanations of how the Liturgy evolved and devotional insights aimed at helping us pray the Liturgy in the way the Fathers intended.
• Paperback, 104 pages, ISBN 978-1-888212-87-7

One Flesh
Salvation through Marriage in the Orthodox Church
Is the Church too negative about sex? Beginning with this provocative question, Fr. Lawrence Farley explores the history of the Church's attitude toward sex and marriage, from the Old Testament through the Church Fathers. He persuasively makes the case both for traditional morality and for a positive acceptance of marriage as a viable path to theosis.
• Paperback, 160 pages, ISBN 978-1-936270-66-8

The Empty Throne
Reflections on the History and Future of the Orthodox Episcopacy
In contemporary North America, the bishop's throne in the local parish stands empty for most of the year. The bishop is an honored occasional guest rather than a true pastor of the local flock. But it was not always so, nor need it be so forever. Fr. Lawrence Farley explores how the Orthodox episcopacy developed over the centuries and suggests what can be done in modern times to bring the bishop back into closer contact with his flock.
• Paperback, 152 pages, ISBN 978-1-936270-61-3

Following Egeria
A Visit to the Holy Land through Time and Space
In the fourth century, a nun named Egeria traveled through the Holy Land and wrote an account of her experiences. In the twenty-first century, Fr. Lawrence

Farley followed partially in her footsteps and wrote his own account of how he experienced the holy sites as they are today. Whether you're planning your own pilgrimage or want to read about places you may never go, his account will inform and inspire you.
• Paperback, 160 pages, ISBN 978-1-936270-21-7

Three Akathists:
Akathist to Jesus, Light to Those in Darkness
• Staple-bound, 32 pages, ISBN 978-1-944967-33-8

Akathist to the Most Holy Theotokos, Daughter of Zion
• Staple-bound, 32 pages, ISBN 978-1-944967-34-4

Akathist to Matushka Olga Michael
• Staple-bound, 32 pages, ISBN 978-1-944967-38-3

For complete ordering information, visit our website: store.ancientfaith.com.

Other Books of Interest

The Orthodox Study Bible: Old and New Testaments

Featuring a Septuagint text of the Old Testament developed by outstanding Orthodox scholars, this Bible also includes the complete Orthodox canon of the Old Testament, including the Deuterocanon; insightful commentary drawn from the Christian writers of the first ten centuries; helpful notes relating Scripture to seasons of Christian feasting and fasting; a lectionary to guide your Bible reading through the Church year; supplemental Bible study articles on a variety of subjects; a subject index to the study notes to help facilitate Bible study; and more.
• Available in various editions. Visit store.ancientfaith.com for more details.

The Whole Counsel of God
An Introduction to Your Bible
by Stephen De Young

In *The Whole Counsel of God*, popular writer and podcaster Fr. Stephen De Young gives an overview of what the Bible is and what is its place in the life of an Orthodox Christian, correcting many Protestant misconceptions along the way. Issues covered include inspiration, inerrancy, the formation of the biblical canon, the various texts and their provenance, the place of Scripture within Orthodox Tradition, and how an Orthodox Christian should read, study, and interpret the Bible.
• Paperback, 128 pages, ISBN: 978-1-955890-19-9

The Names of Jesus
Discovering the Person of Jesus Christ through Scripture
by Fr. Thomas Hoko

In this book based on his popular podcast series of the same name, the late Fr. Thomas Hopko shares meditations on over 50 different names and titles used for Jesus in the Bible. Learn what each name uniquely has to tell us about the character of the Son of God, His role in our salvation, and the relationship we can choose to cultivate with Him.
• Paperback, 400 pages, ISBN 978-1-936-70-41-5

The Rest of the Bible
A Guide to the Old Testament of the Early Church
by Theron Mathis

A beautiful widow risks her life to defend her people while men cower in fear. A young man takes a journey with an archangel and faces down a demon in order to marry a woman seven times widowed. A reprobate king repents and miraculously turns back toward God. A Jewish exile plays a game of riddles in a Persian king's court. Wisdom is detailed and exalted. Christ is revealed.

These and many other stories make up the collection of writings explored

n this book—authentic books of the Bible you've probably never read. Dubbed "Apocrypha" and cut from the Bible by the Reformers, these books of the Greek Old Testament were a vital part of the Church's life in the early centuries, and are still read and treasured by Orthodox Christians today. *The Rest of the Bible* provides a brief and intriguing introduction to each of these valuable texts, which St. Athanasius termed "the Readables."
Paperback, 128 pages, ISBN 978-1-936270-15-6

Christ in the Psalms
by Patrick Henry Reardon

A highly inspirational book of meditations on the Psalms by one of the most insightful and challenging Orthodox writers of our day. Avoiding both syrupy sentimentality and arid scholasticism, *Christ in the Psalms* takes the reader on a thought-provoking and enlightening pilgrimage through this beloved "Prayer Book" of the Church. Which psalms were quoted most frequently in the New Testament, and how were they interpreted? How has the Church historically understood and utilized the various psalms in her liturgical life? How can we perceive the image of Christ shining through the psalms? Lively and highly devotional, thought-provoking yet warm and practical, *Christ in the Psalms* sheds a world of insight upon each psalm, and offers practical advice for how to make the Psalter a part of our daily lives.
Paperback, 328 pages, ISBN 978-1-888212-21-7

Christ in His Saints
by Patrick Henry Reardon

In this sequel to *Christ in the Psalms,* Patrick Henry Reardon once again applies his keen intellect to a topic he loves most dearly. Here he examines the lives of almost one hundred and fifty saints and heroes from the Scriptures— everyone from Abigail to Zephaniah, Adam to St. John the Theologian. This well-researched work is a veritable cornucopia of Bible personalities: Old Testament saints, New Testament saints, "Repentant saints," "Zealous saints," "Saints under pressure" . . . they're all here, and their stories are both fascinating and uplifting. But *Christ in His Saints* is far more than just a biblical who's who. These men and women represent that ancient family into which, by baptism, all believers have been incorporated. Together they compose that great "cloud of witnesses" cheering us on and inspiring us through word and deed.
Paperback, 320 pages, ISBN 978-1-888212-68-6

For complete ordering information, visit our website: store.ancientfaith.com.

We hope you have enjoyed and benefited from this book. Your financial support makes it possible to continue our nonprofit ministry both in print and online. Because the proceeds from our book sales only partially cover the costs of operating **Ancient Faith Publishing** and **Ancient Faith Radio**, we greatly appreciate the generosity of our readers and listeners. Donations are tax deductible and can be made at **www.ancientfaith.com**.

To view our other publications,
please visit our website: **store.ancientfaith.com**

 **ANCIENT FAITH RADIO**

Bringing you Orthodox Christian music, readings,
prayers, teaching, and podcasts 24 hours a day since 2004 at
www.ancientfaith.com

CPSIA information can be obtained
at www.ICGtesting.com
Printed in the USA
LVHW040430260623
750570LV00003BC/12

9 781888 212549